ANGELS

DANCE

AND

ANGELS

DIE

For never was a tale of more woe
Than this of Juliet and her Romeo.

THE
TRAGIC
ROMANCE
OF
PAMELA
AND
JIM MORRISON

ANGELS DANCE AND ANGELS DIE

Patricia Butler

Foreword by Jerry Hopkins

OMNIBUS PRESS
LONDON • NEW YORK • SYDNEY

Copyright © 1998 by Patricia Butler

ISBN: 0.7119.6877.2
Order No.: OP 48062

This edition, © Omnibus Press, licensed from Schirmer Books, an imprint of Macmillan USA.

Printed in the United States of America

Design by Rob Carangelo

Exclusive Distributors
Book Sales Limited,
8/9 Frith Street,
London W1V 5TZ, UK.

To the Music Trade Only:
Music Sales Limited,
8/9 Frith Street,
London W1V 5TZ, UK.

A catalogue record for this book is available from the British Library.

Visit Omnibus Press at http://www.musicsales.co.uk

This paper meets the requirements of ANSI/NISO Z39.48-1992 (Permanence of Paper).

Copyright Acknowledgments

The author and publisher gratefully acknowledge permission to reprint the following material:

Excerpt from *The Town and the City*, copyright 1950 by John L. Kerouac and renewed 1978 by Stella S. Kerouac, reprinted by permission of Harcourt Brace & Company.

Lyrics from "Let's Get Together," by Chet Powers, © 1963 (Renewed) Irving Music, Inc. (BMI). All Rights Reserved. Used by Permission, Warner Bros. Publications U.S., Inc., Miami, Fl. 33014.

Lyrics from "Little Miss S," by Edie Brickell, Kenneth Withrow, John Bush, Alan Aly, John Houser, © 1988 WB Music Corp./Geffen Music/Edie Brickell Songs/Withrow Publishing/Enlightened Kitty/Strange Mind Productions (ASCAP) All Rights Administered by WB Music Corp. All Rights Reserved. Used by Permission, Warner Bros. Publications U.S., Inc., Miami Fl. 33014.

Selections from *Wilderness* by Jim Morrison. Copyright © 1988 by Wilderness Publications. Reprinted by permission of Villard Books, a division of Random House, Inc.

Selections from *The American Night* by Jim Morrison. Copyright © 1990 by Wilderness Publications. Reprinted by permission of Villard Books, a division of Random House, Inc.

Selections from *Steppenwolf* by Hermann Hesse. Copyright © 1927 by Fischer Verlag A.G. © Copyright 1953 by Hermann Hesse. English translation copyright 1929 by Henry Holt & Co., Inc. Copyright 1957 by Hermann Hesse. Revised Translation Copyright © 1963 by Henry Holt & Co., Inc. Reprinted by permission of Henry Holt & Co., Inc.

In going through some old correspondence, I found a note I'd written to Paul Rothchild in which I made the following observation:

> *Have I ever told you how much your unflagging support through this whole thing has meant to me? So far there's hardly a word or thought in this project that hasn't been filtered through you. I think often of the time we've spent on the phone yelling at each other over word choice, sentence structure or tone, me inevitably bawling, frustrated, you getting disgusted. If that ain't love, honey, I don't know what is.*
>
> *Thanks for working so hard to make me sing. You're a great producer and a better friend and I love you more than cake.*

This book is dedicated to the dear memory of Paul Rothchild, a great producer and a better friend. I still do and always will love him more than cake.

TABLE OF CONTENTS

THANK YOU

Throughout the six years it's taken me to put this book together, I always thought the easiest part of the project would be thanking the many people who helped make this dream reality.

I was wrong.

I have found instead that it is nearly impossible to adequately convey, in just a few written words, the love and gratitude I feel toward the people who gave—and in many cases continue to give—so unselfishly of their time and resources to make this book possible. Instead, I will just briefly mention them here, and hope that I have sufficiently expressed my feelings to each of them individually, at other times, in other ways, for them to understand the depth of my feelings.

I would first like to express my great appreciation to Admiral and Mrs. Steve Morrison, and their attorneys, first Brian Manion, then later Louis Reisman. I can't begin to convey my admiration for these extraordinary people. Despite the offensive nature of some of the material with which I approached them, the Morrisons were unfailingly gracious and timely in their responses, as were their attorneys in conveying those responses. I hope my readers will be equally gracious in their opinions of these people who have been through so much for so long.

My agent, Jonathan Dolger, has been the calm voice and steady hand that kept me focused through the years. Years ago, when he was an editor at Simon and Schuster, Jonathan had a close working relationship with Jim Morrison, helping him produce his poetry book *The Lords and the New Creatures*. During that project, Jonathan developed a fondness and appreciation for Jim that I feel served me well in his work with me on this book. I would also like to thank my editor at Schirmer Books, Richard Carlin, another calm voice in the face of my insanity. His assistant, Alicia Williamson, has also humored and helped me for the past year, for which I'm truly grateful.

My dear friend David Deal slaved over the initial edit of this book, which is more than just a turn of phrase considering he received absolutely nothing in return but my gratitude and admiration. His wife, the incomparable Janice Deal, spent just as much time listening to me whine and complain about nearly everything, in return dispensing wise advise, sweet diversion, and a thousand laughs. They are talented writers, good friends, and the perfect couple.

I would also like to thank those who trusted me with their memories and mementos, including Dr. Paul H. Ackerman, Mr. and Mrs. Charles Andresen, Eve Babitz, Mirandi Babitz, Annette Burden, Jim Carnett, Chris Charlesworth, Dana Cordrey, Dr. Arnold Derwin, Pamela Des Barres, Stan Durkee, Charlene Enzler, Boo Ersham, Paul Ferrara, William France, Brian Gates, Bob Greene, Charlotte Greenwald, David Hart, Babe Hill, Jac Holzman, Jerry Hopkins, Randall Jahnson, January Jensen, Christopher Jones, Chris Kallivokas, Nick Kallivokas, Robby Krieger, John Phillip Law, Lisa Law, Rich Linnell, Frank Lisciandro, Kathy Lisciandro, Preach and Bev Lyerla, Ray and Dorothy Manzarek, Barbara Marko, Anne Moore, Jeff Morehouse, Herve Mueller, Thomas Murphine, Julia Negron, Kendall Niesess, Barbara Stewart Noble, Randy Ralston, Bruce Ramm, Thomas Bruce Reese, Dan Rothchild, Paul Rothchild, Raeanne Rubenstein, Ellen Sander, Anne Shores, Bill Siddons, Cheri Siddons, Jay Snow, Richard Sparks, Anne Spinn, Danny Sugerman and Fawn Hall, Penelope Truex, Abner Weed, Cathy Weldy, Officer Darryl Williams, and Gilles Yepremian.

Others who were instrumental in providing access to photos, documents, interview subjects, or any number of the other components vital to a book of this nature include: The American Lung Association; the truly generous and extraordinary people at Audio Mechanics Music and Sound Restoration in Los Angeles, who worked magic with some damaged interview tapes; Michelle Campbell; Capistrano Public Schools; Lenore Coover, R.N., M.S.N.; Edith Edwards, Principal, Weed High School; Noel Eury; Baret Fink; Mike Galante and the other amazing people at Parkway Photo in Chicago; Golden Bough Bookstore in Mt. Shasta, CA, where the Great Spirit prefers you pay by cash or check, not credit card; Larry Gustin, Buick; Dr. William Hendricks; Fredda Isaccs, Warner Books, who unwittingly encouraged me to continue this project when I was first starting the quest; Tess James, a vital conduit to an interview subject, who I could not have encountered without Bradley Kirkland, Tracey Bissell, Barbara Holmes, and the other writers and writer's resources offered by America Online's Writer's Club; Linda Kyriazi; Xavier Leturcq of Haubourdin, France, another America Online acquaintance who translated French documents into English for me; Allison Martino; Pat McGing; Nancy Mitchell, of Pacific Bell, who saved me from threatening phone calls; The National Center for Health Statistics; Bill Nitopi; Richard Nossett, FedEx Man extraordinaire, who toted endless manuscripts through the most adverse conditions; Orange Public Schools; Brandi Price, formerly of Weed High School, a research assistant beyond compare; Mrs. Shirley Rolfe, who instilled in me my love of the biography form; Dan Rothchild; Joe Russo;

Chuck Schiesser, who first turned me on to the subject; Bob Seymore; Dan Salomon, a surprisingly nice guy for such a jerk (kidding, Dan, just kidding); Baron Wolman; Matt Wrbican, The Andy Warhol Museum; Kathy Yager, formerly of McCann-Erickson Detroit; and Henry and Freda Sussman—they, too, know what it is to lose a child too soon.

Of all the things a writer needs to put together a project of this nature, probably the most important is a group of friends who can provide love, support, and occasionally a swift kick. Those who kept me loved and bruised the most were the beautiful and intelligent Rachael Blacker and her equally stunning mother, Kim Blacker; Iain Boyack; John Brannon; my father, William Butler, who gave me my ability and desire to write; Shawn Daly; John and Virginia Dill; Gertrude and Emil Francone, who love me like their own; Maxine Goble; Kaanii Pry Powell; "Uncle" Albert Goldman, who told me I was too stupid to have lived to be 30—he is missed; the ever-patient Sheryl Guyer; Beth Macior, my biggest fan; The Front Porch club—Michael Eldridge, Marianne Ahokas, Jennifer Charron, David Gaarder, Laurie and Tim Worrall, all of whom inhabit my Minneapolis glider dreams; Dolores Meidel; Joyce Olds; Melissa Pretzer; Vince Pusateri; Mike Roettig and Mayme Lou Smith, friends, neighbors, and tireless proofreaders; Kris and Moe Timmerman; Zack Webb; Bill and Debbie Zima and sweet Emma laughing face.

Tom Ridings was the first to back up his moral support with a check to help finance the project. Others who later contributed to my financial well-being are Dr. Ronald Kirschner, known to my friends as Dr. Charm; Harold Gershowitz, my favorite writer, advisor, friend, and erstwhile short-term employer; friend and photographer Baron Wolman; Dan Salomon, who fed and chauffeured me; Tim and Laurie Worrall, and most especially my adopted "mom," Tamsyn Griffith: Without her many contributions, financial and otherwise, this project would have been nearly impossible to complete.

I beg forgiveness of anyone I may have forgotten to mention, and hope they know that, while their name may not appear here, their assistance was truly appreciated.

Patricia Butler
Chicago, Illinois

FOREWORD

When *No One Here Gets Out Alive*, the Jim Morrison biography I wrote with Danny Sugerman, was published in 1980 and became such a big success, going to No. 1 on the *New York Times* list, I decided to reread the book to see if I could figure out why. I never did quite understand, but I did notice something else.

It had been several years since the book was written and during that time, the manuscript was rejected by more than thirty publishers in the U.S. and U.K. (including the two that finally published it). In that time, I guess my subconscious had been chewing over the subject and the thing that I noticed wrong with the book on this new reading was that Danny and I had not given enough attention to Jim Morrison's girlfriend, Pamela Courson, identified when he died in Paris in 1971 as his common-law wife. Jim had called Pam his "cosmic mate"—a phrase that didn't sound so corny in the 1960s—and we still had not taken her all that seriously. For a while, I thought about writing a second book, to tell the story of their romance, and I even started re-interviewing some of her friends, but other book projects came along and I got distracted. Now that book has been written, but not by me. Patricia Butler's exploration of that love story—and her surprising retelling of the Morrison history—should be the final word on the matter.

I want to make it clear from the start that Patricia has become a close friend, though we've never met. Ma Bell and MCI and Sprint and all those other guys have handled our relationship so far. But we are friends, so I suppose it could be said that I'm a biased introducer to her first book. On the other hand, who the hell asks an enemy to write a foreword?

That said, let me add that Patricia has worked six years on this book, and because she's turned up so much new material, my ego insists that the extra time she spent on research is why. I spent two years researching and writing *No One Here Gets Out Alive;* it was finding a publisher that took forever. Patricia, on the other hand, continued to hold a number of full-time jobs while plugging away on this project nights and weekends. She slowly developed relationships on the phone and got her sources to tell stories they never told me, and then, adding insult to injury, uncovered some secrets Danny and I never knew. She even got both Jim's and Pamela's parents to assist in a limited way, no easy task. In this way, over time, the book that initially was to be a biography of Pamela, grew into the noisy sort of psychedelic valentine you hold in your hands.

The question remains: why did I (and numerous other male writers who came along later) miss the story? At the risk of sounding like I'm seeking an excuse, I think the reasons were obvious, and relevant to Patricia's new book. Mainly, Jim deliberately kept his life with Pam separate from his life with The Doors, so they didn't see that much of her. When they later poo-pooed her importance, it was, in part, born of ignorance. I believe they also sometimes resented Pam's presence in Jim's life, because she was a recurring voice that urged him to leave the band and turn his full attention to writing and filmmaking.

At the same time, I was more interested in the music and what it, and The Doors, represented during what most thought would be their brief flash across the pop sky. Jim's incandescent lifestyle offered another diversion. I knew Jim slightly—drank with him, went to Mexico with The Doors for a week, interviewed Jim for *Rolling Stone*—and I never heard him speak of Pam, nor did I meet her while Jim was alive. When I began researching *No One Here Gets Out Alive,* I also learned about the many other women in his life and, while Pam's name kept reappearing, I still did not take her very seriously, nor give Jim credit for having a "real" relationship, however unusual it may have been.

I finally met Pam, only once, a couple of years after Jim died and about a year before she followed him to the grave. She agreed to meet me at the urging of a mutual friend and because, she said, she wanted to know why I was writing a book about Jim. I told her that I didn't think Jim, and the other Doors as a band, had been given the serious attention they deserved, that Jim's behavior had drawn most of the media to focus on the courtroom scenes and drunken escapades. Also, I said, I was more affected by Jim's death than I thought our relationship warranted. So I was curious.

She made no comment, and we ordered lunch. As she studied the menu, I studied her. She had an almost translucent beauty, a radiance. Her slender body, red hair, and pale skin sprinkled with cinnamon-colored freckles, gave her a delicate schoolgirl look. She made you want to take care of her. I knew, by then, that she was not so vulnerable as she appeared, that she had matched Jim outrage for outrage very capably. But she gave little away during that single lunch, leaving only a lasting impression of power and fragility. She didn't want to be interviewed, nor would she agree to see me again. Soon she was dead.

It was not until years later that Patricia Butler picked up the ball that we male biographers had dropped. Patricia called me. We talked. I agreed, enthusiastically, that Pam warranted a full study. Inevitably, as the years passed and Patricia's files began to bulge with unseen photographs and new information, the book changed its focal point and became the story of a romance, the story of Jim and Pam, thereby, finally, giving Pamela Susan Morrison the consideration she deserves, while painting a fuller, more satisfying portrait of the man she loved.

This is not a vicious Sid and Nancy tale, although there are many moments when the crazed rock and roll drama of the time—of all time?—takes hold. Nor is it quite another *Heloise and Abelard,* and not exactly a modern *Romeo and Juliet* although, again, there are familiar echoes. It is instead an original story that, until now, has gone untold.

Jerry Hopkins
Bangkok

PART

ONE

Fortunate Son

A child, a child, hiding in a corner, peeking,
infolded in veils, in swirling shrouds and mysteries.

Jack Kerouac
The Town and the City

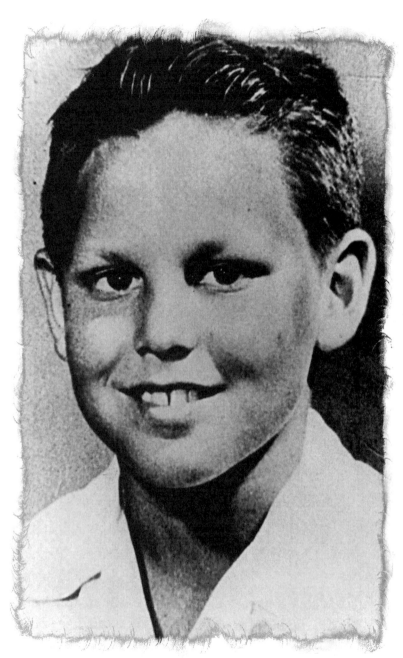

Jim Morrison at about age eight.

Jim looked at the questionnaire Elektra Records executive Billy James had given him to fill out for his first official bio as one of the label's new artists of 1967. The questions were the most basic form of pap, designed to tease little girls into falling in love and spending their allowances—not necessarily in that order. Jim glanced at the list and picked up his pen to address the first question. BIRTH DATE & PLACE: "December 8, 1943, Melbourne, Florida."

The flickering images on the screen show two little boys, possibly four or five years old, rendered in shades of gray by the black-and-white film. Though the movie is silent, they are obviously laughing as they splash in the shallow water by the lake shore. They are trying desperately to climb onto an inflated plastic sea horse, but each time they try, the slippery mount throws them back into the water, where they laugh and splash and try again.

"That was a good time," says Jeff Morehouse, one of the stars of this home movie, along with his friend Jim Morrison. "I can remember that I was really mad that Jim could put his head under the water and I couldn't! He was ahead of me on that. He would splash water on me and then he would duck his head under and I wouldn't be able to do it."

Jeff and Jim grew up together, after a fashion. Because both their fathers were in the navy, the Morehouse and the Morrison families moved frequently but often ended up stationed in the same area. "Both our dads were naval aviators," explains Morehouse, "so we were obviously aiming for different places that carriers go out of; there aren't that many places."

It is said that in life, change is the only constant, and the truth of this adage is felt even more deeply in military families. When George Steven Morrison met his future wife, Clara Clarke, at a navy dance in Hawaii

Cowboy Jim (far left), age five, at Jeff
Morehouse's birthday party, 1949.

shortly after his graduation from the U.S. Naval Academy in 1941, the young ensign wasted no time in marrying the lively and charming mid-western girl. But the military is a demanding mistress, and Steve was forced to leave his new bride shortly after their marriage in April 1942, to join a mine layer serving in the North Pacific.

Steve's next assignment took him and Clara back to his home state of Florida, where he was sent for flight training at Pensacola. Less than a year after the Morrisons' arrival here, their first child, James Douglas, was born. Just six months after Jimmy's birth, Steve once again left his family and returned to hazardous duty, this time flying Hellcats over the Pacific, while Clara and Jim lived in with Steve's parents in Clearwater. It would be a long three years for Clara, watching her son grow and watching her Georgia-born in-laws go slowly about their narrowly prescribed lives as she waited for her husband's return.

With their husbands constantly on the move, many military wives must deal with loneliness, those with children taking on the roles of both mother and father. "Our families were always very close," says Jeff More-house, "because the dads a lot of times would go away, they were at sea. So the moms ran our families every other year, as the sole proprietor of the kids. The mothers banded together quite a lot." Though Clara was overjoyed when the war was over and Steve returned to his family in 1946, their subsequent move to Steve's first official postwar assignment in Washington, D.C., was just the beginning of many moves around the country throughout Steve's—and by extension, the family's—navy career.

Though this sort of existence may seem, on the surface, to be fraught with insecurity, there was a familiarity in the routine that was almost comforting in its constancy, as was the knowledge that others are tolerating the same system. "A lot of people talk about the instability," says Jeff Morehouse, "yet there was a basic stability because we had families that we did move with, so there wasn't complete shock every time we went somewhere. A lot of times we really were in with a bunch of other people we'd known forever. There were a lot of families that did that."

Aside from the constant need to relocate, Jim Morrison's life hardly differed from that of any other typical American boy growing up in the forties and fifties. As second graders, Morehouse remembers, "We would all go and catch frogs, that was a wonderful thing. Hours at the local pond. All of us would be out there catching frogs wildly, and tadpoles. We'd grow the tadpoles into frogs; everybody had that in their house." The boys played in the local woods, using their hatchets to cut down tiny saplings to make an Indian fort. "The other thing we loved to do," remembers Morehouse, "[was] catching these little ringneck snakes. They're maybe only about six or eight inches long, but that was always the big badge of honor if you had a ringneck snake in your aquarium or your jar or whatever you had." And, like so many children of that era, the boys were also enamored of one of television's first superheroes, Captain Video. "We honestly did order the secret rings," laughs Morehouse. "We were all Video Rangers.

"We really did have fairly good times," says Morehouse. "We had pretty good parents, and we did not lead very restricted lives. We traveled a lot. Although a lot of people say, 'Oh, gee, that's terrible—how many schools did you go to?' And I say, 'Hmm . . . I can't count.' But as I say, we had a group of friends who moved with us, a very extended family. So there were a lot of good things here."

Typically, the Washington, D.C., area proved to be barely a resting place, the navy giving the Morrisons only six months to catch their collective breath before ordering them to hit the road once again, heading now for Albuquerque, New Mexico. The family's gypsy caravan had by this time expanded to include Jimmy's new baby sister, Anne. It was on this trip to Albuquerque, on the road just outside of Santa Fe, that Jim later told reporters the family encountered a truck overturned on the road with its occupants, Pueblo Indians, lying about the highway where they had been thrown in the course of a serious traffic accident. As an adult,

Family outing, San Diego, 1954. Left to right: Jeff Morehouse, Jim Morrison, Jay Morehouse, Anne Morrison, Andy Morrison.

Jim would use mystical images to paint a vivid and dramatic picture of dying Indians wailing, the souls of the newly deceased passing into his terrified, four-year-old body. When questioned about the veracity of this story many years later, Clara would simply smile and say, "Jimmy had a very vivid imagination."

The constant address changes did little to impede normal boyhood activities. Jim and Jeff were together again a few years later, in California. "In sixth grade, we would ride our bikes together, we would have dirt clod fights next to the canyon there in San Diego—we were very normal kids," says Morehouse. "We dragged our little sisters and brothers around with us everywhere we went." Jeff had a younger brother, Jay, while Jim was now the eldest of three children, the youngest, Andy, born during the family's time in California. "We were always getting in trouble with them," Jeff remembers. "I remember Jim's parents had this loud whistle when he had to go home, you'd hear that whistle a million miles away." The boys were also inveterate stamp collectors. "Our moms would take us to downtown San Diego," recalls Morehouse. "We'd go to stamp shops, the penny box where they'd have slightly torn stamps and stuff like that. But we bought real stamps, too. I don't think Jim kept his stamps after that year or two, but he had a good little stamp collection."

Jim and Jeff were now attending Longfellow Elementary in San Diego, where Jeff remembers that Jim, in spite of his asthma, was "a very good, sort of a natural athlete, and the best kickballer in the school; that was our big recess [activity]." Jim was also a natural leader, and had been elected by his fellow students to be president of the student body. While Jeff's job was to run the projector, Jim, as president, was required to say a few words to open school assemblies. "I can remember Jim getting ready for those little talks that he'd give, the two or three times we'd have assemblies," says Morehouse, who also remembers sixth grade as the one and only time he and Jim ever got into a fight. Jeff recalls Jim as having "a temper, he could get angry fairly quickly." This was demonstrated one day on the playground when the boys were on opposite sides of a volleyball game. Jeff had just made the point for his side when "[Jim] threw the ball to me, but I was about four feet away and he hit me smack in the face." Though Jim professed his innocence, in the circumstances Jeff was sure Jim was just venting his frustration at having lost the point. "So I tackled him and we rolled around," laughs Jeff. "Hardly did a bit of damage. That was our only fight our whole lives."

The realities of navy life once again separated the boys, who wouldn't come together again until tenth grade in Alexandria, Virginia. It was Jim's tenth "hometown."

While Jeff was enrolled in high school on the East Coast, Jim began his high school career on the opposite side of the country in Alameda, California, where he quickly developed a reputation for being an unpredictable prankster. Characteristically called upon to move with his family to their new post in Virginia by being abruptly pulled from class in the middle of a school day during his sophomore year, Jim said, "Well, I want to go out with a bang." He then walked to the front of the classroom, put a firecracker on the edge of the teacher's desk, and timed his exit to coincide with its tiny explosion.

Jim was soon enrolled as a sophomore at George Washington High School in Alexandria. It's doubtful he ever knew of the presence of Ellen Naomi Cohen, a chubby, rather uninteresting-looking senior and member of the school's chorus. He would, however, run into Ellen later in life when both were working on the west coast—Jim fronting The Doors, and Ellen singing with a group called The Mamas and the Papas under the stage name Mama Cass Elliot.

But if Jim was unaware of Ellen's presence, it's certain that Jim's own presence didn't go unnoticed among his classmates. "Even if Jim had never become famous," says Stan Durkee, who often used to drive Jim to school, "I still would have remembered him." Indeed, the teenage Jim seemed to work hard to be noticed. One day he brought rotting fish on a bus without air conditioning, just to see what kind of reaction he would get (answer: anger and disgust). Another day, when called upon to provide a sentence for translation in Spanish class, Jim walked to the chalkboard and wrote, "We all eat small dogs." Classmate Richard Sparks remembers Jim as being the leader of "a tight little intellectual group that followed him like puppies," an entourage Jim once characterized to Stan Durkee as "my disciples."

Jeff Morehouse was thrilled that he and Jim would be reunited, but was rather taken aback with the changes his friend had undergone. "There was a big change when he came back from Alameda. Even Jim acknowledged it," says Morehouse, "because he and I talked about it when we got back together. He was not anything like the guy I knew in the sixth grade."

Where the younger Jim had been enthusiastic and outgoing, now Jeff found his friend to be "a lot more withdrawn, introspective, wanting to read constantly, especially in the tenth grade when he first came; he was really withdrawn." Though Jim and Jeff, whose families lived only a couple of blocks apart in the area of Alexandria known as Beverly Hills, were spending a lot of time together, it was time spent, says Jeff, "trying to get to know each other. Here was my best friend moving back, and I was all excited, but he was quite a bit different. I wasn't rebuffed or anything, but it was very difficult, because I had pretty much remained the all-American, happy kid, and he had basically gotten very withdrawn, very introspective."

This new Jim had also become a small-time crook, taking up shoplifting and the petty-larcenous game of ducking out of restaurants without paying his check. The little thrill he experienced pulling off these minor crimes lasted well into his adult life. It wasn't until long after he was a famous and wealthy rock star that it stopped, and then only because someone pointed out to him that what he didn't pay, the unlucky waitress or sales clerk he had duped did.

Jim would also now make snide remarks about his father's lack of authority in the Morrison household, once going so far as to say, "In spite of his medals, he's a weakling who let [his wife] castrate him." But for all his contempt for his father's parental ineffectualness, Jim would nonetheless make sure to time his miniature crime sprees to coincide with his father's absences, just in case he got caught. "His parents were rule-setters, that's for sure," says Morehouse, "real disciplinarians." Though the Morrisons were progressive parents in that they had resolved to never raise a hand in anger to their children, their alternative method of punishment was often more painful and the scars remaining far more indelible than any amount of physical beating could produce.

"What it came down to," Andy Morrison told writer Jerry Hopkins, "was they tried to make us cry. They'd tell us we were wrong, they'd tell us why we were wrong, and they'd tell us why it was wrong to be wrong. I always held out as long as I could, but they could really put it to you. Jim eventually learned not to cry, but I never did."

Jim, who now seemed to find it necessary to constantly challenge those around him to the breaking point, devised ways to avoid conflicts with his family's stern disciplinary code by simply avoiding his family altogether. In their house in Alameda, Jim's room had been in an attic turret, which had afforded him a good deal of privacy. In the Morrison's home in Alexandria, Jim set up housekeeping for himself in the basement, separating his living area from the washer and dryer and other usual basement paraphernalia with partitions of flowered sheets. In this way, Jim told friends at school, because the basement had an outside entrance, he was able to go for weeks at a time without seeing his family, which was exactly what he wanted.

"He was good at being by himself," observes Jeff Morehouse. "Jim could go literally weeks on end basically just reading, sitting down in his room. The other thing he would do sometimes is take the bus into Washington on the weekends. He'd wander all day Saturdays, Sundays, just walk around different places; Washington had some really bad areas, poor neighborhoods in lots of places. I went over with him, probably only a couple times, because I did not enjoy it. We would walk down by the river and stuff like that. [Sometimes] he'd just take a bunch of pictures, he had a million pictures. Mostly they were very depressing-type shots. He was interested in that. In those days we didn't have 'vagrants,' we just had poor people. Jim did know some poor people in Washington. He also knew some poor people down in Alexandria. He'd wander around downtown Alexandria—there were some really bad areas, run-down, falling-down houses and so forth—and Jim knew his way around. Sometimes I would ask him, 'What are you trying to learn?' He'd say, 'Nothing, I'm just listening.' That was all he was doing, just listening to these people telling their stories. What makes them happy? How do they do it?"

Jim kept his distance not only from his family but from most of his peers as well. "He dealt with a lot of people through sarcasm and distance," remembers Durkee. "I think he was only really close to a couple of people, and even then I have reason to think he really wasn't close to anybody."

But if anyone might have been considered to be close to Jim at that time, it was probably Jeff Morehouse, who had known Jim for most of his life, and Jim's first steady girlfriend, Tandy Martin, a pretty brunette whose family lived close to the Morrisons and the Morehouses. "I can't remember all the connections," says Jeff Morehouse, "but Tandy was my friend, and then she became Jim's friend, and then they became girlfriend/boyfriend, or as close as Jim could have to a girlfriend in those days. As far as I know, that was the only girlfriend he had. But they didn't have normal dates." Jeff remembers that instead of going to the popular hangouts about town, Jim and Tandy would either go to the movies or take the twenty-five cent bus ride into downtown Washington, D.C.

Finding ways to cut his personal expenses was a high priority for Jim. Jeff Morehouse remembers: "One of the things my mother always gave him trouble for was he never dressed well. He never dressed well because he bought his clothes at the Salvation Army. He bought his clothes at the Salvation Army because he didn't want to spend the money that was given to him except on books and other stuff like that. So he was always getting in trouble for that. When he got his hair cut, which he had to do every now and then by mandate, he found the barber school so he'd get it cut cheap. He cut it himself once or twice, but his mom and dad said, 'That's enough of that! Go get your hair cut! Here's a buck, go get it done.' But he could get it done for fifty cents at the barber school. He was constantly doing that, finding a different way to save his money for books."

Jeff was perturbed that Jim didn't bother to ask Tandy to the senior prom, though the two were considered a steady couple. "Jim had never gone to dances," says Morehouse, "but I thought for sure he was going to ask Tandy to the prom. He didn't! I was sort of mad at him for that." Jeff, whose own steady girlfriend, also part of a military family, had moved away the year before, decided to take matters into his own hands. "I got mad at Jim for not asking Tandy, so I went over and asked her. I didn't care if Jim minded." If Jim did mind, he never expressed the fact to his friends, and Tandy and Jeff enjoyed their evening immensely.

Aside from their slightly less than conventional dating habits, what seemed more disturbing about Jim's relationship with Tandy was the fact that before long, she seemed to bear the brunt of what had become Jim's frequent mood swings. Alternately morosely devoted to Tandy, falling to his knees and trying to kiss her feet in public, or perversely vicious, planning and executing elaborate tricks designed to humiliate her, Jim's erratic behavior hurt, confused, and exasperated the girl. "I asked him why he played games all the time," Tandy recalls. "He said, 'You'd never stay interested in me if I didn't.'"

Jim attributed his mercurial temperament to a problem that he told Tandy he couldn't discuss with his parents and that he demonstrated no interest in discussing with her. At Tandy's urging, Jim agreed to meet with the assistant minister of the Westminster Presbyterian Church to discuss this mysterious problem. But if the session did any good, the improvement certainly wasn't reflected in Jim's behavior, and it's doubtful that Jim ever confided the true nature of his problem to the clergyman.

Whatever Jim's problems, real or imagined, they only seemed to worsen. In fact, he seemed to Tandy to have undergone a dramatic personality change between his sophomore and senior years, a definite change for the worse which did not go unnoticed by Tandy's mother. "He seems unclean, like a leper," Mrs. Martin remarked to Tandy, and she urged her daughter to stop seeing the boy.

But Tandy liked a challenge, and she continued to see Jim until one evening shortly after their graduation. It was on this night, during a party at a friend's house, that Jim's frighteningly erratic behavior turned violent in an episode which would prove to be an eerie precursor to others like it for Jim over the next ten years. Exasperated by his apparently drunken antics during the evening, Tandy chastised Jim, saying, "Oh, Jim, why must you wear a mask? Do you have to wear it all the time?" Jim's reaction shocked Tandy. Before she knew what was happening, he had fallen into her lap, weeping. "Don't you know," he finally managed to gasp between sobs, "I did it all for you?"

Tandy was mortified and at a complete loss. What was he talking about? What had he done for her? Jim, embarrassed and offended by her reaction to his seemingly sincere display of emotion, left the house, only to burst in a moment later to loudly announce "I love you!" to the totally nonplused girl. This was getting a little thick as far as Tandy was concerned; she'd had just about enough of Jim Morrison's dramatic revue for one evening. She turned her nose up at him, expressing doubt that Jim could care for anyone but himself. In a flash, Jim was behind the girl, painfully twisting her arm behind her back and threatening to cut her face with a knife "so no one else will look at you but me." It would be years before Tandy Martin saw Jim Morrison again, another lifetime for each.

As disturbing as Jim's behavior was, even more disturbing is the possible cause, which Jim did not divulge until shortly before his death. It was during preparations for his trial on charges of lewd and lascivious conduct for his behavior onstage at a 1969 concert in Miami that Jim reportedly shared a long-held secret with his trusted attorney and confidant, Max Fink.

In the unpublished transcript of a taped interview with his wife,

Margaret, Max recalled lamenting the location of Jim's indiscretion, asking Jim why, of all the states in the nation, did he have to choose Florida to get into trouble? According to the transcript, Morrison looked Max straight in the eye with an intensity that sent chills through the attorney and replied, "I thought it was a good way to pay homage to my parents."

The cold calculation of Morrison's statement exasperated the attorney, who immediately took Jim to task for this constant, seemingly baseless animosity toward his parents. It was at that point that Jim was said to have reluctantly revealed his painful secret: As a small boy, Max reportedly told Margaret, Jim said he had been molested. Though he did specify that the molester had been male, Jim did not reveal the man's identity, nor did Max ask. Jim cried as he recounted his mother's reaction when he'd told her of the incident, saying she had turned on him, called him a liar. Jim reportedly said his mother's betrayal was something that he could never forgive and was only compounded by another incident that allegedly occurred when Jim was very young, an incident which seemed to have left an equally painful impression on him and added greatly to his growing resentment.

Steve Morrison's absences were, by necessity, so frequent that they were seen as the norm rather than the exception. As is the case with many navy children, Jim had grown to think of his father as nothing but a visitor in his own home when he returned periodically, and of his mother as the primary head of the household and disciplinarian.

It was during one of these absences, Jim said, that he wet his bed; it is unclear how old Jim was at this time. The boy went to his parents' room and climbed into the big bed where his mother was sleeping alone. Clara, waking and taking in the situation, reportedly pushed her son out of the bed and, according to Jim, humiliated him for his lack of self-control, taking him back to his room and forcing him to sleep on the wet sheets. This incident, he said, left him afraid to sleep on the bed at all, and from then on he would curl himself up in a ball on the floor and pray for his mother's death, counting the days until he could get even with her. "After that," Morrison reportedly said, "I never had a childhood."

To kill childhood, innocence
in an instant

When Doors producer Paul Rothchild later heard this account of Jim's supposed revelations, he was thoughtful for a moment, reviewing in his mind his own experiences with Jim's bizarre, often self-destructive behavior and ruthless excesses over the years, before saying, "That certainly explains a lot." But was Morrison's story, reportedly told to Max

Fink in 1969 about incidents that had allegedly occurred from ten to twenty years previous, the truth? It is true, as Clara Morrison once stated, that Jim did have a vivid imagination and had spent years studying and perfecting the art of manipulating the behavior of those around him. Jeff Morehouse backs this up, saying, "Jim would tell a story. He would tell a good story, and I couldn't tell if it was true or not. He had a line, a story, that would just get everybody believing him. I remember in my senior year he told me one or two things, trying to shock me. And I can remember just looking at him because I didn't know if he was telling me the truth or not. And I knew that it was a fifty-fifty call, but I didn't know whether to believe it or not."

Was this story, then, perhaps the product of a calculating, manipulative mind, designed to evoke a desired emotional response from the listener? Or was Jim's revelation a long-held cry for help and understanding? If the story Jim reportedly told Max that day was the truth—indeed, if the conversation between Jim and Max even took place as reported—the dramatic personality change witnessed by Jeff Morehouse and the violent mood swings that Tandy and her mother had observed in the boy could certainly be seen by many as evidence that these claims were valid.

For their part, Admiral and Mrs. Morrison, in a statement prepared by their attorney, "Categorically deny that any of the alleged behavior either on their part or Jim's ever occurred." It is unclear from this statement whether the Morrisons mean for readers to infer that not only were the incidents related false, but that no such conversation ever took place between Jim and Max Fink. While it is possible that Fink made up the whole story, in view of the Morrisons' estrangement from Jim, which commenced with his involvement with The Doors and continued nearly until his death, it seems unlikely that they would have been privy to their son's personal conversations during that period. Unfortunately, the only two people who know the truth about the controversial conversation between Max Fink and Jim Morrison are no longer living to confirm or deny the story's veracity.

Jim quickly worked through the questionnaire, skipping around on the page, pausing to give a few seconds' thought to an answer here, skipping over a question there. Height, weight, and coloring he filled in quickly; the next question he skipped over in favor of the less challenging SCHOOLS ATTENDED: In answer, Jim quickly scribbled, "St. Petersburg Junior College, Florida State U., UCLA."

By his senior year in high school Jim's deteriorating behavior had become obvious to everyone around him. He had grown increasingly withdrawn, showing little interest in what went on around him, preferring to focus all of his attention on voracious and incredibly varied reading and equally passionate writing. He scribbled in notebooks constantly, putting down fragments of thoughts, sketches, and poems. While his grades were nothing

Senior photo, George Washington High School, 1961.

special, his I.Q. was tested at 149 and his grasp of history, literature, and art stymied even his most learned teachers. One teacher reportedly even went so far as to check with the Library of Congress to make sure that some of the books Jim was reporting on actually existed, so obscure were their titles and subjects.

Stan Durkee was in Mr. Gregory's English class with Jim and Jeff during their senior year at George Washington and remembers Jim as being able to give oral reports on most any book at a moment's notice. "[Mr. Gregory] found Jim extremely interesting, he was very impressed with him," says Durkee. "Mr. Gregory would just say, 'Jim would you get up?' And Jim would just stand up and give very sophisticated, very articulate, really extraordinary reviews of certain books, without any preparation." While Jim seemed to enjoy this English class, which was more advanced than most such high school courses, even Mr. Gregory wasn't entirely invulnerable to Jim's moodiness. One day the teacher made the mistake of questioning one of Jim's comments on Joyce's *Ulysses*. It was an innocent enough disagreement, but it angered Jim to the point that he shouted at the teacher, "I spent a *summer* reading that book!" as though this alone should be proof of the soundness of his analysis. The class was stunned by Jim's outburst. "This anger that came out of him seemed so extraordinary!" recalls Durkee. "I'd never seen anyone get angry like that before."

Jeff Morehouse remembers the dispute as being somewhat less serious. "Jim raised his voice, he hardly yelled. But Gregory was really the one taking umbrage with the fact that a student would talk back. Those were the days that we didn't talk back, we weren't supposed to do stuff like that." Jeff, who is now an instructor at the university level, looks back on the incident as being more of a power struggle than an interpretive dispute. "Gregory was wrong. He was being questioned and he didn't handle it very well. He was not used to somebody just questioning another interpretation, that's all there was to it. Nineteen sixty was not the year to question your teacher, but Jim could say something to a teacher, which a lot of us couldn't."

Jim liked to come out on top in these situations, and he usually managed to do so. It was around this time that Jeff Morehouse's father, after twenty years in the navy, was passed over for promotion from commander to captain. Though he would be given two more opportunities to attain the higher rank, being passed over the first time around meant that when he was promoted, he would have to settle for command of a lesser ship, never a cruiser, or an air carrier like the one Captain Morrison commanded. It was, to Julian Morehouse, a crushing blow, leading to his decision to retire, a plan he discussed with Steve at the Morrison house one day. "Well, now that I've been passed over, I'm no longer on the first team," Julian told Steve, "and if I can't be on the first team, I don't want to play." Jim overheard the conversation and later related it to Jeff.

"That struck a real chord with Jim," says Jeff. "He really liked that. And he came back and he told me, 'I really respect your dad for acting on what he feels and thinks.' Jim thought the same way, about lots of stuff: If I can't be number one, I'm not going to play."

But being the best by Jim's standards did not necessarily mean aspiring to achieve the more arbitrary standards set by those who were supposed to be in authority. While Jim may have impressed his teachers in one way or another, and awed his classmates, his grades were surprisingly mediocre, which caused Clara and Steve Morrison a great deal of concern. "You don't really care about my grades," Jim once accused his mother. "You only want me to get good grades so you can brag to your bridge club." But Jim made it quite obvious that he wasn't interested in being a show pony for his parents, trotted out on special occasions and made to do tricks for company, forced to channel his intelligence into acceptable forms that could be held up for agreeable comparison to the children of the other navy families with whom his parents socialized. Instead, he continued his own personal course of study which sometimes coincided with his teacher's planned curriculum, sometimes did not. As far as Jim was concerned, he was learning and that was the point—not which letter grade he could drag home and lay at his parents feet for a rewarding pat on the head.

In spite of his chronic asthma, Jim had been athletic his whole life, even becoming a member of his junior high school swim team in California. Even so, Jeff could no longer interest Jim in school sports. "I was on the rowing team, and he came down and watched me row a couple times, because I asked him to," Jeff recalls. But looking at the team was as far as Jim was willing to go. He also demonstrated no interest in other school activities.

While Jim may have radiated indifference toward school and his classmates, others' feelings about Jim were either black or white, with very few shades of gray in between. He was seen by most as either a freak or extremely cool. "Jim was by no means a leader in high school," says Morehouse, "but he had a bunch of people who were really in awe of him. We all knew what beatniks were, and Jim was the closest thing that George Washington High School had to one, and so that put him on a different plane." The high school did have a couple of fraternities, junior versions of what the teens might expect to encounter when they went on to college.

"It was basically a bunch of the cool guys—self-appointed cool guys," says Morehouse. "Jim told me at one point he was invited into one of the fraternities, but he said, 'I'm not going to join,' and I don't think he ever did. He wasn't much of a joiner."

When Jim took a typically lackadaisical attitude toward filling out college applications, his parents took it upon themselves to enroll him in Florida's conservative St. Petersburg Junior College, arranging for him to stay with Steve's parents, who owned Upton's Laundry in Clearwater, about ten miles from St. Petersburg. Jim shrugged off this decision on their part, but countered by announcing a decision of his own: He would not be attending his high school graduation. "He told me he had to be in Brazil that day," laughs Stan Durkee, "which was his way of saying he thought it was all a bunch of baloney." Jeff Morehouse agrees. "Jim never believed in doing the obvious, and there was no reason to go to high school graduation. He said that to me. I would say such things as, 'Well, my parents would like me to go'; that would be my reason. That wasn't a reason for Jim." His father—now Commander Morrison—was livid at Jim's decision, but Jim remained firm. While the rest of his class marched to *Pomp and Circumstance,* James Douglas Morrison received his high school diploma in the mail.

Morrison's life at St. Petersburg Junior College seemed to echo his high school experience. Like a truly horrendous automobile accident, his bizarre behavior both attracted and repulsed those who came close to him. The worst of this behavior Jim apparently kept hidden from his grandparents, who "had been around Clearwater a long time, lived in a little house down by the library, and were just kind of always shocked and surprised at Jim's 'rambunctiousness' as they called it," says Bryan Gates, a native of Clearwater who also started out attending SPJC, though he wouldn't become well acquainted with Jim until they both transferred to Florida State. Gates remembers that Jim's rambunctious behavior was toned down considerably when he was in the presence of his grandparents, whom he treated with great respect. "He liked them a lot," says Gates, although noting that Jim spent as little time as possible at his grandparents' home. "He was well behaved and respectful [around them]," says Gates, "but he just considered them old. As he put it, 'That's why you don't spend too much time with grandparents, they're old. They don't understand.'" Jim's grandparents would seem to agree with at least part of Jim's assessment. "We just didn't understand him, any of us," his grandmother once said. "There were so many sides to Jimmy. You'd see one, then get a glimpse of another. You never knew what he was thinking."

It wasn't long before Jim found a place near St. Petersburg where

Entrance to the Beaux Arts-Contemporary
Arts, Pinellas Park, FL.

his quicksilver demeanor was appreciated. "The Beaux Arts was really the
beginning in this area of anything that you would call a coffeehouse,"
recalls Bryan Gates. "People not only went there to consider themselves
arty," he says, "but the films were mainly art films, and then [the patrons]
took delight in having coffee and sitting out under some overgrown trees.
That was about the nature of that place. And," he adds, "everybody was
fascinated to a certain extent by the fact that the proprietor was a known,
flaming homosexual about town, so it was kind of daring to go there, to
be seen there."

Thomas Bruce Reese was the charismatic proprietor of the Beaux Arts in Pinellas Park, a small town a few miles south of Clearwater. Founded by Reese's uncle around the beginning of the century, the Beaux Arts—known as Contemporary Arts Coffeehouse and Gallery during Jim's patronage—was a haven for artists of all types: musicians, poets, writers, and filmmakers. "Only thing I didn't have was inventions to fly like Leonardo," laughs Reese. To Jim Morrison, the sprawling two-story coffeehouse was a revelation; he was fascinated by the atmosphere, the clientele, and by the talented, well-educated, and eccentric Reese.

As for Reese, he knew talent when he saw it. Just as he had known Jack Kerouac had a gift from the moment he met the author (though Tom persisted in throwing his fellow Floridian out of the coffeehouse for drunkenness, a state not tolerated in any of the club's artists or patrons), in Morrison, too, Tom saw a raw talent waiting to be honed, and he quickly took a personal interest in Jim. Where others saw instability, Reese saw charisma and a spark of genius together with a smoldering sex appeal. "I did tell Jim what he was exactly," says Reese, "that he was a sexpot and that was it. I didn't use that term exactly, but that's what it amounted to." It was an opinion that Jim quickly learned to share.

"He was aware that he was attractive," the gallery owner confirms. "He had that sexy feeling about him—everybody wanted to go to bed with him . . . whether it was boys or girls, they all were attracted to him." In high school, Jim had hinted to Jeff Morehouse that he had experimented with homosexuality during his time in Alameda, stories that Jeff wasn't sure were true or just calculated to shock. In later years, Morrison would tearfully confess to his attorney that he had been intimately involved with someone in Florida during his junior college years, an individual Jim would only identify as an older man, a nightclub owner whom he considered his mentor, the first person who had really shown him encouragement. Reese, asked if he had been Jim's lover during this time as Morrison had later intimated, hedges. "Well, let's put it this way: everybody wanted to." He chuckles, then adds somewhat coyly, "It certainly sounds like me, doesn't it?" But when pressed to disclose further details of his personal relationship with Jim, Reese grows serious. He is quiet for a moment before saying simply, "I don't think anyone should." It is his final word on the subject.

The Contemporary Arts would prove to be Morrison's first taste of performing in front of a live audience. "My understanding was that Jim had taken quite a delight in going there and making his presence known," says Gates, "reciting poetry beyond what anybody had heard before, and demonstrating his grasp of the poets and arts and so forth, and became, I guess, a bit of a minor celebrity."

Thomas Bruce Reese, 1961.

"He always came on weekends, a very attractive lad. He came with a neighbor boy," recalls Reese, who continually tried to convince Jim to model nude for the club's Life Studies class, offers Jim continually declined. "I had somebody who was head singer, and he had a list of people that wanted to go onstage," he explains, "and Jim would always sign up. You could almost stand up where you were and do your thing, but we had a stage, too, with a mike. But if I remember right, Jim didn't need a mike."

Doors fans might be surprised to learn that these early performances of Morrison's smacked less of Rock God than of Arthur Godfrey. Morrison's "thing" consisted of reciting poetry, accompanying himself on a ukulele. "He would strum somewhat like Ginsburg did," says Reese. "He would sign up in advance, but I always felt he just made [the poetry] up as he went along, based on whatever philosophy he was reading, bringing it up to date, what it meant to him at that moment."

But Jim's interest in the Contemporary Arts extended beyond the opportunity it afforded him to socialize and perform. "I had foreign films, you see, and experimental movies—I had all the ones I could get hold of," recalls Reese. Bryan Gates thought that the amount of flesh shown in some of the foreign films screened at the Contemporary Arts probably helped their popularity. "[The club had] the reputation for showing the French films that had a certain amount of nudity in them, which we adolescents loved in those days," Gates laughs. Tom Reese says, "You paid at the door—when Jim came it was only a buck and you got free coffee. I thought Jim was only interested in music. I didn't realize that he sneaked into all the movies." It was this misunderstanding that appeared to have led to Jim's decision to leave SPJC and transfer to Florida State University in Tallahassee, about two hundred miles north of Clearwater, a move that would ultimately lead him to UCLA.

Reese, whose own impressive academic credentials include a Master of Fine Arts from California College of Arts and Crafts and a Master of Theater Arts from San Francisco State, has always been a true believer in higher education, and vividly remembers encouraging Jim to leave SPJC. "I said, 'Jim, you have ability to do something with music, but I don't know what it is. You're rather musical when you do your lines. They might not rhyme, but they're very poetic and you do them rather musically.'" Folk music was extremely popular at the time, and Reese thought the best course of action for Jim in the circumstances would be to learn the guitar.

"There were three places you could get credit for learning the guitar," says Reese. "One was Florida State in Tallahassee. I told Jim, 'If I were you, I'd love Florida State; there's rolling hills and you're born in Florida and your father's in the service so you can go there practically free.' And so he went there, and I thought because of the damn guitar! And what he took was cinema."

In an ironic twist of fate, at the time Jim began attending FSU, there was a former UCLA professor teaching cinema at Florida State for the first time. This professor immediately encouraged Jim to leave Florida. As Jim explained it to Tom Reese, the professor told Jim, "'We haven't got anything here [in Florida]; no equipment, nothing. Go to UCLA!' And," Reese concludes, "that's why he went!"

While he was finishing his final term at SPJC, Jim happened to meet Chris Kallivokas, who was a high school senior in trouble the night he first encountered Jim. "A bunch of my friends came by," Chris recalls of that night. "They were going to a party and Jim was with them. I said I couldn't go because I had to write a term paper and it was due the next day." Chris and Jim fell into conversation and discovered that they would both be attending Florida State and neither one had finalized their living arrangements yet, though Chris would probably be staying in a house off campus with his older brother, Nick, and some of Nick's friends, including Bryan Gates. "But there was room for one more," says Chris, "so I mentioned that to him."

But first Chris was going to have to make it out of high school. "I had to write this term paper on Lord Essex, and I hadn't done any home-work or research on it," Chris says ruefully. "I'd waited until the last minute and I didn't have any information, just two paragraphs I'd gotten out of the encyclopedia." Chris explained his plight to his friends, and Jim said, "Oh, Lord Essex? I know all about him."

Chris wasn't going to make it to the party, but thanks to Jim he might just make it out of this dilemma. "The other guys left and went to the party," says Chris, "and Jim sat down and wrote a seven- or eight-page term paper just out of recollection. I typed it up, and because it was a formal paper, he created a bibliography, just from memory." Though Chris concedes he doesn't know how accurate the bibliography Jim had created was, it certainly did the trick the next day when Chris handed the paper to his teacher, who happened to have done her master's thesis on this period of British history. "I got an A on the paper, which enabled me to get a C in the course," says Chris, who obviously hadn't done well in the class up to that point. But, after reading his paper on Lord Essex, "[my teacher] thought that I had turned the corner!" That was the last week of school for Chris, who spent the summer hanging out with Jim before they both headed off to Tallahassee in August to start classes at Florida State.

It was during that summer that Chris introduced Jim to sixteen-year-old Mary Werbelow, a friend of Chris's girlfriend. "She came up on several college weekends," says Chris, describing Jim's relationship with Mary, who remained in high school in Clearwater after Jim and Chris left for Tallahassee. "They dated pretty steadily. Jim was an unusual personality. He didn't date a lot of girls." Bryan Gates remembers Mary as "a sweet, attractive girl, open to adventure. That's why she was fascinated with Jim, though many people couldn't understand why a girl who had so many opportunities to have a popular boy as a boyfriend fell for this guy that many around Clearwater considered kind of weird."

But if Mary's attraction to Jim seemed baffling to those who knew them, Jim was quite vocal about the reasons for his attraction to Mary. "He felt that she was a spiritually touched girl, that's what his fascination was," says Bryan. "He thought that she was capable of having visions, and her attitude toward the way the sun would strike trees and so forth—he would go on and on and on with that kind of talk as long as anyone would listen. I remember once he told me he took her into a church one night, late at night, and he was struck by her fascination with the light and the spiritual nature of the structure, and all that sort of stuff. He seemed to be somewhat in awe of her because of what he considered a particular spir-itual capability that he himself didn't have."

The accuracy of Bryan's assessment would seem to be borne out by something Jim once passed on to a friend: *Every man seeks a woman who will absorb his flaws, so they won't be passed on to their children. A maimed man will seek out a strong healthy woman, a deformed man will yearn for a woman of great physical beauty and perfection. The essence of love is not possession, but reciprocation.* It is unclear in its context whether the passage was actually written by Jim, or was something Jim had found that he felt represented his own beliefs.

As had been the case with Tandy, Jim invested all his pent-up emotion in his feelings for Mary, an intensity she found both compelling and frightening. "At that particular time he was really, totally enamored with her," says Gates. "And unlike virtually everybody else he was around, he was polite to her, considerate, never provoked her like he did the other people, and sort of wanted to be not only her friend in the boyfriend/girlfriend sense, but somewhat of her mentor and intellectual coach. It was a nice relationship."

When Chris Kallivokas suggested that Jim fill the vacant slot in the house at FSU, Bryan Gates at first had a hard time remembering Jim from SPJC until someone pointed out the previous connection to him. "When I realized who he was, I just remembered that he was the kid that had the reputation for being a notorious cheater in the Hearts room. Terrible cheater! He figured out that he could renege in Hearts and nobody would realize it." It was an inauspicious beginning of what would turn out to be one of the more solid friendships in Jim's early life.

"[We lived in] a single-family house out in the suburbs of Tallahassee, a mile or so from the campus," remembers Gates of the building one of the Kallivokas boys had rented for the group. "It was a place that became known as Hot Henry's Haven. There were three of us who had committed to live there, and we had gone out looking for various roommates, and Chris was the one who selected Jim."

"We were a pretty unusual group," says Chris Kallivokas. "My brother Nick and Bryan had been in the service already, and through them we had a guy named Beauman, who we called Mother Beauman because he was sort of the guy that took care of everything, he was real neat and organized. Everyone else was typical, the worst sort of college boys in terms of never taking out garbage, never cleaning the house, never worrying about the power being turned off, stuff like that. But Beauman was sort of squared away." In addition to Nick, Bryan, Chris, Jim, and the squared-away Mother Beauman, there was Carl Roach, a gymnast, and George Greer, a friend of Bryan's who didn't actually live in the house but visited often enough to be considered a regular. Chris and Jim, who shared a room, were the youngest in the house, Chris just out of high school and Jim transferring his SPJC credits to start FSU as a sophomore. "We were all Florida guys, very conventional, WASP type of guys," says Chris, "and Jim was very . . . he was *different*. He was always different."

"When Jim moved in he basically had two footlockers full of things," Chris recalls. "Some were clothes and some were his sort of amusements. He had all kinds of little gadgets—a prayer rug, a long gray wool West Point cape, and a little carved stone pipe that had a peephole in it. When you looked in it, there was a photograph of a nude Oriental woman, and when you wiggled it, her hands moved up and down, you know, just like one of those old-fashioned ones, just silly." Besides his more trivial "amusements," Chris recalls the balance of Jim's luggage being "full of books, basically—Norman Mailer, existentialism. He was philosophically on sort of the fringe side of things."

"He had a Beatles haircut before the Beatles," Chris says, "and for a while he wore steel-rimmed glasses that he probably didn't need . . . it was just a stage. And he just had strange clothes, always for shock. At that point in time, kids were really trying to conform, but Jim was just the opposite. Jim was, in retrospect, what I would call a bizarrist. He liked to shock people and cause a controversy."

He certainly caused a controversy when Chris made the mistake of taking him to a tea at Gilchrist Hall he'd been invited to by a girl he'd known in high school. Although Jim had elected to wear a Lincolnesque collapsible beaver top hat for the occasion, Chris recalls the proceedings being quite prim and proper. Until Jim decided to shake things up a bit. "Back then it was not unusual for people to smoke socially, even at something like that," Chris explains. "So Jim took out a cigarette case and offered one of the girls a cigarette. But when he opened up the case, instead of cigarettes in it, he had tampons." Jim always hoped for a big reaction, and he got it. "We were sort of evicted from there," says Chris.

Even when doing something as ordinary as laundry, Jim could manage to draw attention to himself. "Like most guys, we would wait until we were out of clothes to go to the Laundromat," recalls Chris, "and Jim would go to the Laundromat and undress under his West Point cape, and just have his cape on. People would stare at him. He was just a bizarre guy." Jim would try to get a response from almost anyone, no matter what the situation or how great the challenge. "Some girl came calling on us who was a Latter-Day Saint," Chris recalls, "She was on her mission I guess, trying to spread the word. She was very attractive and very religious. Jim created a dialogue with her, indicating interest in her religion. His agenda was, basically, to try to seduce her. I don't think he did, but that was just the way he was."

It was at FSU that Jim began testing some of the theories he had read on the psychology of crowds. "Apparently Hitler had sort of followed [Nietzsche's] belief that you could control crowds with just a few people in the room," says Chris, "so Jim decided that what we should do is go to the local traveling black revivalist tent meeting. They were slapping people on the head and curing them and all that stuff and raising a lot of money. So we were supposed to go into this tent, and we were strategically placed, four or five of us, and Jim was going to make the big move about 'heal me'; I forgot what it was, whether he was acting like he had a bad leg, or crippled. The idea was, when they couldn't 'heal' Jim, we were going to say, 'Hey, we want our money back! This is a fraud!' and start a riot and bust the show up. But instead, two bodyguards reached up and grabbed Jim and took him under the back of the tent outside. By the time we got around he was all beat up. That was the end of that one!"

That wasn't Jim's first or last experiment with crowd control, a subject which he pursued unrelentingly. "If Jim had a theory that a crowd had a unity and a cohesion and a single purpose and a mind of its own that might be discovered," explains Bryan Gates, "he wanted to work through it until he could find it."

Bryan tells of another incident that illustrates the point: "When Jim was at Florida State, we took him to, I think, the first football game he ever went to." (Actually, when they were sixteen, Jim and Jeff had attended the Army-Navy game in Philadelphia with their fathers, an event made memorable in Jeff's mind by Jim bypassing the long lines of uniformed army and navy men waiting to use the urinals and, to their great horror, calmly using the sink to relieve himself. Jeff, the only other person in the bathroom not in uniform, pretended not to know Jim.) "At the half-time," Gates continues, speaking of the FSU game, "Jim realized that the people seemed to be anticipating a show of some kind, and him having memorized some of the early comedy records that used to exist in the sixties, he saw the opportunity to provide the entertainment that this crowd was looking for." The group's seats were located right over one of doorways down into the stadium, and the roof of the exit provided a perfect stage for Jim to perform. "That stadium I think held thirty-five thousand people or more," says Gates, "so Jim was in direct proximity to maybe eight thousand people who could hear him without being amplified. And to watch this one human being, with no more training than to have memorized a comedy record, suddenly obtain the attention of eight, nine thousand people in an audience, get them all under his control, have them, in the short span of two to three minutes, essentially wrapped in the palm of his hand, was just an amazing thing. Only somebody who had his understanding of the psyche of individuals and crowds could've ever accomplished something like that." Unfortunately Jim's performance was cut short when his friends spotted the stadium guards making a beeline in Jim's direction. "We were able to get him out of there before they arrived," says Gates, "and saved him that particular night."

Unfortunately, Jim's experiments in manipulation extended to those he lived with, quickly creating an untenable situation. "I got along pretty well with Jim," remembers Chris, "but my brother and a couple of the others had terrible conflicts and confrontations with him. Some of them were pretty funny, but at the time I guess they were not so funny."

"There was a lot of tension in our house," Chris continues. "Jim was playing mind games on all of us, just sort of experimenting to see if he could get people to do things the way he wanted them done, if he could get people turned around, then kept a journal every day, just a spiral binder, of the results." Most of Jim's experiments were harmless enough, but in the same manner a mosquito constantly buzzing in your ear is harmless. "All Jim would buy is potatoes," says Chris, for example. "He would buy a bag of potatoes once a week and just boil potatoes and eat them. And then he would eat other people's food. We had big cabinets in the kitchen, and it ended up everyone bought padlocks and people were hiding their food from him. And I don't think he was doing it for any reason other than just to mess with us."

It certainly wasn't from the need to economize. Jim received money from both his parents and his grandparents, but he refused to spend any of it. Both Bryan and Chris vividly remember one of the coldest winters that part of Florida had ever seen, when Jim decided he wasn't going to help pay for fuel oil to heat the house. "The fuel oil guy would put in seventy-five gallons of fuel oil and charge us fifty bucks or whatever it was for the winter," Chris recalls. "It was probably thirty degrees in the house, bitter cold, and the guy finally showed up, but because we were college kids, he wanted to collect the money before he put the fuel in the tank. So everyone was digging into their pockets to come up with seven bucks each or whatever it was, and Jim said, 'I won't be needing any this year.'" Jim went on to calmly explain to his nonplused housemates that since his grandmother had recently sent him an electric blanket, he saw no reason why he should contribute money for heat he wouldn't need. This so angered the housemates that they all refused to chip in the money for fuel, and the tank remained empty. But this time, Jim's smugness was short lived. "That night we were all trying to keep warm, and he was sitting there with his blanket," says Chris. "So while he was sleeping, my brother got up and cut his cord."

As exasperating as Jim's behavior was at the best of times, it didn't even come close to what he was capable of saying or doing when he'd been drinking. Chris recalls homecoming night 1962, which started out badly for Jim and only got worse. The first bad news was that Jim would have to wear a tie to homecoming or he wouldn't be allowed to go. Since Jim felt a tie served no purpose whatsoever, he made his point by wearing the tie, but knotting it repeatedly until there was an enormous knot with only about an inch of tie hanging from it. He compounded this by insisting on wearing pointed-toe moccasins instead of dress shoes. Though this should have been sufficient indication that Jim was not going to be on his best behavior this evening, Chris made the mistake of leaving Jim alone with his date and his brother, Nick, while he and a friend went to play a little basketball. Chris and his friend returned a short time later to find all the glass from the front door laying in fragments in the front yard. Jim had apparently said something to Chris's date that Nick had considered so offensive that he had picked Jim up and thrown him through the front door, onto the lawn. "My brother was an ex-Marine, so he was kind of into that stuff," Chris explains. "Jim had been drinking all day, and we'd never seen him drunk before. He got really crazy."

"We all felt bad about it, including my brother," says Chris. The housemates took Jim to the football game with them, Jim drinking directly from a pint bottle throughout the game. Not wanting to bother with their intoxicated friend, the guys left Jim propped on a bench in front of the student union while they went to the homecoming party inside. They hadn't been there long when someone came in and told Nick Kallivokas, "You'd better get out there because your little brother is about to get in a fight with the football team," having mistaken Jim for Chris. By the time Nick got outside, Jim was standing on the bench where he'd been left, surrounded by members of the FSU football team, linemen who were known as The Magnificent Seven. "They were giants," remembers Chris, "and they all had their heads shaved in Mohawk haircuts. The team was called the Seminoles, but Jim was calling them the Semi-holes, and when my brother got there, Jim had his penis out and he was trying to urinate on them."

While Nick rescued Jim from near certain death at the hands of The Magnificent Seven, Jim was starting to feel the physical side effects of a day of drinking, so he was eventually sent home in a cab. When the housemates arrived home at two or three in the morning, they found Jim lying unconscious in the front yard, partially covered by the falling autumn leaves, looking as though he'd been beaten up. "He'd probably thrown up in the cab and the cab driver had roughed him up a little and left him on

First mug shot, Florida, 1963.

the ground," Chris speculates, "so he was pretty pathetic." Chris hadn't seen Jim drink often, "but when he did drink," Chris explains, "it was excessive. He'd go all the way out. I had never seen anyone, or not very often seen anyone, pass out from drinking, but I saw Jim do that a few times."

In addition to occasionally drinking to excess, Jim tended to take physical risks the others found anywhere from daring to just plain stupid, like taunting the football team or leaping between two automobiles as they were speeding side by side down the road. "When you knew Jim, you didn't think that Jim was going to live very long," Chris says. "I always felt that he was a risk-taker. We used to go to parties on Clearwater Beach that summer, [at] typical two-story apartments with wrought iron railings and maybe a pool in the courtyard. And Jim was always wanting to jump from one corner of the railing to another, where if you missed, you'd fall. I wouldn't call it a death wish, but he needed always to have risk."

One of the last adventures Chris remembers participating in with Jim involved an attempt to pay a visit to a girl. Ordinarily this would have been a relatively tame venture, but nothing was simple with Jim. "One of us met a girl somewhere, and she was going to a little Catholic boarding school in downtown Tallahassee," Chris relates, "a two- or three-story red brick building, just like an old-fashioned schoolhouse, and it had one of those fire escapes that was a slide, like a corkscrew. We'd been drinking a little, and we decided we were going to go see this girl. We got there about eleven o'clock at night. Somehow Jim had figured out that we were going to go up the slide and sneak in, sort of the equivalent of a panty raid I guess." It's amazing the truly stupid decisions that seem quite logical after a few drinks. "The slide had dew on it, and Tallahassee's red clay everywhere, so we decided to take off our pants so they wouldn't get dirty, because we had to crawl up the slide. So we laid our pants on a stump, and we got up the slide, and suddenly all the lights came on, and the girls started screaming, and the police came. They caught us with no pants on!" Luckily the police officers had a sense of humor about the matter. "The cops were kind of snickering," says Chris, "I guess they see a lot in a college town."

While Chris found life with Jim to be more fun than frustrating, it wasn't long before the older housemates had had their fill of Jim's bizarre and antagonistic behavior. "He was an impossible person to live with for most people," says Bryan Gates. "He took great delight in provoking people at all times, from early in the morning until late at night. It was fun for him and annoying to them. That was his personality at that time, and some people were able to tolerate it, but the majority of people just couldn't stand to be around him on a continuing basis because there was just too much of that. So, after probably between six and nine weeks, the majority of the guys there had had all that they could take and they voted that it was time for Jim to leave." The vote was taken in front of Jim, who responded by saying that he wasn't going to stay anywhere where he wasn't wanted, and he had plenty of places to go.

The first place Jim found looked promising, a log cabin outside of town which he was to share with another college student, a full-bearded young man of about twenty-three. But when Chris and Jim arrived at the house the next day to move Jim in, they found the area cordoned off with police tape. "The guy had committed suicide, Hemingway style," says Chris, "put a shotgun in his mouth and, with his toe, blew himself off. So of course Jim didn't move there."

Jim's next choice worked out better for many reasons, not the least of which was its highly desirable location. "On the main drag that leads up to the entrance of the college," Chris recalls, "there was a boarding house for girls, and behind it there was one of these old silver trailers with a black tar roof on it." Never one for missed opportunities, Jim moved into the trailer and took full advantage of the amenities. "He actually had a telescope he'd use," Chris laughs. Maybe not a spy *in* the house of love, but at least in its backyard.

The Morrisons had moved to Coronado, California, a suburb of San Diego, shortly after Jim graduated from high school, so Jim had not seen his family in close to three years, a separation which didn't seem to bother him a great deal and which he made no attempt to remedy. "The whole time I knew Jim," recalls Bryan Gates, "he would stay either at the Kallivokas house when he went back to Clearwater or with some other friend. He didn't go back to his grandparents' house at all. He was a real floater, not wanting to get bogged down into any commitment to spend time with his grandparents or anything of that nature. He hitchhiked many times back to Clearwater with me, and he spent most of his time seeing his girl-friend or hanging around with Chris and a couple of people they had known down there a year or two before."

Chris confirms Bryan's account, saying, "Because Jim didn't have much contact with his family, he came home and stayed with me a couple of times during the semester. My mother was an erstwhile writer, and she had this manuscript that she'd probably worked on for years, but she was never going to get it published as an historical reference book, which is what she wanted it to be. But Jim was very good at schmoozing her, so he read it and he told her how great it was. After that, as far as my mother was concerned, Jim just walked on water. He was welcome at our house any time."

"The initial impression I formed," says Bryan Gates of Jim's physical estrangement from his family at that time, "was that Jim was a heck of a lot happier to be living away from his parents than with them, and that he had a set of expectations that he had to meet in order to keep getting money—primarily that he was expected to stay in school. So he met the expectations to get the money, and that was that. Money would come with a set of instructions, most of which Jim ignored. I think his parents were under the impression that he was in much better housing than he really was, perhaps even living in a dorm," says Gates. "At that particular time, before I ultimately met them, my only impression of them was Jim spent a good bit of the time keeping the proverbial wool over their eyes so that he could do what he wanted to do."

During Bryan's last term at FSU, Jim decided that what he wanted to do was hitchhike to California with Bryan. "Florida State had gone from semesters to trimesters, which meant instead of getting out in June, as I thought I was going to, I was going to get out in April," says Bryan. "I had a job beginning in September, and didn't have anything particular to do to pass the time until the employment started. And Jim was aware of that, so sometime in late March or early April, he came up with the idea." Jim's father's ship was due to dock in San Diego shortly, so Clara Morrison had sent her son enough money to buy an airplane ticket to California so he could be on hand for the event. But Jim had a better plan. "What if I don't buy that ticket and instead we use that money to just hitch to California?" Jim asked Bryan. "I had some relatives out there that I hadn't seen for a while," says Gates, "so I said, 'You know, that's not a bad way to spend some time.' We planned to leave late April."

Jim wisely didn't inform his mother of his change in travel plans until he and Bryan were well on their way. "After we got going," says Bryan, "Jim called and told her that he had decided that he didn't want to get on an airplane and just zoom across the country without seeing anything or experiencing anything, he wanted to *feel* the United States, he wanted to *feel* his way across the country." What he *felt* at that moment, however, were the very tangible waves of maternal anger coming through the phone lines. "He was really beginning to feel comfortable being in charge of himself, I think," says Bryan, in retrospect, of Jim's attitude at the time. "He was getting more and more bold, and was about to shake off his own parental restraints. He hadn't done it yet, but that was part of the process. And he pretty well took the attitude that he was going to do it, and if she didn't like it, there wasn't too much she could do about it."

"The entire trip was a series of the sort of encounters that one would imagine based on Jim's proclivity to antagonize people and stir things up," recalls Gates. "The first real experience was his very urgent desire to go back and relive some times he had experienced in New Orleans; I believe he'd been there with his parents, and he'd been given a few moments to himself. That was very interesting to me, because of all things he had in mind, he wanted to stay in what could be characterized as a flophouse." When Jim found a hotel that seemed to be seedy enough to suit his requirements, "he was delighted to find that there was, in fact, a bare light-bulb hanging from the ceiling on one of those long, twisted wires, and an old mattress that had the ticking and the buttons on it," Bryan recalls. "He was just like a kid in the most bizarre candy shop you've ever seen. Everything he'd ever read about and wondered about was coming to life."

Once they'd gotten settled into flophouse life, Jim wanted to make a beeline for Bourbon Street. "The trip down Bourbon Street was fascinating to me," says Gates, "and I think very rewarding to Jim, as he began to encounter much of the kind of life he had been reading about and been led to believe existed, but had never experienced before; he was just absolutely fascinated with whatever oddities we encountered, and he wanted to keep on going and keep on going. 'The fringe,' as he called it, 'we have to press on into the fringe!'"

Jim and Bryan pressed on until they came across a series of bars that were "so much different from mainstream Bourbon Street—I'd never seen anything like them before," says Bryan. What Bryan and Jim had come across was a section of gay bars, more commonly referred to at the time as queer bars. Bryan was rather awed by the alternative lifestyle they'd stumbled across, while Jim was ecstatic, wanting to see more. "We had to move on, move on to other bars in that fringe area," Bryan continues. "One that we went into was called the Copper Skillet. It was the most unusual thing I had ever seen. There were a lot of people in dim light who were obviously very strange, but I kept focusing on the bartender and finally asked one of the other patrons whether this person was a male or a female. I absolutely could not tell, it had characteristics of both. It was explained to me that this was the drawing card for this particular bar, that this bartender was in fact, to a certain extent, a hermaphrodite, but one who capitalized on that and dressed and emphasized both the aspects of his or her conflicting characteristics. And to me that was the most fascinating edge of the underworld that Jim had discovered, that I'd ever encountered."

Bryan had to have known that Jim wouldn't be content to quietly slip in and out of these establishments without stirring up some kind of trouble. Shortly after they'd arrived at the Copper Skillet, Bryan heard Jim in distress from the other end of the bar where he'd gone to try his luck with one of the patrons. "It seems that he had convinced himself that an attractive young blonde lady had taken a fancy to him," says Gates. "Jim didn't realize that she was, in fact, there with other company. When he began to try to make time with this young lady, her female companion took decided umbrage at that, and he found himself being stuck with a little penknife about an eighth of an inch into his chest. Jim had just had his first encounter with what he liked to describe as 'the intensity of lesbian love.'"

The pair continued their journey across Louisiana and Texas to the little Mexican border town of Ciudad Juarez. "Jim was overjoyed to be going there," says Bryan. "He had read about so many of these authors and their experiences in Juarez. Just the idea of walking some of the same streets as his literary heroes had him filled with anticipation." Bryan was decidedly less thrilled than Jim was with their first sight of Juarez, which Bryan describes as "a pathetic, nasty little Mexican border town." But Jim was in his element.

The pair spent the day in and out of restaurants and bars, Jim trying to provoke people in his limited high school Spanish, Bryan reigning him in before any of the locals got tired enough of his antics to do him bodily harm. By evening, Jim was delighted to find that the hotel where they finally ended up was obviously full of prostitutes. Years earlier, when Jim had been living in Alameda, he and his friend Fud Ford read Jack Kerouac's *On the Road* together and subsequently spent hours fantasizing about, in Fud's words, "fucking whores." To Jim, it looked as though his fantasy might be coming true in Juarez. "Now he's hit the high time," says Bryan. "He's in a Juarez whorehouse."

As in the Copper Skillet in New Orleans, Jim quickly convinced himself that a woman, this one of obvious professional standing, had taken a personal interest in him. Although the woman was obviously entertaining clients, periodically disappearing for short amounts of time before reappearing to find the eager American boy still waiting for her, Jim was still convinced that this woman only had eyes for him, and soon he and Bryan would be invited to leave with her. "Of course, as dawn began to approach," says Bryan, "she made it abundantly clear to Jim that her fondness for him, like any other potential customer, revolved around the number of pesos in his pocket, and not his boyish charm. That was somewhat disenchanting for him."

Probably the only people stranger than those Bryan and Jim encountered at each of their stops were some of the people who offered them rides along the way. "About thirty miles west of New Orleans, we were picked up by a foursome who seemed ordinary enough," Gates recalls. "They wanted us in the backseat, so as the car leaves, there's six people in the car: two in the front seat, Jim and I sandwiched between the two in the back. And we'd gone along a ways when suddenly the fellow in the front passenger seat says, 'I guess you all didn't realize that we just got out of prison.'" Again, Jim was delighted, while Bryan was wary, not quite sure if they were being teased. But he was soon fairly certain that there was at least some foundation for concern when the man in the front seat turned around, the revolver in his hand pointed directly at the boys, and said, "You probably don't understand that what we were in prison for was murder." The group went on to insist that Jim and Bryan have a drink out of a big bottle of vodka they had in the car while their fate was decided. "You know it's just people like you that we could've murdered and gone to prison for," said the man with the gun, "and there's nothing to it but to do it."

"Jim is just absolutely going nuts, enjoying all of this so much," Bryan says, "and I am so absolutely horrified by it all that it's unbelievable." Fortunately for the two boys, it was at that point the driver came upon the turnoff that would take the supposed felons in the opposite direction their would-be murder victims were traveling. "So they stopped right there, at this intersection in the middle of nowhere," Gates recalls, "and told us, 'This is about as far as we're taking you boys—get out of here!'" The boys got out of the car, Jim rather more reluctantly than Bryan, and spent the night by the side of the road, waiting for another ride and debating the experience they'd just survived. "Jim's overall reaction to the whole thing," Gates says, "was that they had been fun-loving people who just had a perverse way of having fun with us. My idea was they were probably a bunch of psychotics and we were on the borderline of having been murdered."

It was this fundamental difference in their personalities that got the boys into and out of another bizarre situation when they encountered a woman outside of Phoenix who said she was heading in their direction and offered to give them a lift. Jim was enthusiastic at the prospect of being given a ride by an attractive female, but Bryan sensed there was something not quite right about the situation. As usual, Jim's enthusiasm prevailed. But they hadn't gone far when the woman announced that her reasons for picking them up had, indeed, been somewhat less than altruistic.

"'You know I didn't pick you two boys up to take you to San Diego,'" Bryan remembers the woman telling them. "She says, 'I'm a woman and I want you boys to come back to my apartment, there's some things there I want you to do for me.' Jim was immediately enthralled, his imagination soaring at the possibilities of what might lay ahead of them. Bryan was slightly less enthusiastic. "She made a right turn, off the route," says Gates, "and all I could see in my mind was some giant guy with a club wanting to relieve us of what little money we had left in the world." Jim, meanwhile, was promising the woman he'd do anything she asked, anything at all. No one ever did get to see just what that "anything" might've encompassed, though, since Bryan grabbed the steering wheel and ordered the woman to pull over and let them out. "That in a nutshell was the answer to how Jim and I got along so well," laughs Gates. "He relied on me to keep him from going over the deep end, and I absolutely and totally enjoyed his love of life and his enthusiasm for every kind of bizarre situation that existed."

Jim's mother was less than impressed by Jim's willful exuberance. "He had indicated to me as we approached [San Diego] that his mom was a navy wife," remembers Gates, "and that she was hard to deal with—too prim, too proper, too much emphasis on the formalities of life that had no real meaning to him." When the boys finally reached the Morrison home, Clara was less than thrilled to find that Jim had brought someone with him, something he hadn't bothered to tell her before, though she still treated Bryan in a polite, if distant manner. "I was a nuisance," says Bryan. "She hadn't expected Jim to have anybody with him, and her wishes had been defied as far as him hitchhiking across the country, and I was a party to that defiance." Jim, typically, reverted to a younger, more vulnerable version of his brash self in the presence of his mother. "She was clearly a strict, somewhat domineering, but not unpleasant person," Bryan remembers, "very intelligent and very strong willed, as Jim was. She just wanted him to conform to her expectations."

There was still several weeks until Captain Morrison's ship was to dock in San Diego, and it took only a few days of being with his mother and siblings for Jim to become restless and bored. Instead of waiting for his father in San Diego, Jim and Bryan decided to use the rest of the money they had and take the bus to Los Angeles to "look for some more experiences." Clara Morrison's adamant protests went unheeded, and Jim and Bryan were soon staying with Bryan's two cousins in L.A.

"For the next two or three weeks," says Bryan, "as far as Jim was concerned, we were in Nirvana. Four guys just going anywhere and everywhere throughout the high grounds and low grounds of Los Angeles, everywhere from sleaze clubs to art movies to Pershing Square." Pershing Square was the southern California equivalent of Speaker's Corner in London's Hyde Park. "Jim was absolutely fascinated by all these wannabe oracles, giving advice and exhorting crowds. He hadn't been there more than two or three hours when he's up on a soapbox and has a couple dozen people around him, exhorting them to become true believers and all that sort of thing. He had no fear, he had no reluctances or embarrassments, that was his world."

One of Bryan's cousins was in the process of applying for civil service work, so the foursome spent a good deal of time around the employment office. One day the group discovered, much to their amazement and chagrin, that Jim had signed up to be a farm worker in the pea-picking fields outside of Los Angeles, saying he wanted to practice his Spanish with these migrant workers. "He was on his way and would have gone," says Bryan, "but my cousins and I knew that these people were not exactly the fun-loving sort that Jim was thinking they were, and it was very likely that with his penchant for provoking people and unsettling the norm, he might have been seriously injured had we let him go, so we talked him out of it. But he certainly was ready to go."

Jim's taste of Nirvana didn't last long. "His mother called him and made it clear that he absolutely, unequivocally was expected back in San Diego," says Bryan, "that his father was coming in, Jim would be at that ship, and there were no choices this time. So my cousins and I packed him up in the car and got him back down to San Diego."

Bryan and his cousins stayed around to watch the captain's ship come in. "Jim, I believe, was genuinely glad to see him," says Gates, "probably hadn't seen him in two and a half to three years. There seemed to be no sort of animosity or tension. He was just a young son glad to see a father that he hadn't seen in awhile." Captain Morrison politely thanked Bryan and his cousins for "seeing to Jim's good times," and the group parted ways: Bryan back to Clearwater, his cousins back to Los Angeles, and Jim to spend the next few weeks with his family in Coronado.

Jim was back in Clearwater near the end of July 1963, though Bryan didn't see him again until Jim and Mary Werbelow attended Bryan's wedding that September. "I had a certain amount of trepidation about him coming to the wedding," says Bryan, "knowing Jim's penchant for overturning apple carts of propriety and formality. But as a matter of fact, he was an absolute model, genuinely interested in the ceremony." Bryan concedes that Jim's decorum could, to a large extent, be attributed to Mary's presence. "He was a different person in those years when he was around Mary," recalls Gates. "She was his settling influence, and much of his shenanigans were set aside while he was in her company. So after the wedding, when he took his leave, my understanding was that he was headed back up to Florida State to do some more time, Mary was back in high school, and I had my own separate life to get rolling with."

Though his academic enthusiasm was lukewarm and he had enrolled in the minimum number of classes possible for his last few months at FSU, Jim's involvement in the school production of *The Dumbwaiter,* in which he was cast in one of the play's two roles, truly captured his attention. The play's other actor, Keith Carlson—who would be the first to experience Jim's mercurial onstage presence—remembers Jim as being talented, but unpredictable: "Jim was interesting to work with. Every night waiting for the curtain to go up, I had no idea what he was going to do. He played scenes and delivered lines with an inflection that seemed

Onstage in *The Dumbwaiter*, Florida State University.

totally unmotivated, or at least unexpected. There was a constant current of apprehension, a feeling that things were on the brink of lost control. There was no obscenity during any of the performances, but with Jim, we just never knew." Indeed, with Jim, no one ever did know what to expect in any situation. Unpredictability had become his only predictable quality.

In high school, Jim had confided in Jeff Morehouse that he didn't feel comfortable with who he was, to a large extent, he said, because he felt he didn't know where he was going, he had no vision for the future. But now the pathway was starting to look a little clearer. Jim's experiences onstage, the advice of his cinema professor at FSU, Jim's own sweet memories of his experiences in Los Angeles with Bryan and his cousins, as well as his desire to get away from the restrictions he felt his grandparents were imposing on him, all combined to fuel Jim's desire to go back to Los

Angeles and attend the film school at UCLA. He officially applied for a transfer to California—without his parent's consent—planning to start classes at UCLA at the beginning of the year.

In January 1964, Jim was back with his family in Coronado, preparing for his move to L.A. Though Steve and Clara still objected to this decision, their son was immovable. Jim made an effort to take an interest in his father's work by joining him for a day of maneuvers in the Pacific aboard the *Bon Homme Richard*, one of the largest aircraft carriers in the world, of which Steve was in command. While Jim did cut his thick, wavy hair for the occasion, his father had the ship's barber cut it shorter, matching the captain's own military style. Jim bore this and the rest of the afternoon in silence, though he later expressed deep bitterness when relating the story. To Jim, his father had become the intermittent joke to

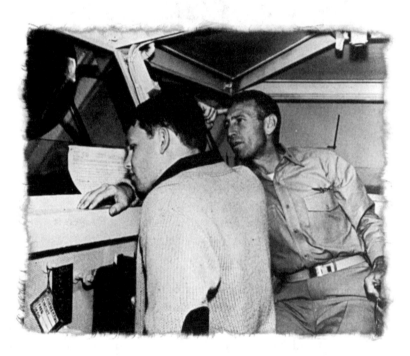

Jim and his father on the bridge of the USS *Bon Homme Richard*, January 1964.

his mother's constant punchline. Captain Morrison may have ruled 3,200 men aboard the *Bonnie Dick*, but in the Morrison household, Jim liked to tell friends, he was no more than the guy who took out the garbage.

A week later Jim Morrison once again arrived in Los Angeles. This time he intended to stay.

"Jim? Billy's ready for your interview if you're done with your questionnaire." Jim smiled at the pretty secretary, a hint of a leer automatically curling the corners of his mouth. He looked at the last remaining question on the page: FAMILY INFO (names of parents, brothers, and sisters). Jim rose to go meet Billy, his eyes still on the questionnaire before him. Hesitating a split second before making his decision, he leaned over and filled in the remaining space with one word: "Dead."

Kindergarten, the first day of school at Cambridge Elementary. There were lots of red shiny cement steps leading up to the kindergarten room. There was a tile mosaic of some kind of animals on the wall by the door. I had never been to school before; I was scared. The other kids who also clutched their mothers' hands seemed very loud to me and they all knew each other, or so I thought. One little girl with carrot red hair and freckles was running away from the door where the teacher stood, but she didn't escape. She fell down and scraped her knee. It started to bleed, but she didn't cry. She kind of yelled, no tears, just bellowed.

T hat little girl was Pamela Courson.
Charlene Estes Enzler's written account of her first day of kindergarten at Cambridge Elementary School in Orange, California, seems to sum up not only Charlene's first day of school but also her classmate Pamela Courson's entire future in the school system: the center of attention for all the wrong reasons and desperate to escape. An odd juxtaposition for a little girl from upstate Weed whose father had so completely embraced the academic system in his own youth. But then again, everything about Pamela Susan Courson's life seems inexplicable, right down to her place of birth.

Though geologists say that California's Mt. Shasta, located near the Oregon border, is nothing more than an inactive volcano, no amount of geological statistics or geographical surveys can dim true believers' notions that the mountain and its surrounding area is now and has always been a center for the sacred and the occult. Stories abound of the Great Spirit that dwells above the tree line, of fairies that flit through the foliage on tiny wings, mysterious lights appearing and disappearing, of otherworldly music that seems to spring from the air at odd moments and just as quickly fades away.

The tiny lumber town of Weed lies in the shadow of the great and mysterious mountain. In a letter to her family, a visitor to the area in 1946 wrote of Weed: *The people in this small town are odd. Even though I had no experiences to speak of the first few days, I was convinced that there was something around the Mountain, because I never felt alone. But it wasn't the nicest type of feeling. I felt as though I were being watched. The stillness was unpleasant, too full of something unseen. I think there may be peculiar forces in the ground . . .*

Yet to residents of Weed, there was more of the mundane than the mystical to life there in the early part of the century. Primarily a man's town, built by men who mastered the forest and braved the elements, there is even today a certain nostalgia evident in Weed, with buildings and ideas little changed from the time Abner Weed founded the town in the late 1800s. In fact, the town itself was still a teenager when Columbus Brymer Courson brought his family there from Texas in the early 1900s when his son, Columbus Jr., was nine.

Though he would later be commonly known as Corky, the only documented evidence of this nickname during Columbus Junior's youth is in his freshman yearbook, where a pensive looking "Cork" is pictured with other members of the Weed High School basketball team, boys with first names like Hotty, Greek, Zip, Shorty, Sophy, Pansy, and Tiny. Either the freshman boys of 1932 believed in nicknames or the parents of Weed had one collectively vicious sense of humor when it came to naming their children.

Tall and athletically built, Courson was a strikingly handsome young man with sandy red hair, a dimpled chin, and piercing blue eyes, who preferred to be called by his middle name, Brymer. A classic overachiever, Brymer was almost impossibly active in school activities and seemed a natural leader. Not only did he play saxophone in the school orchestra, but he directed the group as well. He was not only an excellent student—and member of the Scholarship Society—but he was president of his class two years in a row. He was a member of the Student Council and acted as business manager for the yearbook editorial staff. A gifted athlete, Brymer was president of Block W, the school's athletic club, and lettered in baseball, football, and basketball. "*The flashing play of Kerkes and Barbieri and the brilliant, consistent work of Courson made the 'B' team a contender and threat to the other league teams,*" cheered the school's annual, the *White and Gold,* of the boys' sophomore year basketball efforts. "*Much is expected of the members of the 'B' team next year.*" As predicted, during the following two years Brymer was leading the "A" team.

With intelligence, good looks, and a natural aura of leadership and charisma going for him, Brymer was a young man with prospects, a hot property and a good catch. And he seemed to know it, too. In the "Senior Class Will" printed in the *White and Gold* for the Weed High School class of 1936, he writes, "I, Brymer Courson, leave my conceit to Norman Shelton."

Either this was simply Courson's way of poking fun at his naturally reserved personality, or perhaps maturity and his stint in the navy did something to tame this supposed feeling of self-importance. Either way, friends who knew him as an adult describe Courson as "charming and bashful" and "handsome, with a certain way about him." It was no doubt these qualities that first attracted his future wife.

Five years Corky's junior, Pearl Marie Schmidt—Penny, as she was more commonly known—was a midwestern girl from Chicago, pretty, plump, and vivacious, qualities that seemed to captivate the disciplined and somewhat dignified navy man. Never at a loss for words, Penny had tremendous charm and sea-colored eyes that mesmerized men with their extraordinary sparkle. Corky was no exception.

Very little is known about the couple's early days. Even their closest friends draw a blank when questioned about the couple's background and seem surprised to realize that they know very little of their friends before their arrival in Orange in the early 1950s, and what they do know does not hold up well under scrutiny.

For instance, Madeline Andresen, whose husband, Charles, worked with Corky in the Orange Public Schools, remembers quite clearly Penny's version of her marriage to Columbus Courson: "Corky was in the navy," Mrs. Andresen recalls Penny telling her. "He was in Chicago in flight training, probably doing carrier landings—they had an aircraft carrier in Lake Michigan and it was just an easy, safe place to teach these guys to fly on carriers. And that is where Corky met Penny. They were married in Chicago when Penny was only sixteen."

Despite this account of their marriage, a search of Cook County's records between 1939 and 1950 reveals no evidence of a marriage between Columbus Brymer Courson and Pearl Marie Schmidt during that time, nor is there any such marriage recorded at Great Lakes Naval Training Station or its surrounding counties.

There also seems to be conflicting accounts regarding the biological paternity of Pamela's older sister, Judy, who was born in Chicago in 1941. While the Andresens have no knowledge of Judy's biological father being anyone other than Columbus Courson, Preach Lyerla, a close friend and co-worker of Corky's who also taught in the Orange school system, remembers that Judy's parentage used to provide fuel for fights between the siblings. "They threw that at each other quite often," Preach recalls of the often fierce conflicts that regularly erupted between Judy and Pamela, five years her junior.

But however and whenever Corky and Penny met and were subsequently married, and whatever the circumstances of their elder daughter's birth, what is indisputable is that Corky, who had joined the Naval Reserves after the war, brought his family home to Weed in April 1946, just eight months before Pamela's arrival; he was twenty-seven years old, Penny twenty-three. There was nothing remarkable about Penny's pregnancy, and she gave birth to her second daughter on December 22, 1946, after twenty hours of labor. Filling out the birth certificate the next day, Penny listed her occupation as homemaker, her husband's as a graduate student at UC Berkeley.

Although Pamela's birth in Weed would be viewed by most as nothing extraordinary, nineteen years later Jim Morrison, who had a tendency to find symbolism everywhere he looked, would read much into the event. While Jim also found significance in the fact that both his father and Pam's were navy men as well as in his birthday and Pam's being only days apart in December, the thing that Morrison found most compelling was the proximity of Pamela's birthplace to Mt. Shasta with all its attendant secrets and sagas.

All of the Indian and occult lore surrounding the Great Mountain fascinated Morrison, but he was particularly drawn to the Indian legend claiming that ancient Lizard People had built a massive underground city that extended below the mountain to escape a major Pacific coast meteor shower. The city, a series of connected tunnels shaped like a lizard, was said to have its head in the heart of Los Angeles, its tail under the city of Weed, forever joining the two cities. Jim felt very strongly that because of Pamela's genesis in Weed and her eventual migration to Los Angeles, where the two met, the legend linking the two cities was yet another in the series of signs that he and Pamela had been destined to find each other, were meant to be linked together forever.

But it was not only the union of Los Angeles and Weed that appealed to Morrison. The story of the mythical creatures that were said to have inhabited the underground city also captivated him. According to the legend, the Lizard People were the first inhabitants of the American continent and had colonies all over the Pacific coast. They were said to have revered the lizard and named themselves after the species because they recognized reptiles as a symbol of longevity and control. Inclined to peace and agriculture, they were much further advanced culturally and

Cambridge Elementary School, Orange, CA.

intellectually than modern human beings, characteristics that Morrison particularly admired.

While it's easy to shrug off such a fanciful tale, Morrison seemed to find it enthralling. Seen by many as a somewhat mythical creature himself, Morrison seemed to feel a kinship with the Lizard People. References to reptiles appeared often in his writings over the years, and he jokingly declared himself the lizard king, investing himself with all the powers he imagined would go along with such a position. However lightly ascended, it was a throne he would never be allowed to abdicate.

"Boy, mom, is Pam in trouble *again!*" Paul Andresen was in the same sixth grade class as Pamela Courson at Cambridge Elementary School in Orange and would often come home with accounts of the girl's latest acts of insubordination. "Oh, lord, what did she do now?" Paul's mother recalls asking in exasperation. Apparently on this day Pamela had been throwing rocks in the school parking lot and managed to break the window of a teacher's car. "I guess she was in deep doo-doo over that," chuckles Mrs. Andresen as she remembers the incident.

Pamela (fourth from right) with her
Brownie troop, around 1954.

"Deep doo-doo" had quickly become an everyday state for Pamela
Courson. From her first day of kindergarten when Charlene Enzler
remembers Pamela making an unsuccessful break for freedom, the skinny,
freckle-faced redhead had been making waves. Tandy Martin's mother had
compared the young Jim Morrison to "a leper," and Pamela seemed to
have made an equally ignoble impression on the parents of her classmates.
"My mother *hated* Pam!" recalls Charlene. "She once called her a 'bad
seed.'" Harsh words, considering Mrs. Estes was the leader of Pamela's
Brownie troop!

Charlene remembers those days when her mother was the Brownie
leader, constantly frustrated by the young Pamela. For one thing, Pamela
would never wear the uniform that Charlene concedes was "ugly, dull
brown material with no shape, no style, no saving grace." While she
acknowledges that Pam may not have even owned a uniform, Charlene
suspects that Pamela simply "had the good sense or disposition to pretend
it was dirty each week."

Then there was Pamela's complete indifference to group activities.
"We would all be inside working on a Brownie project and Pamela would
be outside picking dandelions. . . . She was like a butterfly flitting around."

says Charlene. "She couldn't be still, and she just wouldn't go with the group. No matter what we were doing, she'd be doing something else. If we were all holding hands, she wouldn't hold hands. If we were all walking in a line, she'd have to walk on the side or walk backwards!" Enzler says, still exasperated at the memory. "I don't remember her being verbally confrontational in any way, like saying 'No! I'm not going to do that!' She'd just go do whatever she wanted to do. [Her indifference] didn't seem malicious, it was just the way she was."

Preach Lyerla also remembers Pamela as being an insidious sort of rebel, the more subtle of the two siblings. "Judy had the temper and was easily set off emotionally. She could get into trouble, but knew how to kiss it up to find her way out," Lyerla recalls. "Pamela was much more hardheaded. She was the type that would challenge, but she wouldn't take you on toe to toe and yell at you or anything." Unlike her sister, Pamela seemed to have the patience to wait and observe those around her, assessing their idiosyncrasies and then quietly setting about using that knowledge for her own ends. "Whatever infuriated you the most, she would do it," says Lyerla, "but she wasn't brazen or bold about it. And Pam wouldn't apologize either."

"She was like a shadowy figure," adds Enzler. "She was sort of a guerrilla attention-getter: Strike, get the attention, then *whsst*—she was gone!"

But rebels, even those without malicious intent, usually pay a price for their independence, and Pamela was no different. "She was on the outside of us somehow and never played 'with' us, but seemed to be in a world of her own," says Enzler. Charlene looks at a photo of the Brownie troop, her mother beaming in the background, her own hair twisted into tight little curls. "Pamela seems so solemn in that picture and yet she seemed to be a part of the group, to be like the rest of us were, so innocent and pretty." But appearances are often deceiving. "Something always set her apart from us; she was never quite like us," Enzler continues. "She always seemed alone to me, and that's always the way I remember her."

Pamela's physical appearance also set her apart from the crowd. "If someone was really different, you just stayed away from them or ignored them," observes Enzler of behavior at the elementary school level. Painfully thin, with hair the color of an open flame and extremely white skin relieved only by legions of rusty freckles, Pamela's appearance, with or without her ungovernable nature, certainly qualified her as "really different."

"She sat in the corner a *lot*." recalls Enzler ruefully. "I can remember thinking about her sitting there because that hair—that hair always stood out with everybody—that little redhead sitting in the corner by herself with her back to us. Everyone else is whooping it up and having fun and she's sitting in the corner all alone."

In his own way, Pamela's father was also a standout in the conservative city of Orange, located about half an hour southwest of Los Angeles. Preach Lyerla, a longtime resident, remembers Orange County in the fifties as ". . . a very strange place. I mean, we were to the right of Buckley!" He laughs as he recalls the typical reaction he and Corky would receive when others in that Republican enclave first learned of their political affiliation. "[Corky] and I would get invited to parties and people would say, 'Look, look! A Democrat! There's two of 'em! They're liberals! Oh my god—don't breathe around them!'"

But no matter what their political views, no one could find fault with Corky's strong work ethic. From the time they had moved to Orange, Corky had worked hard to provide for his small family, not only as a teacher in the Orange County schools and a member of the Naval Reserves, but also by taking part-time jobs as a short order cook at fast food joints and at nearby Disneyland to help make ends meet. It may be this busy schedule that accounts for the fact that Pamela's father never seemed to be a public presence in her life. Her mother's evident absence from the scene, however, seems more of a mystery.

"I can remember Pamela being very excited once because her dad was going to be at a school function," says Enzler, "but I never saw her mother once—never." Penny's seeming lack of interest in her daughter's activities tended to irk the other mothers who usually shared the responsibilities of helping out at classroom or Brownie activities. Charlene's mother, who seemed to have acted as Pamela's chauffeur on more occasions than anyone else, probably had the most reason to grumble. One incident in particular still rankles.

It seems that one day while Mrs. Estes was driving Pamela home from a Brownie meeting, Pamela decided she'd see what would happen if she tugged at a hole in the velvety fabric lining the ceiling of the Estes' "woody" station wagon, a lovingly maintained car of which Mr. Estes was particularly proud. The result of Pamela's curiosity was the entire head-liner hanging in ruins. "I can clearly remember sitting there watching her rip a strip and thinking, 'Oh, my mom's gonna kill me!' I immediately took responsibility because I was sitting there," says Charlene. "But it wasn't that Pam sat there and thought, 'I'm going to ruin this car,'" Enzler reflects now, "She just saw a hole and started ripping without thinking, 'Gosh, if I do this, maybe I'll get in trouble.'" It was typical of Pamela's mentality to follow her impulses without thinking of the consequences for herself or

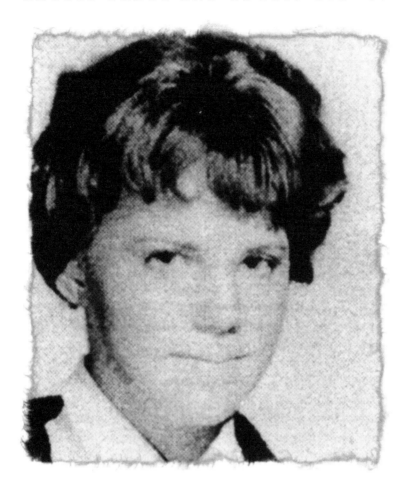

Pamela at Yorba Linda Junior High School.

others, a character trait that Enzler summed up by saying, "Pamela was the kind of child who, if she saw that you had built a house out of blocks, would come over and knock it down, not to be mean but just to see the blocks fall."

In general, Orange in the 1950s was typical of many smaller conservative towns all across the country. For the most part, husbands went to work each morning, leaving their wives at home to tend to the children and the house. Between chores, women would often visit their neighbors for a quick cup of coffee and a little gossip before getting home to prepare the evening meal. After dinner, children would play outside with siblings and neighbors until it was dark and their parents called them in for baths and bed. It was a way of life no one thought to question, as snug as an old pair of slippers, reliable as the daily sunrise. The Coursons seemed to be the exception to this comfortable routine.

Barbara Stewart Noble, whose family lived next door to the Coursons on Mayfair Avenue, remembers well the evenings she spent as a child playing outside with the other neighborhood children—but not Judy and Pam. "They stayed in the house a lot," she says. "[We'd] play at night outside in the summertime, but I don't remember them being part of our play at night or anything."

The Courson children's failure to interact with other children, to stay behind closed doors and not form friendships, invited much speculation on the part of neighbors and Corky's co-workers as to the source of this behavior. All seemed to agree that there was some sort of problem in the home, but no one seemed to know what it was. Fueling this speculation was the fact that both girls had developed a serious truancy problem, despite their father's position in the city's school system. Barbara Noble recalls that in stopping by the Courson house to walk the girls to school in the morning, "Sometimes Penny would say, 'They're not ready yet, they're not going, and they're sick.'" Barbara's mother blamed Pamela and Judy's truancy on Corky at the time, saying that because he was a teacher, his children should be more disciplined. Most, however, were quick to lay the blame on Penny's seeming disinterest. Barbara Noble tends to take a softer view. "I just don't understand how it ever happened, whether [Corky] was just completely overwhelmed with Penny . . . I just don't know."

For whatever reason, by the time Pamela reached high school in 1960, she had no close friends, a history of serious attendance problems, and a record of indifference when it came to class participation. Charlene Enzler recalls that in gym class, Pamela would do anything to get out of wearing the ugly, stiff uniforms the class required. "We didn't have to 'dress out' when we had our monthly 'friend,'" says Charlene. "Pam seemed to have a lot of those monthly friends. The worst part was that you had to yell out 'Menstruating!' during roll call when your name was called, but I guess that didn't bother her too much. She would rather humiliate herself that way than by wearing her gym clothes."

Enzler isn't sure whether this obstinacy on Pamela's part had more to do with her unwillingness to conform to class regulations, or rather that the unbecoming uniform simply offended Pamela's innate sense of style. Even then, fashion did seem to be a big part of Pamela's life. While her dress was always in vogue, unfortunately what was in vogue for the rest of southern California was not necessarily acceptable in Orange. Preach Lyerla recalls, "Pamela at a social event—she would stop the party! People would just look at her because she was wearing the type of clothing that nobody else would dare to. Whatever it was back in the sixties, well that was what she was wearing. But she was always two or three years ahead of what was coming out in Orange County." Lyerla says that Pamela would also try to emulate paintings of big-eyed urchins that were popular at the time. "She was very white and she wore stark white makeup, with the sorrowful stress on the eyes," he says. "She certainly had a mind of her own and was very different."

Another striking thing about Pamela was her sometimes seemingly painful thinness. Very little was known about eating disorders at the time, and even less acknowledged. However, one of Pamela's junior high school teachers unwittingly gave a perfect description of the type of psychological trauma typically attributed to anorexic teens in stressful home situations when he said, "Sometimes it looked to me as though she were trying to make herself disappear."

While most of her classmates ostracized her for being so exceedingly different, Annette Burden liked Pamela for the very fact that she wasn't a typical teen. "Everyone else I knew was just Orange County, run-of-the-mill people," she says, "but I thought Pamela was absolutely great! She was a wild one and just had a wonderful sense of style and adventure, with this spark that was so exciting and fun." Annette remembers that it was Pamela who taught her to smoke and, when Annette ran away from home, it was to Pamela's she went for a night's lodging. "I just stayed there one night," Burden recalls. "Pamela sneaked me into the house. She was the person you'd do that with, she'd understand that you were rebelling and celebrate it."

Annette also remembers being enthralled by Pamela's acerbic wit. "I adored her wry sense of humor. To me she had the appeal of Dorothy Parker—incredibly quick witted, intelligent, observant, cynical, and oozing disdain." She laughs at the memory of it. "She sort of talked out of the side of her mouth a little bit, like she was doing an aside. She'd make some really hilarious snide comment and her mouth would hardly move."

Annette scoffs at those who question Pam's intelligence based solely on her poor performance in school. "I thought she was really smart," says Burden, "but maybe other people didn't because she had that kind of mysterious thing about her. But I knew she was smart because she was so funny, her humor was so wry." Charlene Enzler sat next to Pamela in several of their high school classes and agrees that Pamela, much like the teenage Jim Morrison, was quite capable of doing her schoolwork but

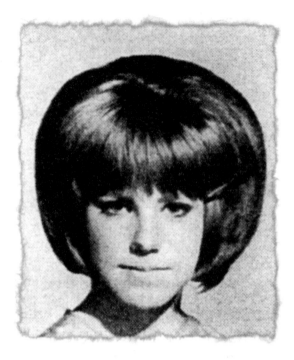

Her photo appears in the Orange High School yearbook in 1964 though Pamela was no longer a student there.

completely indifferent to getting good grades. "She was extremely intelligent—I know, because I saw her papers. She'd do something just brilliant, but then ruin it by drawing pictures all over it so it was exclusively hers and didn't look like anybody else's. She could do the work, she just wasn't *interested* in doing the work." Preach Lyerla agrees and is shocked at the suggestion that Pamela wasn't very bright. "My god, no! I'd say that the only thing I could agree with is that she was a little dingy at times, but we all are. Actually, I've had students in the past who were like Pamela, quite intelligent, but they just have no desire to go along with the same program that everybody wants them to."

Class pictures at Orange High School were taken at the end of one year for distribution at the beginning of the next. Therefore, photos of the 1962–63 junior class were taken in early 1962, when those students were actually at the end of their sophomore year. The photo of Pamela Courson taken for this yearbook shows a typical-looking teenager with the bubble bouffant hairdo that most of the other girls were sporting. "We used to tease our hair into a snarled mass and then use a whole can of Aqua Net hairspray to hold it in place," laughs Charlene Enzler as she cringes at her own photo in the yearbook. But the photo of Pamela that prematurely marks her as a junior at Orange High School doesn't even come close to the reality of her appearance during what would be her last year at the school.

"In high school, conformity was big," says Charlene. She remembers that Pamela, while not exactly blending in with the crowd, still tended to dress in somewhat the same manner as the other girls in her sophomore class. "We all wore pastels and plaids, with full skirts and starched petticoats," Enzler explains, "but suddenly in our junior year, here was Pamela dressed all in black, her once-red hair dyed jet black as well." While beatniks may have been prowling New York's East Village for years by that time, they hadn't yet made it to Orange County. Pamela Courson was their first.

The last conversation Charlene had with Pamela took place in the nurse's office at Orange High School sometime in 1963 and gave Charlene a clue to this startling change in Pamela's appearance. Aside from some classes in common, Charlene had stayed away from Pamela for the most part through junior high and high school, never forgetting the girl's odd and somewhat destructive behavior from childhood. It was quite surprising, then, for Charlene to find herself in a conversation with Pamela Courson and realize that even though she was different from most of the kids in Orange, Pamela was also quite nice.

Pamela was wearing her usual beatnik outfit, and her hair (by this time back to her natural color) was worn long and parted straight down the middle "like a hippie," says Charlene. "Pam said she told them she had cramps, but really she just didn't want to be in school," Enzler recalls of Pamela's reasons for being in the nurse's office that day. This certainly didn't surprise Charlene, but she found the rest of their conversation quite unsettling.

Pamela told Charlene that she had been spending a lot of time at the Rendezvous Ballroom in Balboa, a tiny oceanfront outpost of Newport Beach about fifteen miles south of Orange. At the Rendezvous, Pamela said, she had met a lot of "interesting and very cool people." Charlene recalled thinking that these weekend sojourns seemed typical of Pamela, but all the same, Enzler was a little awed that Pamela's parents would allow their daughter not only to go to the Rendezvous, but to go there alone at night. Tammie Griffith, another of Pamela's classmates, puts Charlene's feelings in perspective by saying, "For any of us to go four miles to Oscar's Drive-In was just incredible, and even then we had to have our parents take us."

But in discussing the Rendezvous with Charlene, Pamela "made it

The Rendezvous Ballroom.

sound like the neatest place she had ever been," says Enzler. "She talked about how neat it was at the beach at night with all these really cool people, and about how the Rendezvous had live bands, and there were a lot of boys there. I thought to myself, 'My mom would *never* let me go near that place!'"

More startling to Charlene even than the fact of Pamela's going to the Rendezvous (and Charlene's realization that Pamela probably had to hitchhike to get there) was Pamela's revelation that she'd gotten drunk. "In those days it was a big deal," says Charlene, "and even if I would have done such a thing, I couldn't even imagine discussing it with someone, because it was considered a cheap, trashy thing to do. *Those* girls did it."

While the Rendezvous undoubtedly attracted its share of *those* girls, for the most part it was a typical teen hangout, "Deliciously dark and smoky and evil," as Annette Burden describes it, "but basically pretty innocent." Though the Rendezvous eventually burned to the ground (ironically, on the night the Cindermen were heading the bill), for years after it was originally constructed in 1930, the oceanfront club was the hub of activity in the area, and Balboa, with its nearby amusement park and the Rendezvous Ballroom as its focal points, had eventually become southern

California's answer to Fort Lauderdale. Annette Burden describes the scene well: "The Rendezvous Ballroom was like Oz to every teenager in Orange County. Parents thought the teen 'scene' in Newport and Balboa happened only during Easter week, but it happened year round at the Rendezvous Ballroom. You'd go there to hear surf bands like Dick Dale and the Deltones, to act real cool while doing the surfer stomp. For Orange County kids of the time, the Rendezvous was a precursor to Woodstock. That's when we first felt the excitement of knowing we really were different from our parents and shared feelings with our whole generation."

Close by the Rendezvous were beatnik hangouts with names like The House of Socrates and Sid's Blue Beat. Since the Rendezvous catered mostly to the surfer scene, it is most likely at coffeehouses such as these that Pamela first picked up the beatnik influence that she brought back to Orange.

Dressing up like a beatnik and spending her nights making the scene did nothing to help Pamela's already disastrous school performance. Corky was now principal of Cerro Villa Junior High School. Though he had an ironclad policy for himself and his staff that all personal problems were left at home, his daughter's behavior often called for immediate attention. Preach Lyerla, who worked closely with Corky at that time, remembers, "I would walk into the office and he would be many times trying to soothe the brow of the people down at Orange High School—'Please let her stay another day' or something. He was constantly on parent conference time with her."

Despite Corky's efforts, Pamela's chronic truancy, combined with poor academic performance and difficult social interactions, prompted the school board to request her transfer. As a result, Pamela left Orange High School in her junior year and inexplicably transferred out of the district altogether, to Capistrano Union High School about twenty miles south of Orange. While Capistrano reluctantly confirms that Pamela Courson did transfer there for her senior year, they concede that she did not graduate.

Apparently restless in Orange, Pamela seemed to have set her sights on Los Angeles. Like her younger sister, Judy had also been transferred out of Orange High School in her sophomore year. In Judy's case, however, the action had been even more abrupt, coming in the middle of the school year. "She left because she couldn't get along with the peer group and she was teased," surmises Barbara Stewart Noble of her classmate's sudden departure. After graduating from nearby Fullerton High School, Judy had moved on to the big city and was making ends meet with odd jobs and occasional work as a model. There was very little Corky and Penny could do to dissuade Pamela from joining her. Relations with her parents had been strained for some time. "I don't think that you could ever say they were really on good terms with Pam from the time that she was fifteen on," comments Preach Lyerla. "They kind of co-existed."

Lyerla acknowledges that her parents were not happy with the situation but felt that with or without their permission, Pamela would do what she wanted to do, just as she always had. "I guess you could call her a runaway in a way," says Lyerla. When she was a baby, Pamela's parents had been forced to put a wire screen over her crib to thwart the adventurous toddler in her many escape attempts. It was a practice they probably wished they'd continued throughout her adolescence. But no matter what their feelings were about the decision, Pamela "ran away" with the financial backing of her parents. "They had pangs," says Lyerla of their decision to help fund the sojourn, "but they didn't want to see her walking the streets or robbing trash cans or anything like that."

As it turned out, they needn't have worried.

CHAPTER

3

Jim Morrison's arrival in Los Angeles in January 1964 coincided with the birth of a generation whose tumultuous course was shaped profoundly by disaster. Only weeks prior to Morrison's arrival, the dreams of Camelot were blown to hell when an assassin struck down John Kennedy on a bleak day in Dallas. The bullets fired that day shattered not only flesh and bone, but the hopes of an entire nation for its future. Americans wept for the fatherless three-year-old saluting a flag-draped coffin; they wept for themselves. And their tears were justified. In short order, the pressures of changing social mores, increased racial strife, and the growing Vietnam conflict engendered a well-founded sense of uncertainty, fear, and doom that permeated the country. So if the voices of this new generation were tinged with more than a little panic, their anxiety wasn't very difficult to understand.

Hey people now
Smile on your brother
Let me see you get together
Love one another right now . . .

It wasn't so much an edict that Jefferson Airplane was issuing in the song later made famous by The Youngbloods, but more a wistful entreaty. Blaming their parents for a world that seemed to have gone horribly off course under adult stewardship, young people were increasingly taking matters into their own hands, desperately trying to stem the tide of violence swirling all around them with a simple, even naive stanchion of good feelings. Writer Annie Gottlieb described the spirit of these young idealists when she wrote, "In our brave new world, we would abolish all that had oppressed in the name of love: inhibition, shame, jealousy, possessiveness, domination, dishonesty, sex roles, even sex differences. That was the dream. There were moments—often stoned moments—when it seemed within reach."

With gathering strength, "youth" became not a measure of years or a liability, but a movement. Years of parental guidance and dutiful, if enforced, Sunday School attendance had hammered home the idea of meek conformity, turning your fate over to a higher power—your parents or God, whichever scared you the most. But now a new religion was suddenly superseding the old, with apostles as unlikely as The Mamas and the Papas and the Airplane:

You can make the mountains ring
Hear the angels cry . . .
You hold the key to love and fear
All in your trembling hand
One key unlocks them both
It's at your command . . .

It's up to you, they were saying; *you can go where you wanna go, do what you wanna do.* And they were! It didn't matter that the streets of Watts were engulfed in flames, that looters and bystanders alike were being shot by police. The Mamas and the Papas were promising a nation of disillusioned, confused kids that they'd be safe and warm if they were in L.A., and no one thought to doubt them. California was suddenly being inundated by dewy-eyed disciples who had come to join the growing sense of community, heady with the sudden realization that they had some say in their own fate, some control over their own destiny. They came to find themselves, lose themselves, or just "be." Generation had blindly followed generation, wearing a deep path. Now, for the first time, a generation was breaking away, searching for a different kind of groove.

Jim Morrison's arrival in Los Angeles that January also coincided with the arrival of the Whisky a Go-Go on the Sunset Strip. Forced to leave the "e" out of its name due to a city ordinance prohibiting the use of hard liquor in the name of a commercial establishment, the Whisky was the first club on the Strip to cater to the burgeoning youth culture. The *New York Times* called the club a "fad" and seemed shocked by the fact that "girls are admitted in slacks and ties are not required for men." But it wasn't women in long pants that these tieless male patrons came to see. It was the bare-midriffed, mini-skirted go-go girls spinning records and dancing in glass cages that caused the biggest commotion. It was a new concept, these women in cages, and one that caught on quickly. Mary Werbelow was one of those who was able to cash in on the craze.

Mary had arrived in Los Angeles not long after Jim, and had supported herself initially by working at the UCLA Medical Center. Jim had been anxious for Mary's arrival, and had envisioned the two of them sharing an apartment, much as they had dreamed of back in Clearwater. Unfortunately, Mary now had plans of her own, not all of which included Jim. She wanted to live alone, she told Morrison. Moreover, she wanted to find an agent and seriously pursue a dancing career. Mary's stubbornness angered and disappointed Jim. Though he had always planned on one of them being a great success, he never thought it would be Mary, and he still didn't.

While Mary was trying to go-go her way to success, Jim was busy pursuing his own interests at UCLA's film school. Morrison had fallen in easily with the film school crowd, finding himself surrounded by many who were just as obsessive and eccentric as he was. Los Angeles in the mid-sixties was nothing if not an oceanside freak show, and many of its stars ended up at the film school at UCLA. Artists and eccentrics, loners and losers, dedicated students and hard core screw-ups—if they possessed talent, no one cared about the packaging. For the first time, Jim Morrison felt at home.

French-born Alain Ronay was one of the first people Jim met in Los Angeles, and describes Morrison at that time as ". . . very shy and withdrawn. But he was very into film. I remember us sitting through *Sleep*, Andy Warhol's eight-hour film. It was like a point of honor to get through it. We were fanatics." Alain would introduce Morrison to many people in Los Angeles, among them a twenty-five-year-old graduate student from Chicago named Ray Manzarek. Ray, who had a Bachelor of Economics degree from Chicago's DePaul University, had started out at UCLA's law school but quickly switched to film. "It seemed to combine my interest in drama, visual arts, music, and the profit motive," explained the pragmatic Manzarek. Ray's refusal to cut a nude scene featuring his girlfriend, Dorothy, from one of his films had initially gained Morrison's admiration, though it would be some time before Ray and Jim became well acquainted.

Among all of his friends at UCLA, the one man who arguably had the most influence on Morrison was Felix Venable. Venable's past could best be described as enigmatic. Theories regarding his life before film school abounded, each more outlandish than the next, but for all the concrete information anyone had on Felix, the man might just as well have sprung into existence spontaneously one day on the UCLA campus. Felix seemed to have no inhibitions or ambitions, ready to sample anything life had to offer and take it wherever it would go, as far as it could go. Jim's reaction to Venable's wildness was reminiscent of his fascination with the flamboyant Tom Reese at the Beaux Arts in Florida. And, more disturbingly, the more Jim was with Felix the more his resulting behavior began to resemble the personality change that had so alarmed those close to him when he was in high school.

"Jim changed radically in school," Alain Ronay once explained to author James Riordan. "In the beginning he was not aggressive at all, but after becoming close with Felix, he changed. He became more and more outrageous until eventually he was just horrible to everyone. . . . He was completely out of hand."

Ray Manzarek also noticed and rather resented the change Felix seemed to engender in Morrison. "Jim was polite, a perfect gentleman who never touched drink or smoked . . ." Manzarek explained to Riordan, "then he took up with this guy—just a plain, evil-minded fuck. And the next time we were with [Jim] socially he was drinking and smoking like a man possessed. And he was starting to act a little weird. It's like those black demons were always there just waiting . . . and this guy happened to come along and swing the gate open and they all came howling out."

It's doubtful that Felix Venable had to do much to persuade Morrison to pass over the conventional boundaries that seemed to define those around him. More likely, Morrison had just been waiting for someone to point the way toward chaos in his new surroundings, for someone to grant him permission to let go. "Jim didn't really start knocking back the booze until Felix was around, but it's not that Felix was some sort of demonic influence," says Michael Ford, another film school classmate. "I think Felix thought he had to succumb to the nineteenth-century Romantic myth that you had to be a drunk and a womanizer in order to be a poet. I mean he might even have been joking, but Jim had a tendency to take jokes very seriously."

Jim also took his filmmaking seriously, and the reaction of his fellow film school students to the movie he produced for his cinematography class was no joke. The poorly lit, badly spliced, rather chaotic work featuring a collection of seemingly disjointed, surrealistic images met with general contempt when it was screened in class. One faculty member went so far as to call it "the product of a degenerate mind." Jim was badly bruised by the stinging criticism and was seen afterward in a campus telephone booth, having a tearful phone conversation with someone. While no one really knows who Jim called to share his disappointment, Mary Werbelow, who today prefers not to speak of her past relationship with Jim, is a safe bet.

Jim had apparently told no one in Los Angeles of his performing experiences onstage at the Contemporary Arts during his time at St. Petersburg Junior College. If he had, it probably would have come as less of a surprise when he started talking about forming a band. Ever since Tom Reese had told Jim that he had "it"—and perhaps even before—Morrison had been fascinated with performing. College friend Martin Bondell remembers Jim's encounter with a woman who had recently seen Bob Dylan in concert. "Jim sat down with the girl and quizzed her intently as to what Dylan sang, what clothes he wore, how he moved, and what the effect of his act was," Bondell said. "He was totally fascinated by it."

Though many remember him as being shy, Jim often went to great lengths to draw attention to himself, just as he had at his previous schools, if only in a negative way. He still liked to do outrageous things, then gauge the reaction he got, filing the information away in his brain for use at another time. He truly seemed to enjoy manipulating the emotions and behavior of those around him, yet rarely in a malicious way. Morrison's attitude was more that of a scientist who builds a maze, then observes and analyzes the behavior of the white mice he sets free within. Morrison once observed that human beings ". . . have no real control over events or their own lives." Just as his provocative behavior when he was a college student in Florida was, for the most part, fueled by his desire to observe his housemates' reactions to it, performing on stage was a way for Jim to create his own world and control the events that took place within it: to set up the maze, herd the mice in, observe their behavior, and—as an added bonus—possibly make a little money in the bargain.

Jim's only real taste of performing since coming to Los Angeles was climbing onstage and provide backup support to Ray Manzarek and Ray's brothers when the Manzareks' group, Rick and the Ravens, would play local bars on the weekends. Just as he had done with other performers at the Contemporary Arts, Jim would join in and contribute what he could—clapping his hands, shaking a tambourine, or providing some improvised lyrics—all the while observing the motions of the band, taking in the unique feel of even those decidedly scant audiences, and storing the information away for another time.

Even though his father had returned from eleven months at sea in November, Jim spent Christmas 1964 with Jeff Morehouse and his family in Los Altos. Jeff was attending Rutgers University in New Jersey, but had flown home for the holiday. They were joined by a few of the other guys whose families had been stationed with Jim's and Jeff's intermittently throughout their lives. Jim didn't mention any plans to go into music, or really much at all about his life in Los Angeles. But what was clear to all present was the fact that, at twenty-one, Jim had already developed a serious drinking problem, which he made no effort to hide. "Though the two of them got along very well," recalls Jeff Morehouse, "Jim drove my mother crazy." Morrison would come down in the morning, grab a water glass, fill it full of gin, and drink it straight. "He really had to have a couple drinks to get going," says Morehouse. "I'd sit there, my mouth hanging open, like 'Wow! You can still stand up!' Because he'd drink first thing in the morning, then he would drink all day, but he didn't act very drunk. My mother scolded him about it, and he'd just look at her and smile." Jim spent three or four very pleasant days with the Morehouse family. Jeff never saw him again.

Once out of college in 1965 (another graduation ceremony he would refuse to attend), Morrison was at loose ends. A degree in cinematography was nice, but the world of filmmaking could be a brutal one to break into. Jim had often spoken of going to New York after his graduation from UCLA, but somehow he never made it, perhaps due to fear of competition or simply lack of ambition.

For all those leaving college during that time, the possibility of being drafted into the escalating conflict in Vietnam (in which Morrison's father, as commander of an aircraft carrier, would play an important role) was a threat that loomed large. Though Morrison would later tease Doors drummer John Densmore by telling him that he'd gotten out of the draft due to a mysterious "Z" classification, it is more likely that the often severe asthma that had plagued Jim since childhood was the source of his fortuitous military reprieve. Another worry behind him.

Jim's increasingly tenuous relationship with Mary Werbelow was also coming to an end. "He was crazy about her," remembers Ray Manzarek, echoing Bryan Gates's observations of the couple's earlier relationship. "Mary was the love of Jim's life." Perhaps that had been true at one time. But as Morrison pondered his own future, Mary's dreams of stardom seemed childish and his own dreams of their idyllic life together outdated.

Despite Jim's doubts, to Mary her dreams of stardom had more basis in reality than Jim's. Ray recalls Mary as "such a fabulous dancer with her little shimmy outfits that they used to wear. Boy, she could sure shake that thing, shake that moneymaker!" All that shaking led to Mary being named Gazzari's nightclub's "Miss Gazzari's," a high honor among the go-go elite. But Jim found Mary's career choice slightly embarrassing.

Recalls Manzarek, "Jim told her to stop doing it. He said, 'Don't do this. Stay in school, study, get your degree, finish up in art.' And Mary said 'No, I want to do this.' And Jim said, 'Look, I'll take care of us, this band is going all the way,' and she said, 'No I don't like your band, I don't think this band is going all the way.' Jim said, 'Yes it is, we're going to be big.' And she said, 'No, I don't think so, Jim. *I'm* going to be big, I don't think you are.' And that was the end of their relationship."

Years later, running into Bryan Gates in Miami, Jim would tell a slightly different story of the demise of his relationship with Mary Werbelow. Recalls Gates: "Jim said Mary simply was not able to handle the swirl of California life around UCLA. When they met the exotic and bizarre people, she didn't have the capacity to just observe it for what it was and let it go, she had to be involved in it." Jim went on to tell Bryan that eventually Mary got involved with what Bryan recalls Jim describing as "a small sect that had their own holy man, and before he knew it she was off to India on a pilgrimage." Jim said that after that he only heard from Mary twice, each time to ask for money to get out of her current situation and get back to the United States. The first time, Jim told Bryan, he sent the money to her immediately. Then, says Gates, "he said several months later he heard from her again with another desperate plea for money, and realized in his own mind that she was so far gone that he was nothing to her anymore than a source of possible economic relief for the travail that she might be in, and he let her go." Gates noted the Morrison seemed genuinely remorseful over the end of the relationship. "He did say that he felt that he'd lost her to that oblivion and, try as he would, he couldn't recover her."

Jim's account might seem odd when looked at in conjunction with his own life choices (and may indeed have been largely the product of his imagination), but it's quite likely that by the time Mary joined him in Los Angeles, Jim had built such a fantasy of spiritual perfection around the image of Mary, that the real, flesh-and-blood Mary couldn't possibly live up to Jim's illusory memories of her. After all, he was certainly not one to be casting aspersions on anyone else's seeming loss of control. When it came to substance abuse, Jim Morrison was the figurative (and later literal) poster child. But whether the cause of their relationship's death was the conflict of Mary's ambitions versus Jim's, Jim's unrealistic fantasies of Mary's spiritual superiority, Mary's alleged immersion in the vices of the sixties, or a combination of these causes and others unnamed, Jim soon found himself with one less reminder of a past he'd just as soon forget.

With nothing and no one to command his time and demand his presence, Jim drifted. He spent a short time with a friend from UCLA, Dennis Jakob, living on the rooftop of the building in Venice where Dennis lived; today the building has been renamed "The Morrison."

"We met in a bar in Santa Monica the summer that he'd finished school," January Jensen recalls of his first encounter with Jim. Jensen had just finished doing his undergraduate work at the Art Center in L.A. where he was studying design, and had then transferred to UCLA to do his postgraduate work. Since Morrison and Jensen were the only two in the bar who weren't "skinheads," as Jensen describes the other patrons, they formed an immediate affinity. "We turned and looked at each other and said, 'Hey.' A lifelong friendship was born.

"Neither one of us were really living anywhere, we were just kind of bouncing around: stay a few nights here, stay a few nights there," says Jensen. "Jim was telling me that he had been writing poems and was thinking about putting them into songs and making some music." Morrison himself would later describe this period as both creative and cathartic: "All of a sudden I threw away most of my notebooks that I'd been keeping since high school and these songs just kept coming to me . . . I heard in my head a whole concert situation, with a band and singing and an audience . . ." And as though remembering the turnout for Rick and the Ravens, Morrison hastens to specify ". . . a *large* audience. Those first five or six songs I wrote, I was just taking notes at a fantastic rock concert that was going on inside my head. And once I had written the songs, I had to sing them." When Ray Manzarek first heard the results of Jim's "note-taking" sessions, he immediately agreed.

Because he remembered Jim often talking of his plans to go to New York after graduation, Manzarek was surprised to run into his old film school acquaintance walking along Venice Beach one day, and even more surprised by Jim's appearance. Jim had never been fat, but as his main sources of nutrition since graduation had been acid and inspiration, Morrison had pared what appeared to be twenty pounds or more from his normally average frame. In addition to his dramatic weight loss, Jim's short hair had grown out until it curled around his face, nearly reaching his shoulders. Morrison had always been attractive. Now he was beautiful.

When Manzarek heard how Jim had been filling his time—and his notebooks—over the summer, he was excited by the possibilities that suddenly started playing themselves out in his mind. And Morrison didn't disappoint. As Jim sat on the sand and sang excerpts from that rooftop concert in his head for Ray, the ever pragmatic midwesterner knew exactly what needed to be done. "Why don't we get a rock 'n' roll band together," he asked Morrison, "and make a million dollars?" What his proposition lacked in poetry, it made up for in prophecy.

"Those were very stoned times," Mirandi Babitz recalls, though with understandable difficulty. "Frankly, we were just high a lot." A child of

Hollywood, by the time Mirandi, whose father was a concert musician, graduated valedictorian of her 1964 high school class she had already traveled the world and was a seasoned veteran of the L.A. scene. To newcomers, Mirandi seemed savvy and sophisticated to the ways of Los Angeles, a city that had become a major focal point in what was turning out to be the extremely painful birth of a new nation. Nineteen-year-old Pamela Courson was among those newcomers, and Mirandi Babitz would prove to be an important role model and friend.

Since her arrival in Los Angeles, Pamela had been intoxicated by the new sights and sounds surrounding her, heady with her newfound freedom. For the first time in her life, she wasn't a freak. Her striking beauty and innate sense of style were no longer shunned as too extreme, but were sought after by many.

Like Jim, Pamela found herself at loose ends, unsure of what direction to take. "We were doing nothing, you know, wandering around trying to figure out what to do in life," Mirandi Babitz remembers of her immediate initial connection with Pamela in the fall of 1966. "Pam and I were both taking art classes at Los Angeles City College. We were the two obviously hippie girls in this class—I had long straight brown hair with bangs and she had long straight red hair with bangs—and we were both incredibly anorexic and little; I think we weighed about 180 pounds between us. I know I was 91 pounds and I don't think Pamela was much over that. She was real cute, you know, a darling little thing. So we started sitting together and talking to each other and we became friends."

Throughout her high school years, no one remembers seeing Pamela with a boy—any boy. Perhaps the boys of Orange County hadn't been quite ready for Pamela's particular brand of feminine charm. The men of Los Angeles, however, didn't even have to think twice.

Tom Baker was a professional actor and not unlike Jim Morrison physically. Lean, clean shaven, dark haired, blue eyed, and hard drinking, Baker and Morrison would eventually become great friends, but it was Pamela who first caught Tom's attention. Babe Hill, a close friend of both Tom's and Jim's, remembers, "Tom liked to take credit for introducing Pam and Jim. It was Tom's story that there was always a little bit of friction between he and Jim—though they liked each other immensely—but supposedly Tom had had Pam before Jim met her and that was supposed to explain some of the friction between those two guys." He pauses for a moment, then, with a sly grin adds, "Then again that may have just been Tom's ego talking." Either way, Jim quickly replaced Tom in Pam's life. Baker would later return the favor after a fashion, replacing Jim in Andy Warhol's sexually explicit hundred-minute film *I, a Man* (originally titled

Tom Baker, c. 1967.

Fuck), in which Tom gained great exposure—quite literally, as he spent much of the movie naked.

Despite Babe's doubts, it could very well have been Tom Baker who introduced Jim to Pamela. There have been many stories about how the two came together in the first place, from outright fiction (as in Oliver Stone's movie, *The Doors,* where a somewhat psychotic Val Kilmer as Jim stalks Pamela from the store to her house, literally dropping in on her front porch. "Don't you believe in doors?" Meg Ryan, as Pam, asks. "They're a waste of time," is his prophetic reply) to considerably more credible accounts, such as former Doors keyboardist Ray Manzarek's account of the event, which he remembers taking place at the Sunset Strip club the London Fog sometime in early 1966.

"Pam walked into the Fog and John Densmore certainly put the make on her and for the next week or so continued to put the make on her. I don't know what happened with that; I'm certain he would have loved to consummate the relationship, though I don't think they ever did." John's former wife, Julia Negron, agrees, saying, "I'd bet every dime I've got that he never slept with her. I can't imagine she'd even spend ten minutes going to coffee with John." But whatever John's fantasies, according to Ray, "Within about a one- or two-week period Jim and Pam had looked into each other's eyes and realized that it wasn't going to be John Densmore at all, it was going to be Jim and Pam."

A friend of Penny Courson's remembers Pamela's mother giving a much different account of Pamela's first encounter with Jim, saying that Pamela had gotten a job in a doctor's office or lab as "some kind of a lab technician, learning-on-the-job type thing." Apparently, Penny's friend says, while Pamela had this job she came down with an illness that necessitated her parents taking her to UCLA Medical Center, where she was treated for "the better part of a year at UCLA." Although Pamela had never shown the slightest bit of interest in any intellectual pursuit up to that time, this supposed illness, according to her mother's friend, apparently sparked the girl's curiosity. "Well, she became very interested in the area of her problem," the woman continues, "and she did not come back to Orange to work; she got a job at UCLA. According to what her mother told me, this is how and where she met Jim Morrison."

"That's absolute nonsense," says Preach Lyerla. "If one of Corky's children were sick or if they were making trips back and forth to Los Angeles at that time, I would certainly have known about it." Indeed the story seems an odd fusion of events from Penny's life, her elder daughter Judy's life, and even Mary Werbelow's. Preach recalls Penny having worked in a lab in Orange at one point, and one of Judy's friends vaguely recalls that Judy once had some sort of job related to health care in Los Angeles. "I guess it's better than saying that your kid ran away from home, hung out in clubs on the Sunset Strip, and took up with some guy in a band," concludes Lyerla.

Despite the high drama of Penny's friend's account, and the certainty of Ray's, Pamela and Jim told a different story to friends. Mirandi Babitz remembers Pamela mentioning that she had met Jim at a campus party either at UCLA or LACC, a story January Jensen confirms as well, based on Jim's version of the event. Though no one gave it much thought at the time, in retrospect it is a story more romantic in its innocence than Oliver Stone's version, more dramatic in its simplicity than Penny's more complicated tale.

"He met her at a party," says January, "but didn't really meet her." Preach Lyerla's observation that Pamela could stop a party just by walking in the room was quite accurate. With her vivid red hair, milky white skin and quick, childlike laughter, Pamela couldn't help but draw attention in any situation. *Barbarella* star John Phillip Law, with whom Pamela would later have a brief friendship, recalls the first time he saw Pamela with her sister, Judy: "Judy was pretty enough, but Pamela—Pamela was *electric.*" Indeed, Morrison, who had been attracted to legions of women and had propositioned (and been propositioned by) a countless number of them, seemed rather nonplused at the first sight of her.

"[Jim] saw her there across the room and wanted to meet her," recalls January, "so he asked around until he found a friend of hers who could arrange an introduction." It is said that breeding will out. The same Jim Morrison who would later, under the guise of Rock Star, swagger up to women he barely knew and say, "So, am I going home with you or what?" reverted to his mannered military upbringing, his gentlemanly southern roots, at the sight of this pale, deceptively fragile looking redhead. It may not have been quite Rodgers and Hammerstein, but it was certainly classic Morrison.

We have started the crossing
Who knows? it may end badly

As quietly and undramatically as that, Jim Morrison had found his "cosmic mate."

January Jensen looked up as the door of the bar opened then closed, momentarily spilling painfully bright Los Angeles sunshine into the smoky, dimly lit room.

"Hey, Morrison," said January as his friend perched on the bar stool at his side. "Long time no see. What's been going on?"

Jim waved at the bartender, who instantly placed a drink before him. Not many kids Jim's age liked an old man's drink like straight Scotch in the middle of the day, so Morrison's unusual usual was particularly easy to remember. Jim tossed back the drink with a practiced flip of his wrist, motioning for another, as he turned to January.

"Oh, you know . . . not much," he said in the quiet, slow voice that made people press a little closer to catch his words. He added, as though in afterthought, "I got this little girl."

"Oh, yeah?"

"Yeah." There was a glint in his eye. "She's wonderful . . ." With one fluid movement he downed the second drink and signaled for another. A sly smile had crept over his face as though he were picturing the girl's soft, pale skin, sea-colored eyes, and hair touched with fire. ". . . She's trouble."

"Well shit, Morrison," January deadpanned, "I guess it oughta work out just fine then."

Jim laughed, then was quiet for a minute, staring down into his glass, again empty. He started to wave for the bartender again, then hesitated. Without looking at his friend he said, "January?"

"Jim?"

"What do you know about love?"

In much the same way Leo Tolstoy thought only unhappy families unique, contented couples tend to be unremarkable. There is little to say about Jim and Pamela in their early days together, not because little was known but because little was noted. Maybe if there had been more drama in the beginning—if blows had ever been exchanged, if the police had ever been called to rescue one from the other—maybe then we'd know more about the relationship between Jim Morrison and his "little girl" during that relatively brief period of tranquility between their first meeting in 1966 and The Doors' first real taste of success the following year.

But the most dramatic thing happening between Jim and Pamela took place only between the two of them. While it may have seemed nothing special to others at the time, to Jim and Pamela the happiness and excitement they found with each other after a lifetime of rejection and disappointment from others must have seemed extraordinary.

If anything might have been considered noteworthy to the outside observer about Jim and Pamela at that time, though, it would probably have been the visual image they presented to the world. Ray Manzarek remembers Jim at that time as being in the best physical shape of his life. After meeting on the beach and making the decision to form a band, Ray had suggested that Jim, who was still living on Dennis Jakob's roof, move in with Ray and his girlfriend, Dorothy.

"There was Rick and the Ravens occasionally on the weekends to bring a little money in from my end," recalls Ray of their financial situation at the time. "And Dorothy got a job with a computer place, taking all the little ones and zeroes off the computer tape they used to use back in the old days. [Then] I came home with Jim and said, 'Honey, Jim's going to move in with us because he's living up on Dennis's rooftop and he's got all these great songs, so we're going to get a rock and roll band together and we're going to call it The Doors and we're going to be rich and famous and successful artists. Everything we've ever dreamed about we're going to do.'" In a situation where most women would have laughed, cried, or simply walked out, Dorothy calmly accepted the change in their living situation, never doubting for a moment that the picture Ray was painting for their future would eventually become reality. "She was duly impressed with Jim's words," says Ray, and they were both impressed with Jim's newfound body image. "He looked just absolutely fabulous!"

While Dorothy worked on computer tapes, Jim and Ray worked on their songs and on themselves. "We ran on the beach," says Manzarek. "We'd go down to Muscle Beach and swing on the rings down there, and just got in great physical condition. Jim was really strong and healthy, hard and lean." At five feet eleven inches, 145 pounds, Jim was considerably more lean than he'd been when he first arrived at UCLA. "It didn't seem skinny," says Ray, "it just seemed like a good, raw-boned leanness. He had a real wiry strength to him. This guy was in great shape!"

At five feet four inches and about 94 pounds, Pamela appeared extremely delicate by comparison. She was a natural beauty with long golden-red hair framing kaleidoscope eyes that have been described as everything from emerald green to deep lavender but were, in truth, ever-changing hazel. Her milk-white skin rarely saw a hint of makeup, and she would frequently burst into unrestrained peals of childlike laughter that showed off straight white teeth. If California had decided to find the perfect girl to represent the state's image, they would have come looking for Pamela.

Ironically, the same striking looks that had made Pamela an outcast in Orange served her well in Los Angeles. Manzarek remembers Pamela bringing a hot rod magazine into the London Fog one day shortly after she and Jim had started seeing each other. "She'd been coming to the club on sort of a relatively frequent basis, and the relationship was blossoming," he says, "and she brought a magazine in and was rather proud to show everybody that she was indeed on the cover of a magazine. She was a babe, a hot babe on a red car. As I recall she had on a two-piece bathing suit. It didn't do Pam justice, that's for sure. Didn't capture the sweetness of her."

"Sweet" is a word that is often employed when people describe Pamela. "She had that sweet, angelic feeling about her," remembers Paul Ferrara. Ferrara was working as a photographer for Gamma Ltd. when he first met Pamela, who was doing more modeling work, this time as a favor for a friend of hers who was a designer. As the photo shoot progressed, Pamela mentioned that her boyfriend's name was Jim Morrison. Coincidentally, Paul had gone to UCLA with Jim and Ray but had lost touch with the two of them in the year since graduation. By this time, The Doors had not yet released a record but they were getting close. "She said, 'You ought to come work for The Doors, or you ought to at least shoot Jim,'" remembers Ferrara, who gave Pamela his business card to pass on to Jim. "The Doors' manager later hired me from that meeting with Pam."

Paul remembers Pamela as having "a fairy-tale quality," as he describes it. "She had that persona," he says. "I think that's what Jim liked about her. She was like one of those people who's so blessed to begin with, whether it's beauty or whatever inside her, I think they're impervious and nothing really hurts them. They kind of walk around with a glowing shield. Pam was one of those."

Early photos of Jim and Pam taken from Pamela's scrapbook show the two gleefully clowning around in a photo booth, Jim wearing a leather jacket, Pamela looking well scrubbed and glowing. But in spite of their seemingly idyllic happiness, at least one person had some instant reservations about the couple's relationship, considering Jim's prospects bleak at best. "What are you wasting your time with this guy for?" Pamela's older sister, Judy, reportedly asked Pamela. "Get yourself someone with money!" Pamela didn't listen.

Longtime Doors associate Danny Sugerman scoffs at latter-day speculation that Pamela was only after Jim for his money for the obvious reason that for at least the first year Jim and Pam were together, Jim *had* no money. "Yeah, when The Doors were at the London Fog, Pamela really wanted to get her hands around that $12-a-night paycheck!" Sugerman laughs. Eva Gardonyi, who first met Jim through her husband, documentary filmmaker Frank Gardonyi, also remembers the premium Jim put on the timing of his relationship with Pamela. "She was there when he had to just do it out of nothing and from nowhere, and she believed in him and he appreciated that," Gardonyi told Frank Lisciandro in his book *Feast of Friends*. "I know that they had been starving together and that was a very important thing. Not when he had money or not when he had fame, but prior to that."

Those lean sweet desperate hours

But no one was "starving" for long. Jim and Ray had quickly set out to do all the things Ray had promised Dorothy they were going to do, forming a band called The Doors that eventually included drummer John Densmore and his friend, guitarist Robby Krieger. Even though the band's early successes were small and far between, Jim and Pamela celebrated each as though it were the ultimate reward. Mirandi Babitz remembers, "The first time Jim actually got some money for singing, he and Pam went wild! They bought Chinese food and had a feast. Anyone would have thought that Jim had brought home a million dollars, but I think his cut had been about twenty bucks!"

It wasn't a lot, but it was all they needed. "That was the great thing about Los Angeles at that time," says Mirandi Babitz, "you could live so cheap. People had these little scrappy apartments so nobody was ever really on the street because you could get by: You could make it on unemployment, you could make it on a waitress's salary." Or on the unpredictable income from a fledgling band.

But with talent, hard work, and a little luck, fortune had turned in

Jim and Paul Rothchild, 1966.

the group's favor. Despite a few setbacks along the way—a contract with Columbia Records that went nowhere, being fired from two clubs on the Sunset Strip, once for disorderly conduct, once for obscenity—the rosy future Ray had outlined for Dorothy quickly began to materialize, and the concert Jim had heard in his head was becoming reality, due in large part to Jac Holzman and Paul Rothchild of Elektra Records.

Producer Paul Rothchild remembered his first encounter with the group: "I was recording director of Elektra Records; Jac Holzman was the owner of the company. Jac's wife, Nina, had seen the group at the London Fog, and she got Jac to come out and hear them." By the time Jac saw the group perform, The Doors had already been fired from the London Fog and had moved down the Strip to the Whisky a Go-Go. "Jac was inclined to sign them," Rothchild continued, "but he wasn't quite sure. So he had me come out when they were playing at the Whisky, opening for the group Love, one of Elektra's acts."

After sitting through The Doors' first set, Rothchild was not at all impressed with what he'd heard. "It was the worst set of music I'd ever heard in my life!" he recalled. But experience had taught him that anything that warrants a first look almost always warrants a second look. "I kind of knew that the record company always gets to hear the bad set, a law of God," he said, "so I stayed for the second set and heard one of the greatest sets of music ever. That night was like a microcosm of The Doors to come, the best and the worst it would get. A few weeks later I was in the studio with them."

Shortly after Elektra had expressed their interest in the band, Jim's seemingly spontaneous decision to confide in the audience at the Whisky one night during a performance of "The End" that he wanted to kill his father and fuck his mother led to the group's swift and involuntary departure from the club. But what the Whisky didn't want, Gazzari's was happy to take on, so the group simply moved a little further down the Strip where they were met by increasingly enthusiastic audiences.

In September 1966, their agreement with Elektra finalized, it took The Doors only two weeks working with Rothchild and engineer Bruce Botnick at Sunset Sound Recording Studios to produce their first album. However, as rapid as the recording process was, it had not been completely trouble free. Jim had caused minor problems when he dropped acid before recording "The End," and further complicated things by breaking into the studio one night and blasting the contents of a fire extinguisher over everything in the room. But even though Jim's drinking was on the rise and he was using hallucinogenics the way others used breath mints, Jim was in relatively good physical and mental condition and gave a tight, if sometimes understandably tentative, performance in the studio. Rothchild knew he was watching the formation of a major star. Yet despite Jim's obvious talent and his demonstrated ability to deliver what was asked of him, Morrison's erratic behavior rang an alarm bell in Paul's mind. Near the completion of the album, during mixing Paul turned to Robby Krieger and said, "We'd better get as much of this stuff from Jim as possible, as fast as possible, because he's not going to make it."

In anticipation of the album's release, in November the group made their first trip to the East Coast. In her 1992 book, *Linda McCartney's Sixties,* McCartney recalled the first time she photographed the band at Ondine's, a small club in New York City. "No one in New York had ever heard of The Doors. They had never performed outside of Los Angeles and hadn't released any records." she wrote. "It wasn't Jim Morrison's looks that struck me first about him. It was the poetry of his songs and the way he would get completely lost in the music. He had this habit of cupping his hand behind his ear so that he could hear his vocals in the way that traditional folk singers did."

In fact, nearly a year and a half since he first stood on stage with Rick and the Ravens, holding a powerless electric guitar, Morrison finally seemed to have found his bearings on stage. Often too shy to face the

The Doors backstage at Ondine's, 1966, before the release
of their first album.

audience during the group's earlier sets at the London Fog, Jim would
instead sing with his back to the spectators, giving the appearance of
singing not for those who had paid the price of admission, but for deep,
personal reasons he was reluctant to share with those around him. While
this only added to his dark and mysterious persona, the truth was that Jim
was simply insecure about his own limitations. He had performed onstage
before, in Florida at the Contemporary Arts. But there he had recited
poetry, his own and others', and played the ukulele. With The Doors,
however, Jim was broaching unknown territory, singing in public, and was
not sure that his voice was up to the challenge of fronting a band. "We
had a discussion one night after a lame set and confronted Jim with his

The house on "Love Street" (before renovation),
next to the Canyon Store.

shyness," says Densmore. "We were used to facing each other in rehearsals, and Jim wasn't secure enough yet to break that circle of energy."

But those insecurities quickly vanished as the audience reception grew warmer. Now it was obvious that when Jim stepped behind the microphone, he owned the stage and reveled in the attention of those held rapt by his presence there. In an early review of the band for the UCLA *Daily Bruin*, Bill Kerby wrote of Morrison, "He has more natural disdain, more utter contempt for his surroundings than anyone I have ever known. But when he stands, throttling his microphone, staggering blindly across the stage, electric, on fire, screaming, his is all there, waiting, daring, terrified, and alone. And digging it."

Returning from New York, Jim and Pam decided to take the next logical step in their relationship by moving in together. With the Elektra deal solidly in hand, and Jim's continuing income from the band seeming more secure as a result, the couple moved into one of three small apartments in a house on Rothdell Trail, perched on a hillside just above the Country Store. While the Country Store still thrives, the house on Rothdell Trail—more commonly known to Doors fans as "Love Street"—remained for years a sad, empty shell, stripped to its foundations and left vulnerable to the elements and to fans who make pilgrimages there on a regular basis. But there was a time when it was the perfect place to live.

"The place in Laurel Canyon was dirt cheap," remembers Mirandi Babitz. "There were like three apartments, and Jim and Pam were in one floor of it, in the middle part. I'm sure they weren't paying more than sixty bucks a month, because that's all any of us was paying." Jimmy Greenspoon of Three Dog Night lived with Danny Hutton, two doors down from Jim and Pamela, and a number of other stars of the music scene lived in the neighborhood as well. "Gene Clark of The Byrds was around the corner, and Roger McGuinn, David Crosby, and Chris Hillman were across the street," says Greenspoon. "John and Michelle Philips were right there, and Cass Elliot was a little further up the street. So was Frank Zappa and his family." There was a feeling of community and creativity that flowed through the area almost as fast and thick as the drugs provided by the local dealers, who also lived in the Canyon near the store. "Everybody would be running back and forth to each other's houses exchanging brownies and drugs," Greenspoon recalls. "On the weekend, everybody would leave their doors open and you'd hear this amazing amount of music just flooding through the air."

Soft parade
Love Street brigade

It was this musical invitation that lured self-proclaimed groupie Pamela Miller from her friend's Canyon apartment to the Morrisons' doorstep one day. Enticed by the strains of "The End" from the not-yet-released album *The Doors,* Miller, curious who would be lucky enough to possess a demo pressing of the album, crept down the hill and peeked in the window of the apartment from which the music seemed to originate. She was greeted by the sight of Jim Morrison, wearing nothing but black leather pants, bending over and peering into the refrigerator as he hummed along with the music. She eventually got up the nerve to knock on his door, and the next thing she remembered was being ordered out of the house by "Jim's redheaded girlfriend," who had walked in, unfortunately, just as Miller was demonstrating to Morrison how supple she was with a back-bend that had sent her purple velvet minidress over her head, a move "the redhead" obviously felt was a little more than neighborly. Pamela Miller retreated to the sounds of smashing vinyl as Pamela Courson took her displeasure at Jim's wandering eye out on their defenseless record collection.

This was the flip side of Pamela's sweetness, the steely side that few ever saw and those who were the object of it never forgot. "That chick's got an arm you wouldn't believe!" Jim reportedly told Danny Sugerman

Mirandi Babitz and Clem in 1967.

once as they ran from one of Pamela's fits of pique. It was partly this paradox that so intrigued Jim and attracted him to Pamela. This tiny, sweet, angelic morsel who loved him, supported him, played with him, respected his art, and when provoked, wouldn't hesitate to haul off and punch him in the face. Actor Christopher Jones, who would later incur the wrath of Pamela, laughs wryly at the recollection of Pamela's response to an imagined infidelity. "Remember that scene in the movie [Oliver Stone's *The Doors*], where the duck got pounded into the ground?" he asks. "Well, that was Pamela, and I was the duck!"

Though in later years Pamela Miller—under her married name, Pamela Des Barres—wrote about a couple of other brief encounters with Jim, those encounters never amounted to much. "He turned out to be a very one-woman man," she wrote in her 1987 memoir, *I'm With the Band*. "As far as I know, he spent the rest of his life with the redhead . . . I guess he loved her madly and vice versa."

There's a palace
in the canyon
where you & I
were born . . .

Though anything but dull, life on Love Street with Jim and Pam proved to be somewhat less than ideal for Mirandi Babitz and her boyfriend, Clem. "We lived with them there for maybe three weeks," she says. "It was odd, really strange, because I never felt comfortable around Jim. I thought he was weird, he was like . . . *black*. But I think Pam liked that, liked that sharp edge." Indeed, despite her childlike innocence, Pamela's own sharp edge, like a sword sheathed in the plushest velvet, would often surprise even Jim, who knew her best. After all, *he* was supposed to be the dangerous and complex one.

Mirandi remembers watching Jim and Pamela take great pleasure in trying to scare each other, popping out of dark shadows, waving knives, or playing chicken in the car on the steep cliffs of canyon roads. They were like two children left unattended, reveling in their youth, their freedom, and each other, sometimes risking their lives for an even greater thrill. "They were going to play until there was no sand left in the box," says Paul Ferrara.

"They would go up to Mullholland and roll the car toward the cliff!" Mirandi exclaims, even now exasperated at their defiance. "They did really weird stuff to scare themselves; they liked the rush. And it wasn't just Jim. Pam was like that, too. She liked that." In fact, Mirandi says, it was quite possibly Pamela who egged Jim on to ever more daring stunts, teasing him into proving his fearlessness.

With others, from his childhood friends to his fellow band members, Jim had grown used to easily coming out on top in these games of one-upmanship, but not with Pamela. If he pointed the car at the cliff on Mullholland and put it in DRIVE, it would just as likely be Pamela's foot pressuring the gas pedal as his own. It was just this defiant attitude that differentiated Jim's obsession with Pamela from his past similar feelings for Tandy Martin and Mary Werbelow: When confronted with Jim's often erratic behavior and sometimes violent mood shifts, Pamela, undaunted, knew how to give back as good as she got and didn't hesitate to do so. This wasn't just a girlfriend, Jim was quick to discover, this was a roller-coaster ride! Together they would laugh, scream, cry, and laugh again at the absurdity of their screaming and crying. They would smoke grass, which was Pam's favorite, or drop acid, which was Jim's trip of choice. Then they'd go to UCLA for B-12 shots so they could get themselves together enough to do it all over again. And why not? They were young, beautiful, in love, doing what they thought they wanted with their lives, and even starting to make some money doing it.

. . . we lived & died
& laughed & cried
& the pride of our relationship
took hold that summer

"They were two halves of the same person," a friend once observed. And they'd come together at last, instantly melding into one. The other members of The Doors agreed. "They were like the same person, you know?" says Doors keyboardist Ray Manzarek. "They were the opposite sides of the same coin, the same person as a male and as a female. . . . They were perfect for each other." Guitarist Robby Krieger concurs, saying, "If it were possible for Jim to have a mate for life, we all felt that Pamela was that person." And drummer John Densmore noted that it was only Pamela who ". . . had the fire to be Jim's match."

As 1966 came to a close, the two wandering souls who had felt so incomplete on their own such a short time before had finally found a home with each other, both literally and figuratively. No longer simply Jim Morrison and Pamela Courson, they were Jim and Pam, seemingly endless and inseparable. "There was a true teenage sweetheart love affair going on between Jim and Pam that started before he was famous," says Paul Ferrara. "But once he got famous . . ."

J im, what are you doing?"

It was June 1967, and The Doors were once again in New York City, enjoying a successful three-week run at the Scene. Tonight the mood was jovial as the band members, their girlfriends, and assorted others sat at a large table in a restaurant, savoring a few rare moments of relaxation in what had already been an extremely hectic year. But suddenly Pamela noticed that in the midst of the merriment, Jim had become perfectly still and, with a wide grin seemingly glued on his face, was staring unwaveringly at Robby, who was busy eating on the other side of the table.

"Jim?" Pam asked again, when he didn't respond to her first query.

Without breaking his stare or dropping his smile, Jim said out of the corner of his mouth, "Everybody stop what you're doing and smile at Robby."

A few puzzled looks were exchanged, but everyone did as Jim asked, and in seconds everyone was smiling and staring at Robby. The guitarist, unconcerned, continued to shovel his dinner into his mouth. After a few moments of this, Pamela, talking out of the corner of her frozen smile without looking away from Robby, said, "Jim, why are we doing this?"

"I want to see if he stops chewing with his mouth open and smiles with his mouth open," Jim replied.

Sure enough, under the beaming gaze of his friends and co-workers, Robby smiled wide, his half-chewed dinner plainly visible in his mouth.

The whole table cracked up.

There was a lot to smile about by the summer of 1967. *The Doors,* the group's self-titled first album, had been released by Elektra in January. Going all out for its promotion, the record company had rented a giant billboard that towered over the Sunset Strip, picturing a dark and moody lineup of Ray, Jim, Robby, and John next to the legend "THE DOORS BREAK ON THROUGH WITH AN ELECTRIFYING ALBUM." The four band members were photographed in any number of stances on and around the billboard—standing under it, climbing up to it, perched symbolically on top. No other band in history had ever been promoted via billboard, and Elektra was determined to get as much mileage out of this groundbreaking event as possible.

The album itself was received with enthusiastic praise on some sides, indifference bordering on contempt on others. A typical example of this can be seen in two reviews from opposite sides of the country. Pete Johnson, in the *Los Angeles Times,* wrote: "Jim Morrison, lead vocalist . . . is somewhat overmannered, murky, and dull. The best example of his faults is 'The End,' an eleven-minute thirty-five-second exploration of how bored he can sound as he recites singularly simple, overelaborated psychedelic non sequiturs and fallacies. Many of the numbers drag and there is an abundance of banal lyrics."

It's hard to believe that Richard Goldstein was reviewing the same album when he wrote in *New York* magazine: "'The End' is eleven and one-half minutes of solid song. Its hints of sitar and tabla and its faint aroma of raga counterpoint are balanced by a sturdy blues foundation. Anyone who disputes the concept of rock literature had better listen long and hard to this song. . . . Morrison's delivery (during the murder fantasy it approaches gospel wailing) tells us to absorb first, and search later. The Doors are a major event for Los Angeles. Their emergence indicates that the city of Formica fantasy is building a music without neon, that glows anyway." This contradictory reaction to the first album would set the tone for the rest of The Doors' career: Love them or hate them, their music provoked a response.

Unfortunately, "Break On Through"/"End of the Night," the single that was released with the album, seemed to be provoking less of a response than either Elektra or The Doors had hoped for. Though a hit in Los Angeles, the record stalled at number 106 on the national charts, a failure that couldn't help but discourage the group. But so much time was spent with performance dates calculated to promote the album that the band had little time to dwell on failures, real or perceived.

Their itinerary for the first six months of 1967 was exhaustive and exhausting, centering largely in California. They played gigs up and down the state, performing with groups including The Grateful Dead, The Junior Wells Blues Band, The Young Rascals, The Byrds, Buffalo Springfield, and Jefferson Airplane. They headlined at Gazzari's and returned to the Whisky in triumph. As the old saying goes, there's no deodorant like success, and anything that Jim might have done or sung to offend the Whisky's management was long forgotten, or at least forgiven, with the help of the crowds the group could now command.

In mid-March the band traveled back to New York for a return engagement at Ondine's. Preceded by stirring reviews similar to Richard Goldstein's in *New York* magazine, The Doors were greeted by enthusiastic and very curious audiences. Who was this madman fronting the band? Though at this point Jim still looked very much the college boy in his buttoned-down shirts and corduroy pants, once he took possession of the stage, any visions the audience might have harbored of a harmless young man were blown to hell and back.

I'm human
But I'm not an ordinary man
No No No

The *New York Times* reported that the audience for one Doors concert, ". . . sat in rapt attention to every visual and vocal gyration of The Doors' lead singer, Jim Morrison, as if in homage to some primitive ritual." At the end of the piece, the reporter added, as though in afterthought, "The other members of the group . . . are essentially instrumentalists." It did not sound like a compliment.

It was an issue that had emerged quickly and would resurface continually throughout the Doors' career: Was it "The Doors," or was it "Jim Morrison and The Doors"? Jim's feelings were very clear on this: The Doors was a solid unit made up of four equal parts, and God help the announcer who made the mistake of singling him out when introducing the band. The Cleveland DJ who did just that was startled when, the second the words "Jim Morrison and . . ." escaped his lips, Jim himself ran out onstage, grabbed the microphone away from the man, and yelled, "Hold it! Wait a minute, wait a minute! Ladies and Gentleman, THE DOORS!"

But for four individuals, trying to remain a cohesive unit is difficult, even under the best of circumstances. "They were all strong and different personalities," explains Bill Siddons, who joined the band as road manager in May 1967. "Ray was the controller and Jim was the wild artist and Robby was the space cadet and John was the little old lady." Another Doors insider was less optimistic in his assessment of the group's interpersonal dynamics. "It was a bad marriage from the start," he said. "Jim always felt there was a tremendous resentment of him by the others, which was natural. Jim got virtually all of the acclaim and attention, and the others were pretty much obliterated. There were egos involved, and each was of an entirely different temperament."

Ray Manzarek (who was born in 1939, not 1935, as is often reported) was older than the others by at least four years, and had in fact seemed to emerge as the leader of the group, even the father figure, a role Jim often relied upon, as he had with Bryan Gates, and just as often resented, as with his own father. While Jim was still living with Dorothy and Ray, Manzarek once made the mistake of suggesting to Jim that he get a haircut. How could Ray have known about the occurrence on the *Bon Homme Richard* when Captain Morrison had ordered his son to trim his already bristling hair? How could Ray have known of Jim's bitterness over the incident? But while Ray may have never known the possible trigger of Jim's rage, he certainly felt the bullet. Jim responded to Ray's suggestion by screaming at him, *"Never tell me what to do!"* Message received. "I'm never going to try that again!" Ray told John Densmore.

Though it now makes Manzarek uncomfortable to be considered the "businessman" of the group ("It probably has to do with that 'Let's get a rock and roll band together and make a million dollars,'" he complains. "If I hadn't said that line, I would've been okay"), but the fact is that while Ray and Jim may have shared an initial vision of the group as artists with a message, Ray's vision was obviously more firmly rooted in reality than Jim's.

"I had a bachelor's degree in economics, so it wasn't very difficult for me to say, 'Wait a minute, let's keep an eye on the business side of things here,'" explains Manzarek. "Of course we're doing this for the art and the spirit and all of that, but we're also going to make a record, put the record out, and we're going to get as much money from the record as we can . . ." Keenly aware of the grave losses other artists had incurred by losing sight of the realities of art as commerce, Ray was determined that the same fate would not befall The Doors. "The Doors could sell records and make money at the same time," he says. "Make art and money. So yeah, I was certainly aware of the business aspects of it."

In sharp contrast to Ray's cool nature and ordinarily even temperament, John Densmore was easily upset by Jim's bizarre antics and made the grave mistake of constantly showing his displeasure, which in turn compelled Jim to constantly try bigger and better ways to drive John insane. "John didn't think it was an artistic statement to not show up for work, or to say 'fuck you' to the audience, or to do a lot of the things Jim did," explains Bill Siddons. "Robby was more able to roll with the punches."

Robby Krieger was easygoing, amiable, and probably came closest to being Jim's intellectual match, though he tended to keep this fact to himself. Krieger's sense of humor was sharp, sly, and dry as toast, but his quiet, shy demeanor often masked this fact from those who didn't know him well. His good nature made him a favorite target of Jim's jokes as well, but unlike John, Robby had the ability to laugh at himself and could usually appreciate Jim's often odd sense of humor—like the incident at the restaurant or the night in New York when Robby was awakened from a sound sleep in his hotel room by a telephone call from God. "Krieger, this is God," announced a dignified voice that sounded surprisingly like Jim's, backed by decidedly undignified giggles that sounded much like Pamela's. "I'm just calling to tell you that you've been removed from the human race."

Despite Robby's laid-back attitude toward life, it still must have rankled a bit to see Jim getting the lion's share of the attention that came the group's way. A few years ago, when asked by a journalist about the song "You're Lost Little Girl," Krieger uncharacteristically snapped, "I can tell you this much—Jim didn't write it, *I* did!"

Krieger was, in fact, the frequently unrecognized hit-maker of the group. In keeping with the "all for one, one for all" stance The Doors had taken from the beginning, authorship of their songs was always attributed to "The Doors" as a whole, rather than broken down by who had first hummed the melody, who had actually penned the lyrics. In fact, much of their work comprised contributions, large and small, from all the band members. But because Jim was the face in front of the band, the voice that gave life to all the songs they played, it was common for audiences and the public in general to attribute creation of all the group's songs to Jim. True, it was Jim's poetry and unpredictable performances that gave The Doors their personality and a reputation for being darker, deeper, more substantial than the average rock group. But it was the song that flew from Robby's pen in a matter of minutes one day that would reverberate endlessly around the world and shape the group's destiny.

"Light My Fire" was released by Elektra in April 1967, backed by "Crystal Ship." After Ray had admonished the group to come up with some new material in early 1966, Krieger had gone home and written "Light My Fire" together with "Love Me Two Times" in "about an hour or so," as he recalls it. Robby had presented the new material at the next rehearsal, saying, "I think it's a hit!" Jim contributed his own typically Cimmerian touch to the song's second verse, John supplied a Latin beat, and Ray provided the trademark organ solos that introduced and bridged the song. Just as Robby had predicted, a little over three months after its release, "Light My Fire" became The Doors' first number one hit. In a little over three years, it would become Jim Morrison's swan song.

TWO

Treatise on the Steppenwolf

. . . sometimes the idea runs through my head that I am living an extremely dangerous life, for I am one of those machines which can explode.

Friedrich Nietzsche, 1881

CHAPTER

6

L ater Pamela couldn't remember what they had fought about exactly. Had it been his drinking? That was certainly a common bone of contention. Had he lingered too long under the libidinous gaze of an admiring stranger? Had she? That had started to become more commonplace as well. It could've been just about anything. It could've been nothing at all.

In later years, the memory of the anger's aftermath would linger with Pamela, if not its exact cause. Jim had stormed out of their New York hotel room, leaving her lying there, a chill creeping over her that had little to do with her nakedness. She got out of bed and grabbed the first thing handy to cover her tiny frame, Jim's red hooded sweatshirt. Pamela pulled it over her head and was instantly enveloped by his smell as the fabric passed over her face. For a moment she buried her nose in the soft folds and inhaled deeply, pulling him inside through his unique aroma of whiskey and tobacco and something nameless that identified him as unconditionally as a fingerprint.

Where was that asshole?

Pamela opened the door and cautiously looked up and down the corridor—all clear—before stepping out. She walked silently down the hall, wearing nothing but the red sweatshirt, which came almost to her knees. Little Red Riding Hood in search of her wolf. Reaching the next room, she slipped silently inside without knocking.

Obviously their gig at the Scene was pulling in the crowds. Ray, Robby, and John were sitting in front of a table piled high with the cash taken from the night's performance. But their eyes weren't on the money, nor did anyone seem to notice Pamela standing just inside the doorway. Instead, all attention was riveted on Jim, who stood brandishing a glowing cigarette lighter ever closer to the pile of money, threatening to turn it all to ashes.

As silently as she had entered, Pamela left the room.

There was once a man, Harry, called the Steppenwolf. He went on two legs, wore clothes and was a human being, but nevertheless he was in reality a wolf of the Steppes. He had learned a good deal of all that people of a good intelligence can, and was a fairly clever fellow. What he had not learned, however, was this: to find contentment in himself and his own life.

The Steppenwolf Hermann Hesse wrote about could have just as easily been named Jim as Harry. *Steppenwolf* was, in fact, one of Morrison's favorite books, perhaps because he did see himself in its pages. Like Harry, Jim was intelligent and clever, though psychologically at odds with himself. And like Harry, Jim was having an increasingly difficult time finding contentment within himself and his rapidly changing life.

In August 1967 the band was back at Sunset Sound to begin recording sessions for the aptly named *Strange Days,* the group's follow-up to *The Doors,* which had peaked at number two on the national charts. "Light My Fire" had given the band not only the number one hit they'd wanted but also the recognition Jim always felt they deserved. However, instead of being happy with their success, the more popularity the group gained, the worse Jim seemed to feel.

Attorney Max Fink once expressed the opinion that Jim never forgave Robby for writing "Light My Fire." Jim was garnering all the attention fronting the group not because he was a great singing talent, he thought, but because of his good looks and his unpredictable nature. The other three members of The Doors each had very tangible talents— keyboard, drums, and guitar—while Jim was supposed to be the word man. But when The Doors took the stage, more often than not it was Robby's words the audience was screaming for, not Jim's, even though Jim was the one they wanted to see and hear give those words voice.

"He'd have great periods of insecurity where he'd feel he was a fraud," said a friend. It was good to be wanted, good to be admired; Jim had certainly striven to be the center of attention, in one way or another, his entire life. But now that all eyes were on him, something about the experience rang false. "He knew that he wasn't getting through to people on the one level that he wanted," says January Jensen, "and that on the other level, he was coating everybody with this celebrity status. He felt uncomfortable, very uncomfortable." Record executives and club owners admired his ability to pull in a paying audience; women admired his good looks and his mysterious ways; audiences admired what appeared to be his headlong dash toward an abyss that most were too terrified to even imagine, let alone endeavor to experience. They all wanted him for one reason or another, but none of the reasons felt quite right.

Just as he had made it a point to befriend the street people of Washington, D.C., when he was in high school, and had tried to join the migrant farm workers when he visited L.A. with Bryan Gates, as Jim's fame grew he liked to hang out in the poor sections of Los Angeles and mingle with the people there. "These people are truly happy," Morrison said of his sojourns. "They eat, they screw, they work at menial jobs. They go nowhere, but they don't question." It was an irony that didn't escape Jim. Most people would assume that Jim had everything he could ever wish for, yet, said a friend, "He envied these poor Mexicans for finding the happiness that eluded him."

It had been a fine fantasy once, growing up to be loved and admired, sought after, wealthy, adored. But somehow with all the admiration and wealth came not contentment, but a sense of falseness and the growing need to obliterate intruding reality. Obliterating reality for Jim usually meant grabbing the nearest bottle. And it was when Jim had been drinking that the funny, charming, generous, gentle person most people knew to be Jim Morrison disappeared and, in his place, appeared the Steppenwolf.

Paul Rothchild remembered a day not long after Jim died when, for Paul, the singer's battle with alcoholism was drawn sharply into focus. "I was driving in the car listening to the news radio, and along comes this interesting feature. The announcer says, 'Have you ever been to a bar with a bunch of your buddies and everybody's had a drink and they start feeling pretty good? And then you all have another drink and start feeling *pretty good* and have another drink and people are pretty loaded—except for one guy, who's not getting loaded. Then you have a fourth drink and you're all smashed except for this one guy who's not very high. And then this guy has one more drink and all of a sudden he turns into a maniac and he either starts beating people up, or he becomes very loud and verbally abusive . . .' And I'm screaming at the radio, *'Yeah! I knew that guy! I knew that guy!'"*

The host of the radio show went on to explain that a study had just found that these people were born without the enzyme necessary to metabolize alcohol properly. "What happens," recalled Rothchild from listening to the report, "is that the alcohol builds up and builds up and they don't get high, because of course you get high not from the alcohol, but from the metabolization of sugar back into sugar. And then all of a sudden there's so much alcohol in the blood that the brain short-circuits and they go schizophrenic on you. And oh boy, that was Jim, right there. But until he reached that point, he could be drinking and he would have no outward appearance of being drunk. But then, like a switch flipped, he would turn into an absolute maniac."

"That was it! That was it! Very succinct," is Paul Ferrara's reaction upon hearing Rothchild's description. "Everybody thought that Jim was always on drugs, but he was really just drunk," says Ferrara. "They'd all go, *'Yeah, man, what's he on?'* I'd say, *'Three bottles of scotch.'"*

Being drunk is a good disguise.
I drink so I
can talk to assholes.
This includes me.

As wild as Jim could be in public when he'd been drinking, with Pamela he was often a different person, just as Mary's presence at his side in Florida had kept the beast in him at bay. "They were real quiet when they were together," remembers Paul Ferrara. "When Pamela was there, it was like he was with his wife, you know. But boy, when she was gone . . . ! We used to get thrown out of places. There was a whole list of places in Hollywood we couldn't go in with Jim. They'd say *'No! Get that fucker out of here!'* The Troubador was one—he couldn't go in the Troubador."

If Jim had been drinking in public and Pamela was with him, says Ferrara, she wouldn't hesitate to let him suffer the consequences of his behavior alone. "We went to the Jupiter one night, Pam, Jim, and I," Paul says. "It was opening night for Blood, Sweat, and Tears, their first gig. We were in this little balcony, and Jim was screaming. Of course he was drunk—he would not do something like that when he wasn't drunk. When he wasn't drunk, he was the gentleman, he was the angel dude. But he had his threshold, and once he passed it, he was obnoxious. There's no doubt about it. And eventually he would just pass out, pee in his pants, and we would carry him home." That night the ushers threw Jim out of the theater, but Pamela insisted that Paul stay with her and see the show. It had been Jim's decision to drink, it would be Jim who suffered for it, not them. They found Jim after the show, curled up in the back of a stranger's car, asleep.

"He was like the world's heaviest drinker," says Ferrara. "He just drank everything in sight, and eventually it would make him shitfaced. And that's when he got into all the trouble."

Drummer John Densmore was feeling the effects of Jim's ever increasing substance abuse, going so far as to ask Vince Treanor, who replaced Bill Siddons as the group's roadie when Siddons was promoted to manager, to pour out any liquor he found so Jim wouldn't be tempted. Vince wouldn't be the first or the last baby-sitter assigned, without success, to save Jim from himself. But such tactics were pointless. If Jim wanted to take drugs, including alcohol, he had any number of people not only willing but anxious to down a few with him or fetch a few for him. And if John didn't like it, well, Jim had his own way of showing contempt for John's concerns.

Robby and John had taken an apartment together in Laurel Canyon, near Pam and Jim's place. Densmore remembers coming home one day after one of the *Strange Days* sessions to find their apartment in shambles. "We wondered for about thirty seconds who'd done it," John writes in his 1990 memoir, *Riders on the Storm*. But it was unmistakably Jim's work, possibly the result of "one final acid trip before truly commiting to booze." But Jim hadn't worked alone. "Pam had joined him in the excursion," writes Densmore, "and they'd ventured next door to our apartment and freaked out. Jim got the idea to piss on my bed." John was characteristically livid. Robby, just as typically, found the whole thing incredibly funny. Of course it wasn't his bed Jim had pissed on.

Pamela's willingness to follow Jim's lead when it came to drug and alcohol use was starting to wane. As he had with Mary Werbelow in the beginning, Jim took great delight in having someone he could educate and influence, and Pamela was the perfect pupil, anxious to try anything Jim suggested, excited by the newness and danger of it all. But the drugs that appealed to Jim most—hallucinogenics and, especially, alcohol—didn't always agree with Pamela. Acid trips tended to turn into nightmares of crawling bugs and walls dripping with blood. Ray remembers an incident in a motel in San Francisco, when he and Dorothy had a room next to Jim and Pam's. "They dropped some acid," he says, and "[Pam] did not exactly go into the cosmic bliss one could go into. She said, '*Blood! I'm seeing blood everywhere!*' She plummeted into the depths of blood, obviously a real scary trip. That was probably the last time Pam ever took acid."

While their habits may have differed, Jim and Pam were merely traveling separate lanes of the same treacherous road. "She was into her downers, and Jim was into his downer," says Rothchild. "Her downers were primarily things like hash and grass, and his downer was alcohol." Ray concurs. "The opiates were more her thing," he says. "Actually Pam was the first person we ever knew who had opium. I'd never smoked opium before; that came from Pam and Jim. We played a gig in San Francisco and were staying in Sausalito. And Pam produced some opium. And I thought, 'Oh, hey! Look at this! Holy cow! Opium!'" Ray, Dorothy, Jim, and Pam all lit up. "[It was] very mellow, very nice," Ray recalls.

"Mr. and Mrs. Nice," 1967.

It wasn't that Pamela was adverse to Jim's downer—alcohol. After all, she'd started drinking in high school when she would spend weekends at the Rendezvous Ballroom. But when it came to escaping reality, alcohol was slow, boring, and, even worse, fattening. Even as early as 1967 it was easy to see what Jim's alcohol consumption was doing to his once lean body. "The quality of his flesh was disgusting to me," says Mirandi Babitz. Mirandi had a unique vantage point from which to observe Jim's physical state since she had fitted him for some of the leather pants he'd taken to wearing. "Even when he was thin he was pudgy," she recalls. "It was the alcohol! He always had that slight layer of bloat, even when he was a thin guy."

Pamela, on the other hand, knew that Jim appreciated her leanness; he had even referred to it in "Twentieth Century Fox," a song he had written especially for Pamela, about a modern woman who was neither pudgy nor punctual. At five feet four inches, Pamela's weight fluctuated between ninety-four and ninety-eight pounds, nearly twenty pounds below what was considered at the time to be ideal for a woman of her height. January Jensen remembers Jim speaking with great pride of Pam's tiny build, and Jim's close friend, Babe Hill, who initially began working for The Doors as filmmaker and photographer Paul Ferrara's assistant, confirms this, saying, "He talked about it all the time." It's doubtful Jim realized that the svelte look he found so attractive stemmed back to Pamela's ongoing bouts with anorexia rooted in childhood, or that Pamela would, at times, starve herself for days in order to maintain the figure he so admired. To him, her size made her seem like one of the mythical sprites that frequented Mt. Shasta—ethereal, magical—and it made him feel powerful by comparison. The fact that she had more than once nearly knocked him unconscious during some of their more tumultuous fights in which harsh words were not the only things thrown seemed almost beside the point.

It was, unfortunately, these fights Jim and Pam had that people tend to remember best about the relationship. Anne Moore was a rock journalist in L.A. and became friends with Jim later in his career. But long before she met Jim, Anne had heard stories of the tempestuous nature of his relationship with the volatile redhead.

"He and Pam fought for nothing special," she says. "They'd do it just to be fighting. They could be blissfully happy and suddenly let go with a wordy fight, or a physical, knock-down-drag-out fight. I never could figure out whether he wanted a chick that ballsy or not; she seemed very strong." But it was precisely this strength that Jim admired in Pamela because he himself lived with the self-certainty of his own inherent weakness. *"I'll just this about all that,"* he wrote of their lopsided union, *"I was the mouse who caught the cat."*

It was obvious that Jim's fights with Pamela were largely fueled by alcohol. But while Pamela would take Jim to task for his drunken behavior, the other members of The Doors, who were also being regularly challenged by Jim's alcoholism, remained silent. After all, Jim was a poet and rock star, and romantic tradition almost demanded that he live a life of excess in order to fulfill either of these roles. But in reality, Jim was just Jim, an intelligent and talented young man with a problem, who was falling apart, drop by drop, and dragging everyone else under in his wake. Even so, this slow-building self-destruction was largely ignored by those around him, a fact that John Densmore has referred to as "the secret, unspoken pact to cover up the fact that something was wrong in the band."

But Ray Manzarek defends what he considers a decision not to interfere with Jim's personal life. "We didn't get a rock and roll band together to watch over each other's every move," he says. "We got a rock and roll band together to create music. I mean it wasn't as if he was drunk all the time or anything. Most of the time he was perfectly sober and normal and lucid and intelligent and bright, witty, and charming."

It was true, Jim certainly wasn't drunk all of the time. But he was drunk enough of the time to pose a serious problem. "You never knew whether Jim would show up as the erudite, poetic scholar or the kamikaze drunk," said Rothchild. The fact that *Strange Days* was taking far longer to record and was far more involved than the first album had been didn't help. Always the perfectionist, Rothchild was doing take after take just to get a single sound, a single rhythm, a single feeling just the way he wanted it, and the continual takes and retakes were starting to wear on everyone's nerves. Because of the tedious nature of much of this work, Jim would only show up when his presence was absolutely required and not before, and even then he would often keep the others waiting, sometimes for hours. When he did finally show up, writes Densmore, "there was incredible tension in the room for a while, but no one expressed his anger over Jim's rudeness or tardiness."

"So what do you do?" says Manzarek, exasperated. "You're dealing with a person who goes from one extreme to the other. Totally capable of doing his work, a marvelous guy, lot of fun, he'd come into the recording studio, we'd laugh and joke and have a great time, and once out of eight to ten sessions he'd come into the studio drunk as a skunk." But one in ten was enough to cause delays and stress within the group, particularly those times when Jim found something even more serious than alcohol to distract him.

"Once [Jim] came in with a girl, who'd given him too many pills on top of it," remembers Ray. "So you've got Paul Rothchild, Bruce Botnick, Ray Manzarek, John Densmore, and Robby Krieger trying to figure out, 'What the fuck do we do in this situation?'" Jim later told Pamela that the "five to one" odds he wrote about in the song of the same name referred to exactly that configuration: Paul, Bruce, Ray, John, and Robby all, in Jim's estimation, pitted against him.

In many ways, Jim hadn't changed at all from his days at FSU. He was still pushing people's buttons, testing their limits, and watching their reactions. But those around him *had* changed; they'd grown up. Jim was no longer dealing with Bryan and Chris and the other college boys at Hot Henry's Haven who could cut the cord on his electric blanket and tell him to find another place to live. Now he was dealing with contracts and commitments, with the expectations of total strangers, with hundreds of thousands of dollars and the lives of far more than just the other three band members all dependent upon the actions of just one person: Jim Morrison.

"It's not as if Jim's totally insane or anything," says Manzarek, of Jim's condition. "He's slurring his words and kind of staggering around. And you want to say, 'Jim what are you on?' And then you see the girl, and then the girl holds her hand out and there's a bunch of pills. Jesus! But it's still Jim and he's still lucid and he's still talking to you, except he's slurring and staggering and a little goofy. And you think, 'Is he going to get better? Is he going to get worse? Let's call the paramedics in case he gets worse. But maybe he'll get better and say, *'C'mon let's go! I wanna sing!'* Okay, he wants to sing. What are we going to do, close the session down?"

Instead, no one spoke, no one rebuked, no one discussed, a classic situation with those who find themselves in a relationship of any kind with an alcoholic. "It feels like there's an elephant in the room but you don't mention it," Jane Woititz writes in *Adult Children of Alcoholics*. "There's elephant shit everywhere . . . but you pretend it's not there." Jim did his thing, when he could, when he would, and the others waited in silence, hoping for the best but ready for the worst. "It was a strange relationship in that this man was not a blithering idiot who was totally out of control all the time," says Manzarek. "Just the opposite. And the fact that he took too many pills in one evening with a girl and wasn't actually able to get a vocal didn't mean that he wouldn't get one tomorrow. And if he does, you know, fine. And if he doesn't . . . sure enough, tomorrow would come and there'd be Jim, or two days later, and he'd be absolutely straight and fine and Jim Morrison."

As Manzarek observed, when Jim was drunk, his condition seemed to control him and those around him. But when he was sober, he was able to easily charm anyone who met him. On the first of several excursions to Orange to visit the Coursons—trips he liked to characterize as "visiting the in-laws"—Jim was determined to put his best foot forward to impress Pamela's parents. Being an upstanding young citizen was one of the acts he could pull off especially well when he wanted to; Chris Kallivokas's mother could attest to that.

Wearing an uncharacteristic suit and tie, his hair cut a little shorter than normal, Jim mixed easily with Pamela's parents and a few other close friends who had been invited over to the Courson's home for cocktails. Since everyone was drinking martinis, Jim asked for one, too. Corky mixed the drink, and as people were milling about, Jim sneaked into the kitchen, where Penny was preparing hors d'oeuvres. "Mrs. Courson," said Jim in a conspiratorial tone, "don't tell anybody, but I just can't stand this!" And he poured the martini down the drain, partially refilling his martini glass with water. While the impression given was, as Jim intended, that of a self-conscious teetotaler, the fact was that Jim simply would have preferred a straight scotch but had the good sense not to ask for one in the circumstances. The Coursons were predictably charmed by their daughter's boyfriend.

Paul Rothchild had known, in a peripheral way, that Jim had a girlfriend but, he said, "I didn't become really become aware of [Pamela] until the second album. She was around a great deal more then. Every time he saw her coming into the studio, my friend [assistant engineer] Fritz Richmond used to call out, 'Here comes the most beautiful girl in the world!' And she was. She was very beautiful." But while Paul was as charmed by Pamela's beauty and apparent sweetness as anybody, he also sensed something under the surface that made him wary. "I have a thing called red signal danger, an alarm lights up in my head," he said. "And to me she was dangerous. There was nothing but trouble there." But as Jim had explained to January Jensen, trouble was just what he'd been looking for in a woman.

The vision of Pamela as nature's child had also begun to change with Jim's success. The more well known her boyfriend became, the more Pamela tried to dress and act the way she thought the girlfriend of a successful rock star should. "The first time I met Pamela, I remember she was makeup-less, lovely, in a very kind of all-American way, a bit of an innocent," remembers Bill Siddons. "And then every time I met her, she was a little different and a little wilder from that point on." But Siddons could see in Pamela's escalating wildness a desperate attempt to keep up with Jim's intensity. "In my personal opinion, she was almost kind of dragged along into Jim's world, and she kind of went, 'Okay! I'm on this boat, I guess I'd better paddle!' And I think that kind of happened to Pamela, and I saw her get just a little more outrageous as time went on."

But as outrageous as both Jim and Pam could be at times, whether together or apart, there was an underlying sweetness in their relationship, a longing for a lovingly stable alliance that neither seemed capable of maintaining for any length of time. "It wasn't Mr. and Mrs. Nice," recalled Rothchild of Jim and Pam's relationship. "It was weird, but with a surface attempt at Mr. and Mrs. Nice." Says Mirandi Babitz, "It was like 'Let's go to the Morrisons for dinner—and see the plates fly!'" Yet at the same time, there remained a tender devotion that, while not always obvious to the outside observer, ran very deep. Their love for each other was a constant thread that appeared throughout Morrison's writing, and even some of their fights were immortalized in the pages of Jim's notebooks.

Jim's writing had always been one of the few constants in his life. No matter how often he had moved with his family, no matter where life or circumstance might take him, Jim would always carry notebooks with him in which he could put down his observations and work out passages of poetry, some of which would later make their way into the songs of The Doors. Nothing was more important to him than his writing, and there was no one he wanted more to share this work with than Pamela.

"I remember one time we were going down from my place in the city, in San Francisco," says January Jensen. "We were on a holiday, going down Highway One headed to L.A., taking our time. Jim always carried a notebook with him because he was always writing whatever came into his head. And every time we'd come to a restaurant, a general store, or a gas station, he'd have to stop and call Pam." January, Babe Hill, and Paul Ferrara, who were also along for the ride, would tease Jim unmercifully about his obsession with this woman, so Jim would make up excuses for the phone calls. "He'd say, 'I gotta call the office,'" January laughs. "The office, hell! I would watch over his shoulder what he was writing in the notebook, because after he talked to Pamela, it would give him inspiration, good or bad, and then he'd start writing. And I could always tell he'd talked to Pamela."

Why does my mind circle around you
Why do planets wonder what it
Would be like to be you

"Sometimes when she was angry, I guess, she'd curse him," Eva Gardonyi said in *Feast of Friends,* "but never, ever, thought of him as a bad poet. She always gave him quite a lot of attention and admiration, and he also showed a great deal of kindness and loving behavior toward her." Jim had taken a somewhat jaded view of life from an early age, particularly after The Doors started becoming successful and the real world intruded on Jim's fun. But with Pamela he always had an appreciative audience. *"There was preserved in her the fresh miracle of surprise,"* he wrote of her, and it was true. Where Jim looked around the world and saw dark corners and lurking shadows, Pamela, observed Gardonyi, ". . . was easy to burst into laughter and look at life in that love-child, you know, that sweet-child manner." They were opposites to the extent that they came together at full circle and became one fixed point there.

"She was quick, Pamela, and she had a clarity of a child with very good intuitions, and an innocence that Jimmy loved in her a great deal, that childish innocence," says Gardonyi, with whom Jim lived briefly at one point while Pamela was in Europe. "And even though she was at times impossible to be with, he would say, 'She's a sweet child.' Somehow he just needed to take care of her. Actually it was quite touching. She was one of the few people he trusted enough to bare himself." Everyone loved different pieces of Jim Morrison, and he revealed those pieces in turn, depending upon his audience of the moment. But with Pamela, Jim could put aside that caution and be himself, for better or for worse.

Many loved him as a refined and clever and interesting man, and were horrified and disappointed when they had come upon the wolf in him. And they had to because Harry wished, as every sentient being does, to be loved as a whole and therefore it was just with those whose love he most valued that he could least of all conceal and belie the wolf.

"With her, at home, he could just be Jim," said Paul Rothchild. "He could have smelly feet and be a human being and she accepted it." Even so, Rothchild observed, Pamela also wouldn't hesitate to jerk Jim back into line if his behavior became too outrageous. "And he'd like that," said Rothchild. "That was fun for him because very few people were willing to go on the offensive with him. I guess he liked that about her. She just had enough guts to go on the offensive."

"Pamela said something to me in Paris that never left me," says Bill Siddons of the few days following Jim's death. "She said, 'There were a lot of people who pretended to be close to Jim, but I was the only one who had the nerve to stand up to him.'" Bill immediately recognized the truth in her statement. "All the rest of us just kind of went, 'Okay Jim, whatever you want, Jim, we'll work around it.' But Pamela didn't. Pamela just went, *'Fuck you, buddy! You'd better do this!'* She screamed and yelled and jumped up and down and didn't take any shit from him. So inevitably he went back to her. Because he knew that she was willing to lose him."

CHAPTER 7

I want you *out of here!*" This revelation was delivered at the top of Pamela's lungs and punctuated by a plate shattering against the wall behind Jim's head. He looked at the dent in the wall, then at Pamela—furious, pale, and shaking—across the room. No matter how close he came to getting his head bashed in, he still had to admire the girl's pitching arm.

"Pam, honey, we'll never get anywhere if you don't tell me what you want," Jim said calmly, solicitously. He knew that nothing made her more furious than not being taken seriously when she was in a mood like this.

"I hate you, Jim Morrison, and I want you out of here *now!*"

"I'm sorry, did you say something? There's some hysterical woman screaming in my ear and I can't hear a thing. What did you say?"

He could tell she was casting about for something else to throw. Then, seeming to think better of it, she instead walked into the bedroom and quietly closed the door behind her. Ah, what new move was this? The approaching sound of sirens in the distance a few minutes later answered his question. It was only when the sirens ceased their screaming and there was a heavy knock on the door that Pamela emerged from the bedroom, a satisfied smile on her face.

"Jim, honey, I think you have visitors."

Pamela opened the door to two of L.A.'s finest. Each was young, freshly scrubbed, and surprised as hell to see Jim Morrison standing in the room.

"Officers," said Pamela, "this man won't leave. I've asked him again and again, but he refuses to go." No need to tell them that Jim lived there, that it was Jim who paid the rent. If Jim didn't bring it up, why should she?

Unfortunately, her desire to see Jim thrown to the ground, hand-cuffed, and, hopefully, pistol whipped was cut short. "Hey, aren't you Jim Morrison?" asked the younger of the two in awe. "My girlfriend and I saw you guys at the Whisky last year; you were great!"

"Excuse me!" Pamela interrupted what appeared to be the instan-taneous formation of a new fan club. "I called you guys to get him out of here. Remember?"

"Oh! Pam, *honey,* did you want me to leave?" Jim's voice was puzzled, a tad hurt. Pamela wanted to smash his smug face in. These cops were actually buying this crap! Only someone who knew him as well as she did would see that beneath his polite, charming exterior, Jim was drunk.

The older officer turned to Pamela as though she was the intruder in this situation. "Ma'am, there's nothing we can do unless he refuses to leave. Will you leave the premises, Mr. Morrison?" he asked, turning to Jim.

"I had no idea she wanted to me to leave!" Jim exclaimed, his face a study of innocent consternation. "She's shy, you know, and sometimes it's hard to tell what she wants," he confided, giving the officers a knowing grin as though to say *'Women! What're you gonna do with 'em?'* The officers chuckled, letting him know that they all shared this common burden. They were just three buddies, good ol' boys having a joke at the little lady's expense. Pamela was eyeing the pistol in the hip holster of the nearest officer, gauging her chances of getting all three of them before the other cop could take her out. She was a pretty good shot, but still, it didn't look good.

Jim sauntered nonchalantly to the door, his adoring fans trailing behind. He stuck his hands in his jacket pocket as one of the officers opened the door. Suddenly Jim stopped, hesitated a moment, then turned, saying, as though in afterthought, "Oh, by the way, officers . . ."

Casually he withdrew his hand from his pocket, pulling out an enormous wad of parking tickets. Pamela's already pale skin blanched paper-white as she saw what Jim was about to do. Neither Jim nor Pamela paid much attention to street signs, tending to park their cars wherever they happened to stop. In fact, ever since The Doors had started to make real money, both Jim and Pam had more than once parked in some odd location, forgotten where they had left their car, and rather than look for it, simply bought a new one. The tickets the two accumulated were sent off to Bob Greene, accountant for The Doors, for payment. The mess of paper in Jim's hand represented several hundred dollars of unpaid fines in Pamela's name that Jim had been planning to send on to Bob. Pamela knew now that they'd never make it that far.

As he pressed the tickets into the hand of the nearest officer, Jim's smile was that of someone who knew he was about to throw the winning pitch in a particularly close game. ". . . These belong to her."

It was several hours before Pamela heard the guard call out her name. "Your boyfriend finally posted bail," the stout matron announced as she led Pamela out of the crowded cell and down the hall. "He's just in time, too. Ten more minutes and you were going to be sent over to Sybil Brand. They don't let you spend the night there without a strip search, you know."

If Pamela noticed Jim's face smiling at her in the waiting room, she gave no indication. Instead, she walked past him and out the door without speaking. She was half a block away before he caught up with her.

"Hey, no thanks for bailing you out?" His chuckle was tentative in the face of her stony silence. Was this the time? The one time he'd gone too far?

"I hate you," her tone was even, matter-of-fact.

"C'mon, Pam! You've gotta admit it was pretty funny!" His tone held the shadow of a doubt, like that of a third grader whose teacher had somehow failed to see the humor of the snake he'd placed in her desk drawer.

Pamela stopped short, spinning on her heel to face Jim, oblivious to the curious stares he was drawing. Let them stare! She was certainly used to it by now. "They were going to strip search me, Morrison! You call that funny?"

He looked at her freckled face, flushed with frustration. God, she was beautiful! Why did he keep doing these things to her? Why did they keep doing these things to each other?

"Well, I hope you made them buy you a drink first."

She stared at him a moment longer, the stupid grin on his face faltering slightly. Why did she put up with this shit? "I really hate you," she said, and resumed her angry stride.

"Aw, Pam, c'mon; you know I was just kidding," he called after her. "C'mon!" He quickened his step to catch up with her, grabbing her arm to slow her down. His voice grew husky, seductive, "Love my girl." Suddenly he was Jim Morrison, Rock Star, an entity he knew from experience that no woman could resist.

"I hate you."

Well, maybe one.

Just off the sidewalk ahead, Jim spied a funky-looking vendor displaying his wares. Plastic statues of the Madonna of every size and description were lined up like a virginal chorus line. Jim ran ahead, grabbing the largest statue and throwing whatever money he had in his pocket at the vendor. From the man's delighted grin, Jim was sure it had been more than enough. Cradling the three-foot statue in his arms, he ran awkwardly back to Pam, planting himself firmly in front of her.

"Please accept this as a token of a penitent's devotion," he said with a gallant, theatrical bow.

"I hate you," she said softly, eyes downcast at the figure resting on the sidewalk between them. But Jim could see the little smile on her face.

"You don't hate me," he whispered as he leaned over and placed a soft kiss on her lips.

She waited a couple of beats, letting him suffer. "All right, maybe I love you," she finally admitted as she walked away, leaving him standing next to the Madonna. "But," she yelled back at him, "I hate myself for it!"

Jim laughed, grabbed the statue, and ran after Pam. One arm around the Madonna, one arm around Pamela, Jim and his girls made their way home.

& I'm still here
& you're still here
& we're still around

CHAPTER

8

O nce upon a time, back in the early days, it was time for Ray and Dorothy to get married." Ray Manzarek takes the third-person approach when speaking of his own wedding to Dorothy Fujikawa in December 1967, a time when, as Manzarek puts it, "Ray could support Dorothy in the manner to which neither one of them had ever become accustomed."

"So anyway, come marriage time," Ray continues. "Jim and Pam are firmly couple-ized, and it's time for Ray and Dorothy to get married. We have our license and we've had our blood tests and we're all set and ready to go. Being the good hippies that we were, the last thing in the world we were going to do is have some kind of a regular ceremony, nor did we want to do a 'flower child on the hill.' We'd been living together for five years, so the marriage itself was just a formality as far as the state was concerned, in which we sort of took each other's name, put rings on the finger, and said we are now officially an entity, a couple on the planet.

"So we went downtown to City Hall and got married on a judge's lunch hour along with approximately seventy-four other couples—fifty Chicano couples, twenty-four black couples, and one hippie couple: Ray and Dorothy, with Jim and Pam as best man and bridesmaid. We were the only longhairs in the place! One by one, [couples] would go into the judge's chambers and come out within two or three minutes. And then the next one, and then the next one, and then the next one. In the morning we'd gotten a ring, because we knew we had to do the 'with this ring I thee wed.' So we went to a five-and-ten store on Broadway, which is the big Mexican shopping street, and got the most garish snake ring I could possibly find. It was absurd! The most ridiculous thing I've ever seen! It was a coiled snake with a phony turquoise diamond in its skull. This is the ring we will use for this official ceremony."

Dorothy and Ray, who had the ring in his pocket, were already there waiting when Jim and Pamela arrived at City Hall for the brief ceremony. "Jim didn't know anything about [the ring]," Ray says, continuing with his story. "So into the judge's chambers. The judge said, 'Is it a two-ring or a one-ring ceremony?' I said, 'It's a one-ring ceremony.'

"So the ceremony proceeded as usual. 'Do you, Raymond Daniel Manzarek, take Dorothy Aiko Fujikawa, to be your lawful . . . ,'" Ray remembers the judge intoning. "'Okay now put the ring on her finger and say *with this ring* . . .' So I pulled this ring out of my pocket and Morrison just bursts out laughing! He had to put his hand over his mouth when he saw the thing. His eyes started to water, earwax started coming out of his ears he was trying to stifle it so hard.

"After the ceremony, into the cars, off to Olvera Street where we ate lustily of enchiladas and margaritas and drank the afternoon away," Ray concludes. "We got married on the Winter Solstice, so it couldn't have been a lovelier wedding, couldn't have been a better day. Jim and Pam were in fine form. They had a great time."

Ray reasoned that it was this simple and festive nature of his wedding to Dorothy that may have first sparked in Pamela plans for her future with Jim. "Pam saw how absolutely easy it is to get married," says Manzarek. "My god, there's nothing to it! You just get your blood test, get your certificate, go stand up in front of a judge, and boom! You're done."

If nothing else, Jim and Pamela certainly had the "get your certificate" part of the proceedings down cold. On Wednesday, June 26, 1968, Jim Morrison and Pamela Courson went to Los Angeles City Hall and took out what was rumored to be their second marriage license, though the first one, said to have been picked up in Mexico shortly after the couple first met, no one remembers ever actually seeing. But any thoughts of a June wedding expired along with the marriage license, which was allowed to languish and die, unused.

"It was like a game," January Jensen laughs. "What should we do today? Well, let's get a marriage license!" Cheri Siddons concurs. "They would try," she says. "They would be really proud and they'd say, 'Well we have a marriage license and we're gonna get married.' Then boom! One of them would go and throw the other one in jail or something. You know they always sabotaged it somehow."

Later, in court papers filed after Jim's death, Pamela would state that one of the reasons she and Jim never actually followed through on these marriage licenses was that The Doors' management wouldn't allow it, though she stated that she and Jim did agree to a common-law arrangement during a Doors tour in Colorado in 1967. "Jim and I had discussed marriage on several occasions before this trip," Pamela testified, in writing, "but felt, as did his managers, that the attendant publicity to a publicly registered marriage would have a detrimental effect upon the image they were trying to develop for him." Apparently it was one thing for Ray, Robby, and John to get married, but for the band's sex symbol to do anything as seemingly safe and normal as taking a wife was deemed potentially harmful for the group.

While this explanation does make a certain amount of sense professionally, Paul Ferrara finds it hard to believe. "That's a typical response for any male sex symbol shit," Ferrara scoffs. "If you get married, the little girls won't come. But I think that's pretty passé as an example of why anyone wouldn't get married. And I don't think that Jim would ever, in a million years, do anything that The Doors' management wanted him to do."

In fact, most who knew Jim and Pamela well agree that Pamela's story of a common-law arrangement in Colorado was likely little more than a matter of legal necessity to protect her interests after Jim's death against claims on the estate that prevented her from drawing a widow's stipend. Ferrara, for one, never doubted the deepness and sincerity of Jim's feelings for Pamela, and Pamela's for Jim, but feels that Jim simply wasn't ready for, nor saw the necessity of, any sort of legal entanglement. Another of Morrison's associates concurred, saying, "I don't think Jim would have married anyone. He had ambivalent feelings about women at best."

Ferrara attributes Jim's ambivalence to a less abstract reason. "I really don't think he wanted to marry Pam because he really had Pam just exactly the way he wanted her at that point," Paul explains. The thought of getting married brought on nightmare visions of not only emotional fidelity, which Jim could probably handle, but physical allegiance as well, which was anathema to Jim. "If you get married you can't go to New York and have a girlfriend and go somewhere else and have a girlfriend," says Ferrara. "In fact he did love Pam, but wasn't ready to marry her. But he was going through motions and actions to make her feel more comfortable with the situation."

One of the things Jim had done toward this end was finance a retail venture for Pamela, a hip boutique on La Cienega, not far from The Doors' office, that the couple decided to call Themis, after the Greek goddess of justice and law. It was, after all, only just that Pamela get something for herself out of Jim's involvement with The Doors. She had certainly had to live with enough of the negative effects.

"You're talking about a woman who's living with someone who's larger than life, and there aren't really too many definitions of what's going

Pamela's business card from Themis.

on," says Ferrara. "And her position in that life was a constant battle to maintain some sort of dignity as an entity. She could be totally eclipsed and overpowered by what was going on with him. But he was strong enough to allow her to have her life, and that's why he financed Themis and all the other things that she might want to do, because he wanted her to be alive and vital. I'm convinced of it."

"I thought it was the most extravagant gift a man could give a woman," says Bill Siddons, of his first visit to the store. "And Jim loved giving her the gift, he loved that Pamela was having so much fun with it."

To others, though, the store seemed like nothing more than a plush money pit. "John and I went over there," recalls Ray Manzarek, "and walked into the place while they were working on it and said 'Holy shit! This has gotta cost a fortune!' Soft young men with soft moist eyes wearing soft garments and flowing hair were stapling feathers to the wall. Jesus Christ! What is going on here?"

That's what Mirandi Babitz wondered the day Pamela called to tell her old friend that she was opening a new boutique, a store that would be in direct competition with Mirandi's own.

Mirandi and her boyfriend, Clem, who was British, had moved to England in 1967 and had been married there. Clem had previously done some leather work in Chicago, and Mirandi knew how to sew, so the couple began designing clothing together. It wasn't long before some of the hippest shops on London's Kings Road—Granny Takes a Trip, Hung On You—were selling Mirandi and Clem's designs and taking special orders as well. "I started meeting groups like The Who and The Rolling

Stones and all kinds of people because we made clothes for everybody in the rock world," Mirandi recalls."We were pretty good."

The couple returned to the States in 1968 and opened a boutique on the Sunset Strip. "I didn't see very much of Pamela until they started coming in and then I started making clothes for Jim," says Babitz. Pamela showed an immediate interest in her friend's shop and asked Mirandi about the details of opening and operating the boutique. "It wasn't like everybody was opening a boutique," says Babitz. "I mean there were like three in L.A. I had mine, and the next thing I know Pam calls me up and says kind of guiltily that she's going to open this boutique and Jim's giving her all this money and she's going to design clothes." That was, says Mirandi, "pretty much the end of my feeling comfortable with her."

Part of Mirandi's resentment of Pamela's actions stemmed from the fact that, unlike Mirandi, Pamela didn't have to scrimp and save to open her shop. "I was twenty-one," Babitz says, "and I had done this whole thing entirely on a shoestring, scraping together the money." But Pamela only had to ask, and whatever funds she needed were instantly at her disposal.

"Jim was always giving her stuff," says Paul Ferrara. "Money, clothes, cars, dogs, anything she wanted. He was crazy about her, and so he pampered the hell out of her. She would want something, and he would just call Max and say 'Give her whatever she wants, Max.'"

January Jensen recalls a typical incident that illustrates the point: "One night we were going to the airport. Jim had just bought Pamela a new Porsche, so she drove us. We got to the airport, running late as usual, and we jumped out of the car." Pamela suddenly remembered something she wanted to say to Jim, so without looking, she threw open her door and yelled to Jim and "a car came along and hit the door of the Porsche at about thirty-five miles an hour," says Jensen, and sheared the door completely off its hinges. Giving Pamela cab fare and a kiss, Jim dismissed the damaged car, telling her, "Just get a new one."

Later, rumors would circulate that Jim had sunk anywhere from $100,000 to $1 million (an unlikely sum) into Themis, but the expenditure seemed to bother everybody but Jim. "Money meant nothing to Jim, it really didn't," says Ferrara. "It was immaterial to him if he spent one dollar on her or a hundred thousand dollars, as long as she was happy."

In fact, Jim was notoriously open handed not just with Pamela, but with all of his friends. "One time I was making a little movie, and I got to a point when I was looking at it on a Moviola," Ferrara recalls, "and I needed $5,000 to make it into a thing where I could take it into the labs and everything. And Jim looked at it on the Moviola and he goes, 'God, this is great!' And I said, 'Yeah, I've been trying to save up the money,' and he says 'How much you need?' I told him, and the next day I had a check in my hand."

Jim's attitude was that his financial success was a fluke; therefore whatever he received was, in his words, "free money," money he didn't really feel he'd earned, but was there to be enjoyed all the same. "Tommy Tucker sang for supper," Jim once told January. "We're gonna have a feast!"

"You'd have to come from an upper-middle-class background to have that attitude toward money, wouldn't you?" observes Babe Hill. "If you came out of the ghetto, money is money and you're going to spend it on yourself, on your own luxury. If you come out of an upper-middle-class family where you've never starved or anything, money is nothing to you. And that went for both [Jim and Pam]." It's true that neither Jim nor Pamela had ever wanted for anything material in life. Both had come from families who may not have always approved of their children's activities but always funded them. "Only one job the guy ever had," says Hill, "and that's being Jim Morrison." It was a full-time job with long hours, but it paid very well.

Jim, Babe, Paul, and Frank Lisciandro worked on various film projects together, and they had an office, which they liked to call the clubhouse, conveniently located just above Pamela's store. Even so, Pamela discouraged Jim's friends from hanging out there. None of Jim's drinking buddies represented the upscale kind of clientele she was hoping to attract, and she didn't want them cluttering up the place.

Pamela would go on buying trips to Europe and Africa, stocking the store with the most unusual, exotic—and expensive—merchandise she could find. "It was *extremely* expensive!" says journalist Anne Moore. "I remember seeing a belt down there that I ended up just going home and copying. It was just leather thongs and some beadwork, and I think they were asking something like $85 to $95 for this thing. That was a hell of a lot of money then! That would be like four or five hundred dollars now! And I'm sure she wasn't buying it at any cut cost or anything. I'm sure she was just buying what she wanted." But again, Jim wasn't concerned about Pam's expenditures, even though he would complain about it in a good-natured way to his friends. "We used to sit up there in the clubhouse and he'd complain about, 'God, all the money she's spending on that place!'" says Babe Hill. "But he said it in such a way that you could tell he was really proud of her. Like a man talking about his wife who's frivolous or something. He loved her very much."

The wives of the other Doors patronized the store, though Julia

Densmore Negron notes that most of the stuff was a little ahead of its time. "In L.A. in those days, we were wearing stuff like landlubber jeans and T-shirts. Pam had all these pants from London with the real high waist, crushed velvet bell-bottoms, like something The Who would be wearing. All the stuff she brought in was like fashion for Europe, but it wasn't quite over in L.A. yet." Even so, says Negron, "She talked us all into buying tons of it."

To Pamela this must have seemed the ultimate joke, getting The Doors' wives to spend large amounts of their husbands' money in her store. A solid wall of animus had sprung up between the other members of the group and Pamela, mostly because Pamela encouraged Jim on a regular basis to leave the band, feeling that The Doors were taking advantage of Jim for their own gain and keeping him from doing the kinds of creative and artistic work for which he really wanted to be known. For this reason, Babe Hill noted, when Pamela went on her buying trips, "I think she took kind of a perverse pleasure in spending not Jim's money, but The Doors' money."

Jim fielded veiled criticisms from the other band members, and not so oblique warnings from their accountant, about the amount of money he was allowing Pamela to go through. In their eyes, it was nothing but a waste because the store couldn't possibly turn a profit. To Jim it was something that gave Pamela a feeling of security and independence. He was proud of her for undertaking it, and if she spent every last dime of his money and The Doors' money, too, so be it.

Jim was given the perfect opportunity to demonstrate his support for Pamela and her store when he was approached by the oversized, glossy fashion magazine *Show* to participate in a piece they were doing on "Celebrities and Their Favorite Designers." Jim chose Pamela.

"It was up to the person who agreed to do this to pick the locale," says Raeanne Rubenstein, the New York photographer who was hired to shoot the layout for *Show*. "Sometimes it was their home and sometimes it was the designer's shop or studio. As I recall, each location was different. But Jim wanted to do it in Pamela's shop in California."

Pamela's storefront, located in what was called the Clear Thoughts Building, was white stucco, and the intense California sun reflecting off the surface that day was hot and blinding. For Raeanne and the reporter who accompanied her, stepping into the dim interior of Themis was like slipping into a cool dream. Embedded among soft pheasant skins, tiny mirrors on the ceiling reflected back the dancing flames of dozens of candles. The walls dripped with rich tapestries and extravagant feathers in every hue. Mounds of plush pillows invited one to sit and be enveloped by the rich surroundings and the heady fragrance of incense. The racks of elegant clothing in soft fabrics from exotic locales seemed almost incidental.

"It was small and dark," says Raeanne, "which made a huge impression on me because it had been so incredibly bright outside. It was the exact opposite of breezy and sunshiny. They had dressing rooms with tie-dyed curtains, and they had lots of pillows; you sat on the floor when you were there. It was dark and romantic, very poetical. It certainly didn't remind you of southern California. It reminded you more of a Greenwich Village poetry den, or someplace in Paris maybe."

Raeanne and the reporter were greeted by Pamela and Jim, who wore a Mao jacket of velvet. "They had invited some of their friends to come," says Raeanne, "and they dressed them up in other equally sort of flamboyant clothes."

Jim and Pamela (who would be referred to as "Pamela Roselilly" in the subsequent magazine article) had definite ideas of what they wanted to do and show and, says Raeanne, "We just followed the leader, which was them." She adds, "Jim appeared to be very involved. He acted like he was very happy."

The shoot lasted for eight hours, during which, Rubenstein says, "Nobody seemed to be in any hurry to leave." In the course of the day, Raeanne was able to form a very strong impression of Jim and Pamela, separately and as a couple.

"Pamela was great!" she says. "First of all, I thought she was beautiful! But she was also really sweet, just a darling." As for Jim, she says, "He was very cooperative and nice. I found him to be friendly, warm, kindhearted, outgoing—you know, all the good things. I thought he was very anxious to give Pamela what she wanted, and what she wanted was this boutique, so he would do anything he could to help her make it a success."

Jim was also impressed with Raeanne, and the two remained friends after that day. Jim would invite Raeanne to dinner when he was in New York, and when he wasn't, he would send her bits of his poetry, books that he had self-published. "He sent me one that had a blue cover with one of those string closures," she recalls. "And inside all the pages were loose and there was a poem, but you could read it in any order just by shifting the pages around. They weren't bound. And the idea was that the poem was to be made up by the reader. That one really made an impression on me."

Raeanne had a hard time reconciling the Jim Morrison who had become her friend with the Jim Morrison she would read about in the press. "It was really a fascinating thing because I would see him on one

The Themis Photos.

The Themis Photos.

The Themis Photos.

© Raeanne Rubenstein

The Themis Photos.

day, and then he would go out and do some outrageous thing that would get reported in the newspaper the next day. It was really difficult to equate the person I knew with the one who was always getting himself in trouble."

The entire shoot at Themis, says Rubenstein, "was a wonderful experience." It also produced some of the most beautiful and enduring images of Jim and Pamela ever captured on film. Though Jim's face was just beginning to show the effects of his alcoholism in its roundness, he still projected a dreamy, brooding handsomeness that nicely offset Pamela's fire-and-ice beauty. Perhaps most notable about the photos is that in most of the shots, Jim in some way positioned himself to be in the periphery, making sure that Pamela was the center of attention. "I got the impression that he was very proud of the fact that she wanted to do this," says Rubenstein, and his efforts to make Pamela the focal point of the layout attests to that pride.

"They were a type of couple that I wasn't unfamiliar with from those days," Raeanne observes. "They seemed to have a kind of sweetness and gentleness about them, and a kind of ethereal quality, like they weren't quite there. I thought they were great in that sort of romantic, dreamy way that people tended to be then if they were sort of the lucky ones, which Pam and Jim really were. It's just too bad they couldn't have appreciated it more."

But it was difficult to say whether or not Jim and Pam appreciated what they had, simply because they kept to themselves as much as they could, even when they were out in public. Ray Manzarek recalls that if Jim and Pam were having dinner with the others, the two of them would participate in the group discussion for a little while but would inevitably drift off into their own private conversation "about people we'd never heard of and didn't know." Julia Negron is struck by the memory of Jim and Pam at a Christmas party Julia and John hosted one year. "They sat on the steps together like a suburban couple from down the street," said Negron. "I remember thinking, 'How nice!'"

But they had their separate lives as well. Jim had his group of friends—Babe, January, Wes Farrell, Paul Ferrara, Frank Lisciandro—whom Pamela would see on occasion, and Pamela had her set of friends—a more sophisticated, fashion-conscious group—whom Jim avoided whenever possible. "Pam was always a bit of a mystery to me," says Negron. "Besides the fact that she was rarely around, she seemed quite sophisticated with all her jet-set friends and her clothing store." With such disparate tastes, Negron wonders, "Who could even imagine what their home life was like?" No one seemed to know for sure, and neither Jim nor Pam seemed eager to share details.

"What was Pam doing when she wasn't with Jim?" Ray Manzarek wonders aloud. "I didn't know. What was Jim doing when Jim was not with The Doors? Half the time I didn't know."

And that was, undoubtedly, just the way Jim liked it.

CHAPTER 9

The man drew deeply on his cigarette and glanced again at his watch. He waited. Planes arriving and departing LAX roared periodically overhead. He drew back further into the shadow of the building as he watched people coming and going. He scanned each young, male face, mentally comparing it to the description O'Grady had given him. O'Grady had worked with Max Fink in the past, and Fink thought the kid was a prostitute, but who knew? Didn't really matter. Blackmail was blackmail, no matter who was turning the screws.

It was nearly time now. "Don't worry," O'Grady had told him, "This kid won't be late. He thinks he's meeting Jim Morrison." According to O'Grady, Morrison had told the kid to meet him in the alley behind the motel for the payoff. Sure enough, the man watched as the kid who'd been described to him appeared, right on schedule, hurrying into the alley to what he thought would be a profitable meeting with a rock star. The man quickly pulled on a pair of leather gloves. He knew his job: educate the kid without actually killing him. The details were Fink's problem and O'Grady's, not his. All he had to worry about was making sure the kid got the point. He stepped from the shadows and entered the alley.

Jim waited by the phone. Maybe this was the time, the time he'd finally blown it for good. Of course at this point there wasn't much he could do about it. He'd handed the problem over to Max now, and he'd have to trust Max to handle it. After all, it wasn't the first time Max had come through in similar circumstances.

The last time, of course, had been more embarrassment than threat, starting much less dramatically with some phone calls, messages left at

Max's office. "Just ignore it," Jim had instructed Max, trying to be nonchalant. But Max had seen the fear in Jim's eyes and knew there would be more calls, more urgent messages. There were.

"Really, Max," Jim had insisted. "It's just this guy I know. He probably wants me to get him some concert tickets. You don't need to return his calls, I'll take care of it." Max had waited, certain Jim was hiding something. Whatever the truth was, Max had a feeling it was going to be bad. Next time Max would take the call directly.

He hadn't had to wait long. The caller was a nightclub owner in Florida who said he'd known Jim when Jim was still attending college there. "Listen, I just want to talk to Jim," the caller had implored. "If you'll please just give me his phone number. I just need to talk to him, that's all."

Of course Max wasn't about to give this guy anything and had insisted instead that the caller tell him just what his connection with Jim had been. So the man had done just that, in far more explicit detail than Max had found comfortable.

When Max had confronted Jim with this story, Jim had admitted that it was all true. "I did it for my career, Max." Jim's eyes had begged understanding. "He was the first person to really encourage me, give me confidence. He knew I could be a star when everyone else thought I was just a freak." Jim's eyes hadn't met Max's, hadn't been able to face this humiliation head on. "I did it for my career." His voice had sunk to a whisper. "I'm not a queer."

But that had been long ago, and no real threat, not like this time. Now Jim waited again for the ring of a phone. He walked to the window and looked out to the street below. A couple walked by, happy, laughing, seemingly carefree. Their joy looked so effortless. What was their secret? How did they do it? How did anyone do it? What did they all know that Jim didn't?

Why didn't that phone ring?

It was over a week now since Jim had shown up at Max's Beverly Hills home at 2:30 in the morning to ask the attorney's help with this current situation. "It was only that one night," Jim had insisted. Max had watched his client intently as he'd outlined the situation, and suddenly he was sure Jim was lying. This was no one-night stand. Jim had a history with this boy; Max would have bet on it. Wisely, he'd kept these thoughts to himself.

"I gave him a couple of grand; I thought he'd be satisfied with that and disappear."

Max closed his eyes, taking a moment to compose himself. Shit! For the smartest person Max knew, Jim could certainly be stupid. The worst thing you could do was give in to a blackmailer; Jim should know that. As Max had watched his client—his head bowed low over his coffee cup, hands slightly trembling—the attorney had thought again of Jim's words that last time: *"I'm not a queer."* Despite this new circumstance, Max didn't really doubt those words. It had never occurred to him before any of this happened that Jim might be light—he'd certainly had enough women—and nothing that had happened since had changed this opinion. At most, Max thought, Jim was just confused, and embarrassed and uncomfortable with that confusion. He didn't know what the hell he wanted to be. Given his past, that seemed hardly surprising. But others might not be so understanding, and this kid was threatening to go public with the details of his relationship with Jim, whatever that relationship had been.

"He's been leaving me messages at Elektra," Jim had explained to Max. "Subtlety's not his thing, you know?" He'd given a weak grin. "He made it clear enough that I'll pay or he'll talk." He'd paused and tried the grin again. "I guess either way, I'll pay, won't I." It hadn't been a question, just an acknowledgment of reality. After all, it would be Jim's word against that of a street prostitute. "And I'm not exactly the sweetheart of the media," he'd added.

Max had had to laugh. What an understatement! The Doors' concerts in New York and Phoenix had resulted in rioting and arrests. Jim wasn't exactly being hailed in the mainstream press as a national treasure.

"Besides," Jim had continued, "even if the press bought my denial, I'll never get the smell of this thing off me. You think the fans will forget it? You think the record company executives will forget it? It's not exactly the image they've been trying so fucking hard to create for me, is it? I could kiss my solo career goodbye." Max knew that Jim had been trying to get out from under The Doors for over a year now to branch out on his own, but so far the band wouldn't let him go.

A silence fell between them, Max lost in thought, Jim in despair. And then suddenly Max had had a plan.

And now Jim waited.

The man emerged from the alley, alone. Adjusting his jacket and peeling off his gloves, he checked his watch then squinted up at the sky as another plane roared off into the blue. He put a cigarette to his lips and lit it, extinguishing the match carefully between his fingertips and tucking it into his pocket. No trace. He checked his watch again and walked away.

A short time later the phone on Max Fink's desk rang. Max picked up the handset, listened without speaking, and replaced it a few seconds later. He sat for a moment, staring at the phone, drumming his fingers on the handset before picking it up again and dialing.

Jim answered on the first ring and listened intently for the news he'd been waiting to hear. He said nothing for several moments, all the energy in his being seemingly focused on the words that were being spoken on the other end of the line. "I understand. Thank you," he finally said. "I'll never forget this."

The following day a private messenger arrived at Max Fink's office, bearing a magnificent set of golf clubs in a lambskin carryall. The card, addressed to Max, said simply, "For the only father I've ever known."

Christopher Jones was driving into the parking garage at the Chateau Marmont one afternoon in 1968 when a beautiful redhead suddenly jumped on the hood of his car.

Jones was becoming a familiar face around Hollywood. That year, he had starred in the youth-oriented *Wild in the Streets,* in which his character took over the country and put everybody over the age of twenty-nine in concentration camps. With his low, mumbling style of speech and his dark, pensive good looks, Jones was already being hailed as the next James Dean. So if he was surprised at all by this sudden gorgeous apparition staring at him through the windshield of his car, it was probably more by her opening sentence than her unconventional approach.

"What's your name?" she said, pointing at Chris.

"Chris," he replied. "What's your name?"

"Pam."

"Pam who?"

"Pam Morrison. Jim Morrison's my old man." Jim, she explained, was upstairs.

"Now isn't that interesting," Chris said.

Jones and Morrison not only had similar physical qualities, but also a similar feeling of impending danger about them. Even so, Jones was no homewrecker, so when Pamela asked him if he was free to see her the next evening, he said, "I thought you were married?"

"Not really," Pam told him. "Not legally anyway. Jim can do what he likes, and so can I."

"Well then," said Jones, "why don't you meet me here tomorrow?"

It was, after all, the sixties, and love—or at least a warm facsimile of it—

was supposed to be free. But while the female half of these spontaneous couplings may have been living in the sixties, they had, for the most part, grown up in the far more staid fifties. For these women, the strong ideals of marriage, home, and family with which they had been raised were not as easy to put aside as they seemed to be for their male counterparts, whose sexual upbringing had consisted more of "Do what you want to do but don't get caught" than anything else. Now these guys could do what they wanted to do *and* get caught, and it wouldn't make any difference.

"We were constantly trying to stake little white picket fences around these guys," says Mirandi Babitz. "But it was a real tug of war. The whole thing of being in that crowd, which was the hippest of the hip at that time, was that we were supposed to be doing this free love thing, but we didn't want to! All the guys wanted to do it. They thought it was just great, because they got their steady girl and anybody else who walked by. That was the cool way to be. And our job, as women, was to be cool about it, to say, 'Oh yeah, that's fine, we think that's swell.' Which we didn't! But we didn't even have a right to get pissed off."

Whether she had a right to or not, Pamela got pissed off whenever she pleased, and Jim certainly gave her enough reason. Even dividing and subtracting the stories of his alliances to take into account baseless gossip brought on by his good looks, easy charm, and celebrity, Jim's sexual exploits were still impressive, if only for sheer volume. But in spite of their numbers, every woman that Jim ever looked at, laughed at, or lusted after had one thing in common: the absolute certainty that the only thing standing between themselves and a lifetime of happiness with Jim Morrison was Pamela.

High in the Hollywood Hills is an enormous white mansion known in the sixties as the "Rock and Roll Castle," which was owned by *Barbarella* star John Phillip Law and his brother, Tom. It was at the Castle that many of the in-crowd's greatest and most notorious names came to live and play. The Beatles stayed there for a while, as did Bob Dylan, who wrote some of his most memorable songs in the neat little room he occupied on the second floor. Andy Warhol's crowd frequented the Castle when they weren't in New York—Severn Darden, Edie Sedgwick, and The Velvet Underground, with their statuesque German lead singer, Nico. Morrison, too, often haunted the halls and walked the ledges of the Castle, putting on shows meant to impress and horrify.

"Everything at the Castle was theater," said Paul Rothchild. "Jim was a colossal madman pursued by his own demons. He was a tester, too, like Dylan, but much more cruel. Jim took Nico up in a tower, both naked, and Jim, stoned out of his mind, walked along the edge of the parapet.

Hundreds of feet down. Here's this rock star at the peak of his career risking his life to prove to this girl that life is nothing. 'This is theater, I'm doing this theater for you.' He asked Nico to walk the same line and she backed down."

. . . Hanging
from windows as if to say: I'm bold
do you love me?

Nico was tall and brooding and mysterious and, like Jim, larger than life (not to mention larger than Jim: "Nico could've broken Jim in half!" John Phillip Law laughs). She was also several years older than Jim, though not immune to girlish crushes. "He had a fetish for red-haired shanties . . . you know, Irish shanties," Nico once said. "I was so much in love with

© Lisa Law Productions

Nico at the Rock and Roll Castle, 1969.

him that I made my hair red after a while. I wanted to please his taste. It was silly, wasn't it? Like a teenager."

It might've been silly, but Nico wasn't the only woman who seemed to feel that Pamela's hair was the secret of Jim's attraction to her. Several women fashioned their hair after Pamela's long red style, and seemed puzzled when Jim didn't immediately transfer his allegiance to them. So instead, they would try to dress like Pamela, talk like Pamela, starve themselves thin like Pamela, behave like Pamela, or if Jim had recently complained about Pamela's behavior, do what they could to treat him in exactly the opposite manner. But still, maddeningly, he kept returning home.

"I took it very, very seriously in the beginning because I thought for a long time that I was going to catch him," says Anne Moore.

Moore was a journalist writing for the type of teen magazines that loved to feature Jim in their pages. Anne met Jim not in her capacity as a writer, though, but as a guest at a backstage party after a Doors performance at the Forum in 1968. "It was one of those things where we saw each other across the room," says Moore, somewhat reminiscent of Jim's first meeting with Pam at a campus party. But now Jim was far more self-assured and didn't hesitate to walk over and introduce himself to Moore. "It just clicked," she says. "It was like we'd known each other from before."

Anne didn't see Jim again for several months, until they both attended a party at the Whisky sponsored by Elektra Records to introduce one of their new bands, the members of which happened to be friends of Anne. "I went with some friends," Moore remembers. "It was extremely crowded, they were pushing everyone they could in. Jim and John and Ray showed up, but it was so crowded even they couldn't get seats. And the next thing I know, Jim is sitting on the floor behind me." Anne didn't breathe through the entire performance, so acutely aware was she of Jim's presence just inches away.

"Here are my best friends up onstage," Anne laughs. "I've been waiting all these years to see them up there, and it was like, *I can't wait for them to get off the stage, because if Jim leaves before I can turn around and say something, I'll kill myself!*" She needn't have worried. Jim was just getting up at the end of the band's set when Anne turned around and stuck out her hand in his direction, saying, "Hi, I don't think you remember me . . ." But Jim took her hand and said, "Hi, Anne." The two talked for a few minutes, then Jim leaned over, kissed Anne on the cheek, and said, "You're going home with me tonight, aren't you?"

"I'm no fool!" Anne laughs. She told her girlfriend to get lost, and

Jim and Anne walked the few blocks to her apartment. "And that was the beginning of a two-and-a-half-year friendship," she says.

After that night, Jim would drop by at odd hours for home-cooked meals, to talk, or to spend the night. Though she was aware of Jim's relationship with Pamela, Anne's common interests with Jim, as well as his frequent visits, encouraged her to think that she was usurping Pam's place in Jim's life. "And then it got through my little thick skull that I wasn't," says Moore. "And I decided that I would just continue the relationship the way it was—seeing him every so often, talking when we saw each other, having sex when we saw each other, just enjoying each other's company—and get the most out of it that I possibly could, and enjoy it."

It seemed a common theme: Women would get involved with Jim, do everything they could to woo him away from Pamela, and when that failed, finally resign themselves to getting from Jim only the small pieces of himself he was willing to share. In return, Jim could be generously romantic, lavishing gifts and poems and letters full of ardent words of love on whichever woman caught his fancy at the moment. He would be gentle and sweet and kind and loving, and then—in an instant—he would disappear, leaving behind nothing more than souvenirs of his affection.

"When he was with you, he was really with you, you were the only person in the world," observes Moore, "but then he could move on to the next person and forget he even knew you until he was with you again."

That was perhaps the most insidious side of Jim Morrison, this ability to step into a different personality with the ease of someone stepping into a comfortable pair of slippers. He adapted to the expectations of his audience, both onstage and in his personal relationships. In this way he was able to sustain and keep separate what to him may have seemed several casual affairs, but to the women involved often became the great love of their lives. Jim didn't seem to realize that others were taking his attentions very seriously, or by the time he did realize it, it was only because something in the situation had gone wrong and the woman involved in his secular passion play du jour was not playing her part as written.

A good example of this was a West Coast journalist who had apparently convinced herself that Jim's intentions went far beyond the physical relationship they had briefly enjoyed after she had interviewed him for a popular music magazine. Unhappy with his inattentiveness, she reportedly started calling Jim at his office and, when her calls stopped being put through to him, she began to seek him out in person, most notably at a party given by Elektra, which Anne Moore remembers as the only time she saw Jim lose his temper in public.

"It was a great party," Anne recalls. "I came in and Babe and Jim came in, and we were all sitting around the refreshment table talking. They had just gotten back from fishing, and Babe had just gotten an earring for the first time, which I just thought was so neat." The lighthearted conversation was interrupted when the journalist came in and spotted Jim. "She was following Jim around and wanted to talk to him," says Moore. "And finally he just turned around—probably the only time I've ever seen him mad—and said in a very matter-of-fact voice, but no denial that he's pissed, 'Leave me *alone!* Stop following me around like a damn puppy dog! I don't want to talk to you! I don't want to have anything to do with you!' And he stormed off. Babe and I suddenly got very interested in the guacamole!"

Anne had never seen Jim react harshly to anyone, ever. "I'd seen him be polite to crazy fans, seen him with all kinds of people I wouldn't have had any tolerance for. So the very idea of seeing him snap like that—that's why I remember the dialogue." Jim fled to the bar, the determined woman in hot pursuit. "The next thing we knew, he's saying something else to her," Moore says. "And I couldn't tell exactly what that was, but I could certainly hear raised voices."

It is said that Jim later took another tack with the woman, this time setting up a situation he was sure would cause her to lose all interest in him: He asked her to marry him. This might not sound like the best way to get rid of someone who is obviously obsessed with you, but Jim added his own bizarre twist to the proposal, a clever ploy that would probably have worked for someone else.

"I want to marry you," Jim reportedly told the woman, "but you must understand that I love Pamela and she will always be a part of my life. So if you and I get married, Pamela will, of course, have to live with us." It was a brilliant strategy, designed to make a woman stalk off in righteous indignation at the sheer audacity of such a proposal from any man. But what Jim didn't count on was the fact that he wasn't just any man, he was Jim Morrison. The woman accepted his proposal. Despite the fact that Jim subsequently left the country with Pamela, the journalist even now remains convinced that he had every intention of returning to her in California, the two of them then spending the rest of their days residing together in wedded bliss, with Pamela apparently living serenely in the guest room.

Pamela's reaction to these relationships of Jim's varied. She seemed to find the type of warm, deep respect he showed for someone like Doors manager Bill Siddons's wife, Cheri Siddons, with whom he shared a lovingly platonic friendship, far more troubling than his sexual liaisons. "He made me feel very special," says Cheri, who remembers sitting with Jim in Long Beach one afternoon and discussing her pregnancy. "He was asking me a lot of questions, like did I feel differently yet and what was it like. He was so really, really involved all the way through; he was very hurt that I didn't make him the godfather to the first child and he told me he wanted to be the godfather of my second child. And he said, 'That one will be a boy,' and it was a boy." Unfortunately Jim didn't live long enough to see the child's birth, but Cheri never forgot their conversation that afternoon, which she feels was typical of their friendship. "I felt very admired, almost pedestal-admired, and it was very flattering," Cheri says. "He just had that way about him. He was just very, very wonderful when I was around, so I guess I had that really delicious part of him."

Pamela seemed to find the friendship less appetizing. "I'm a very outgoing person on many levels," Cheri says, "and I made the normal approaches with Pam, but she was so cold that I eventually just gave up. There was so much resentment and coldness that came out of her, and detachment." Pamela's coldness might have come from her resentment of Jim's obvious respect and affection for Cheri, or it may also have been the fact that, as the wife of The Doors' manager, Cheri was seen as part of the group from which Pamela wanted Jim to extricate himself. Either way, the effect was a chilling one for Cheri.

Conversely, when New York journalist Patricia Kennealy showed up at Pam's apartment in Los Angeles to inform Pamela that not only had she had an affair with Jim, but had, she claimed, aborted his child as well, Pamela responded with nothing more than mild curiosity. "How interesting," she reportedly said. "I've never met one of Jim's women before." Pamela later mentioned the meeting in passing to her mother, expressing regret that Patricia hadn't kept the child.

"You know it's funny," Siddons adds, "because my understanding and my memory is that Pamela *was* the only one. I mean I knew there were other ones—of course you'd have to be blind not to know there were other ones—but I knew ultimately Pamela was always the only real one."

Sometimes Pamela was the real *annoying* one, and at those times, Jim's other relationships also provided him with sympathetic sounding boards for his troubles with her. After all, what more compassionate and receptive ears could he find than those of the women who saw Pamela as their only stumbling block to bliss? "The only person he ever really talked to me about was Pamela," says Anne Moore, "and that was mainly when he'd come over after having a fight with her, and he'd be wanting to let off steam and wanted someone to talk to who wasn't going to give him any hassle. That was one thing I *really* worked very hard at was *not* giving him hassle."

Pamela felt no such compunction about making Jim's life easier; he had enough hangers-on and paid flunkies to smooth his way for him. "They argued, you know," observed Eva Gardonyi. "They both had their grievances, like 'You done that to me, and for that I done that to you.'" But, she concedes, no matter how serious the rifts, no matter how swift the retaliation, "Somehow they always seemed to have gravitated back to each other after every little escapade."

Probably the most well-documented "escapade" that never happened was the rumored affair between Pamela and actor John Phillip Law. Law's star turn as the gorgeous blond angel with Jane Fonda in 1967's *Barbarella* had made him a high-profile celebrity in the late sixties, as well as an excellent means at getting back at an unfaithful boyfriend.

"I went out with Pam a few of times and that's all," says Law, somewhat baffled by the stories of grand passion that have been built up around this brief relationship. Law met Pamela when her sister, Judy, rented a room in the house he owned in West Hollywood. Initially, John was unaware of Pamela's relationship with Jim. "All I knew was that she was Judy's sister and she was cute," he says, "and she responded to me, so we ran around a little bit. I remember going over to Jim's house one time and going out to dinner a few times, and not much more than that."

Law acknowledges now that he was probably an unwitting, though not unwilling, pawn in a private game between Jim and Pam. John had only seen Pamela a few times when he left the States for a job in Europe. "The next thing I know she and Jim were really hot and heavy and I never did see her again after that," he says. "At the time, I wasn't aware of how serious she was with Jim. That was sort of between them, I stayed out of that. But I'm sure Pam just used me to make Jim jealous. That's about as much as there was to it."

Pam's relationship with John Phillip Law had just been a little game to get Jim's attention. But if Pamela knew or imagined that Jim's breach of faith in their relationship had been drastic enough, her means of revenge could be equally drastic. Paul Ferrara was one of Jim's best friends and remembers somewhat painfully the night Pamela seduced him.

"Jim went off on some goddamn tour and I was left home," says Ferrara. "I think Pam knew that Jim was with someone else that night. That's the thing that probably wore her down to a frazzle, the fact that she could not ultimately control him when he left the house. So she was just very lonely and kind of down, and she figured, well, he's sleeping with whoever, so I'll do something too. It was almost like she was getting back at him. So she asked me over for dinner. I think we smoked pot—she liked to smoke pot a lot and so did I, but Jim didn't—and she just got real close

**Room 32, Alta Cienega Motel. "He likes to stay there
to work himself up before a performance . . ."**

and cuddly and one thing led to another. It's not something I'm real proud
of, but it happened."

Jim returned home the next day, and by the time he saw Paul, Pamela
had told Jim of their liaison. "I heard you were with Pam last night," Jim
said to Ferrara in a casual tone of voice. "Oh, god, I guess so," was all
Paul could manage to say. That was the end of the conversation, and the
subject was never broached again. Another round of the game had been
played, but it was getting increasingly difficult to tell who—if anyone—
had won.

We're perched headlong
on the edge of boredom
We're reaching for death
on the end of a candle
We're trying for something
That's already found us

"There was some psychological drama that they were working out between
the two of them," says Cheri Siddons. "Their relationship was so intense."

Christopher Jones didn't know what might have gone on between
Pam and Jim at the Chateau Marmont that day to prompt Pamela to ask
Chris out, but as long as she wasn't married and wanted to see him, Chris
was certainly happy to oblige.

The West Hollywood apartment on Norton Avenue Pam and Jim shared.

The Doors were playing at the Hollywood Bowl on July 5, 1968. Jim was staying across the street from The Doors' office at the Alta Cienega Motel that day because, Pamela explained to Chris, "He likes to stay there to work himself up before a performance." So Chris was spending the afternoon with Pamela at Pam and Jim's apartment in West Hollywood.

"From that apartment I saw, she didn't blow a lot of money," says Jones. It was a one-bedroom place, and I think the only thing I saw in there was leather pants and some sort of sheepskin coat of his. The whole place smelled like a sheep farm. And there was a picture on the wall: Somebody had taken a photograph of Jim with a ship superimposed over it because he sang that song, 'Crystal Ship,' and he sort of liked that. The rest was bare. They weren't extravagant." The most unusual thing about the place for Chris was the contents of the refrigerator. "Pamela opened the refrigerator and she showed me all these beef hearts, wrapped in butcher paper," says Jones. "Jim always eats hearts," Pamela said, as though this should explain everything.

There were no phones in the rooms at the Alta Cienega, so Jim was at a pay phone when he called Pamela that afternoon and asked her to come pick him up and take him to the concert. "He's never done that before," Pamela said to Chris. "Should I go pick him up?"

"Fuck no, don't go pick him up!" Chris told her, so she didn't. Jim called several times, "really pissed off," according to Jones, but Pamela never went for him.

The Rolling Stones were going to be in the audience at the Bowl that night. Mick Jagger had spent a little time with Jim at the Alta Cienega earlier in the day, and they had hit it off. Pamela later told Chris that she thought Jagger had given Jim a hit of acid before The Doors took the stage at the Bowl, but if he had, the trip didn't seem to be reflected in Jim's performance, which was good but far more subdued than usual. Jim knew that Pamela had spent the day with Chris, and when she didn't come pick him up at the motel, he was just as sure that she would be bringing Chris to the concert. As though to curry her favor, onstage he wore an intricately embroidered vest from Themis that Pamela had given him.

After the show, Pamela brought Chris backstage, where he stayed in the hallway talking to his friend, Wes, while Pamela went to see Jim in the dressing room. "Wes was a friend of Jim's, too," says Jones. "He looked exactly like Fabian. They called him Dirty Dirk because he'd get on airplanes and make it with stewardesses because they thought he was Fabian. So he and I were standing in the hallway, and suddenly Pam sticks her head out the door and she says, 'Come here.'"

As soon as Chris entered the dressing room, Jim reached for Pamela and sat her down on his lap. "He just sat there grinning at me, with Pam on his lap," says Jones. "Pam was looking at me kind of nervous. But Jim knew about us at that point, and he was trying to get it up on me. But I just stood there and smirked at him, you know, who are you kidding?"

The Doors left to tour Europe less than two months later, and Pamela came along, choosing mostly to stay in London while the band toured. Jim and Pam seemed content enough together there, and Jim felt he had won this round of their private game. Ray was impressed by the domestic bliss the couple seemed to have fallen into at their furnished flat on London's Eton Square.

"We visited them before we left London," says Manzarek, speaking of himself and his wife, Dorothy. "Jim and Pam made us a wonderful breakfast, a full English breakfast of incredible English bacon and really beautiful yellow, golden-yolked, sunny-side-up eggs, English toast, the Polish strawberry jam, and good, strong French coffee. It was the most domestic I'd ever seen them. And I thought, This is going to work out! This could work out! This is good!"

But it wasn't good for long. Back in the States, Jim began rehearsals

Christopher Jones, 1967.

for the group's new album, *The Soft Parade* (the first album on which The Doors would claim individual songwriting credits due to a dispute over lyrics), and Pamela once again began seeing Christopher Jones. "She'd broken up with Jim," says Jones. "He wasn't her boyfriend at the time." Jones was getting ready to fly to London to begin filming *Looking Glass Wars* with Anthony Hopkins. Pamela loved to travel and Chris hated to travel alone, so Pamela flew back to London with him.

They stayed in a suite at the London Hilton. When Chris wasn't busy working on the film, he and Pamela would go shopping, or go gambling with the film's producer. It was a good time for a couple of weeks until Chris made the mistake of writing a letter to his ex-wife.

"I was very sneaky in how I did it," says Jones, "but it wasn't a love letter or anything. My ex-wife and I have a daughter, so I was just communicating. But I went over to my manager's room and put the letter on his phone for him to mail it. Pam went over and got it, opened it, and read it!"

Pamela was furious at what she considered to be Chris's breach of faith, and she flew into a rage, which culminated in her hitting Chris in the face with the hotel key and storming out of the hotel with her things. He didn't hear from her again for a month.

The Doors embarked on a tour of the States in November, and still Pamela hadn't come home. Their breakups before had always been minor ones, quickly healed, but this was stretching out for weeks, and Jim felt he had to take action. Without telling anyone where he was going, he left for London to get Pamela back.

"Jim left town and didn't show any of us the respect to tell us that he was leaving, how long he would be gone, when he was coming home— he just disappeared," says Bill Siddons. "So Buick came up, offered us a bunch of money, unheard of money, to do something with a song that Robby wrote, and they all kind of went, 'Well, gee. We'd really like to have Jim's vote here, but it's a lot of money and it's really big and could be important, so fuck it, let's go!'"

While The Doors were making the deal of the century without him, Jim was in London contacting the few people he was sure would know of Pamela's whereabouts. It wasn't long before he located her, and the couple reconciled on at least a provisional basis. "One o'clock one morning," say Jones, "I've moved into a mews house in London and the doorbell rings. I go down to see who it is, and it's Pam." Jones had heard through mutual friends that Jim had come over to London to get Pam back, so he asked her, "Where's Jim?" Pamela told Chris that she and Jim had been out drinking at a nearby rock club, Jim had gotten drunk, they'd gotten into a fight, and she'd left him there, crying.

"So you just left him sitting there crying?" Chris asked. "Why don't you go get him?"

"No," she said, "let him cry. He likes it."

As always, Jim sobered up eventually and was able to convince Pamela to come back to the States with him. It was upon their return that Jim found out about the deal with Buick.

"I thought it was an interesting idea," Manzarek says of the Buick deal. "The car they wanted to use it for was the Opel, a small little ecologically correct car, a little four-cylinder, two-seater automobile that they worked on with the German Opel company. It wasn't obviously a big Buick or anything like that."

Whatever impression Ray might have had to the contrary, the car that was actually being promoted was not the sporty Opel, but the Buick GS455, a 370-horsepower muscle car that *Car Life* magazine called a nice car to "take home to mother, or to the dragstrip on grudge night."

"I said, 'Fine, go ahead and do it,'" says Manzarek, as did John and Robby, though Manzarek says the deal was called off when Jim returned and expressed his objections. "Jim said, 'No no no, I veto it!' Fine. Let's cancel it. So Elektra had to call Buick and say sorry! A preliminary yes is now an official no." But that yes had already been translated into television, radio, and print ads, as well as a billboard on the Sunset Strip, visible from The Doors' office. "They couldn't take it back," says Siddons. "They'd already agreed to it."

"So it was the 'Almighty Dollar' that focused the surfacing split between Jim and the rest of us," writes John Densmore in his book *Riders on the Storm.* "Jim was being deceived by the three soulmates with whom he had made a pact back in Venice, California, without any business people present."

They deserted me, deserted the cause, message
or word for another god.

"That was the end of the dream," says Bill Siddons. That was the end of that era of Jim's relationship with the other members of the band; from then on it was business. That was the day Jim said, 'I don't have partners anymore, I have associates.'"

A few months after returning from London, without Pamela's knowledge, Jim had Max draw up a will in which he made Pamela his sole beneficiary. It was as binding a commitment as Jim felt he could make at that time, and he assumed it would protect Pamela legally in case anything should happen to him. Jim signed and had Paul Ferrara witness the will in Max Fink's office in Beverly Hills on February 12, 1969 (coincidentally, Ray's thirtieth birthday).

There has been some controversy over the years caused by Fink's later stating that he never drew up a will for Jim, but Paul Ferrara remembers otherwise. Paul was often with Jim when Jim would stop by Max's office to sign this or that or take care of other business, so Paul thought nothing of it when Jim handed him a paper at Max's office one day and said, "Here, sign this." Says Ferrara of the document in question, "I can't see how this could be bogus, and I can't imagine that Max said that he never did this unless he was losing his mind!"

Ferrara also doesn't understand the speculation that Jim would not have excluded others in his life from his estate. "Pam was the all-inclusive person he would leave anything he had to," says Ferrara. "Nobody else was really warranted giving anything to, I don't think anyway. I don't

Introducing automobiles to light your fire.

BUICK MOTOR DIVISION

The Gran Sports. From Buick 1970.

They're the cars you've been asking us to make.

This one's the GS455 equipped with the Stage I performance package. If it's performance you want, the GS455 Stage I has it.

A 455 cubic-inch engine. With a high-lift cam and four barrel carburetor which breathes through real air-scoops to add performance.

A cooling system that should never overheat.

And four on the floor is available. Or an improved 3-speed automatic transmission.

Maybe it's the name Buick, with all the goodness and confidence that goes with that name, that really gets you.

Whatever it is, the GS455 Stage I has it. And so do all the Light Your Fire Cars from Buick 1970. See them.

Now, wouldn't you really rather have a

1970 Buick.

"C'mon Buick, Light My Fire."

really think Jim believed he was going to die, number one; he was scared of it. But I do believe that his will was intended to make Pam happy. And to prove to her that he did love her."

Seventeen days after signing this legal love letter, Jim Morrison committed professional suicide.

THREE

Living Without Life

The village idiots in her bed
Never cared that her eyes were red
Never cared that her brain was dead
In the hours that her face was alive
It was the thing just to be by her side

You got a lot of living to do without life . . .

Edie Brickell
"Little Miss S"

Jim and Pam had a fight that morning."

By this time, Bill Siddons might have been making this statement about any morning of the week, any week of the year. If Jim Morrison had become famous for his unpredictability onstage, offstage, Jim and Pamela had become equally famous for the predictability of their fights. But the fight Siddons is referring to in this instance took place on the morning of March 1, 1969.

"They were supposed to be coming to Miami," says Siddons. "I had rented them their own home in Jamaica to hang out for a week's vacation after the Miami gig, and then, after the vacation, we were going to do a number of other dates on the East Coast—the first real tour I'd booked as opposed to weekends. We were taking a chance to see if Jim could actually work for a week as opposed to two or three days. And we had all these wonderful plans!

"We had an 8:00 A.M. flight to Miami, and we were all meeting at the airport," Siddons continues. "Jim and Pam didn't show up. So I put the guys on the flight and said, I'll find Jim and follow. Finally Jim and Pam show up in a limo, but not in time to catch the flight. They're having a fight, and Pamela leaves and goes home. So it's me and Jim going to Florida, and I'm scrambling to get us there.

"We found a plane that went through New Orleans, and in New Orleans we stopped and went to the bar at the airport and had a couple of drinks, then got on the plane from New Orleans and went to Miami. By the time we got to Miami, I noticed that Jim's face muscles had slackened, which is the only way I could really tell how drunk he was. So I knew he was real drunk on the way to the gig.

"The gig was kind of out of control already for business reasons. I had my detectives down there who were my security force, and when we got to the gig, my head of security ran up and said, 'Bill, you got big problems here. This guy's fuckin' around with you, his ticket sales ain't right.' So we went into the hall. The backstage scene was kind of chaotic. There was some hippie group of people there; I don't know how they got in or why they were there, but they were carrying this lamb which ended up in the pictures of the *Live* album sleeve. The whole thing was pretty much out of control. Out front, there were 14,000 people there, when there were only supposed to be 8,500. I wasn't getting paid; I was just worried about getting paid. And the promoter's brother was this karate expert who threatened to kill me—it was just this complete madness scene.

"And the guys went onstage. I put them on. I could tell Jim was drunk. I didn't think he was like, gone, but he was drunk. And they went onstage and they started to play. And I'm fighting with the promoter, and I'm hearing this song start three times, and I realized things were pretty weird. And I walked out and there was like seventy people onstage, and I ran up and Vince [Treanor] was kind of panicked about what was going on onstage, but it seemed benign to me. I'm trying to remember the details of it. . . . There was a bunch of people onstage, and then the stage broke— a lot of shit happened when I was fighting with the promoter, so I'm not really clear on how much of what was happening onstage I was actually there for, but it wasn't very much of it."

What Bill missed was the dissolution of a dream turned nightmare. After the few false starts Bill had heard from backstage, Jim's attempts to sing "Back Door Man" turned into a drunken harangue, aimed ostensibly at the audience but more likely directed inward, at Jim's own inability to get his personal life under control, which was underscored for him by Pamela's absence in Miami. Their relationship was out of control. His career was out of control. His life was out of control.

"*You're all a bunch of fuckin' idiots!*" Jim accused the audience. Jim had wanted to be a poet, but he thought people would take his words seriously if he got their attention by becoming a rock star first. "*You let people tell you what you're gonna do . . .*" Jim had tried his best to leave the band, but here he was, onstage with them again. "*. . . let people push you around!*" Jim had wanted to go after Pamela, but he had to be in Miami with the band. "*Maybe you love gettin' your face shoved in shit . . . you're all a bunch of slaves!*" Who was he really talking to? Who was he really talking about? "Pamela had control over Jim in real life," journalist Eve Babitz once wrote. "He made his audiences suffer for that." But if the audience was uncomfortable with what was happening onstage, it was clearly Jim who was suffering now.

Things went from bad to worse. As Jim's tirade continued, someone from the audience threw a gallon of fluorescent orange paint at the stage, hitting members of the band. There was no going back to the music now, so Robby and John left their instruments and started to leave the stage, the left side of which began to sag. Meanwhile, Jim was calling for action. *"I wanna see some people up here havin' some fun! I wanna see some dancin'. There are no rules, no limits, no laws, come on! Won't somebody come up there and love my ass?"* Before the police could stop them, several members of the audience were onstage. One of the fans poured champagne over Jim's head, soaking his hair and his shirt, which he removed. "Let's see a little skin! Let's get naked!" he urged the fans, many of whom immediately began throwing off articles of clothing. Morrison had swapped hats with a police officer, donning the policeman's cap and putting his own floppy black hat on the policeman's head. Jim now reached over and grabbed the black hat, sending it sailing into the audience. The policeman followed suit, taking his own cap off Jim's head and sending it flying into the crowd, a rare moment of fun between Jim Morrison and a law enforcement official (though the officer would later blame the cap's loss on Jim and demand payment from Bill).

When it looked like the shirtless Jim was going to try to doff his leather pants as well, Ray yelled for Vince to stop him. Vince immediately got behind Jim, putting his fingers through the belt loops of Jim's pants and twisting, making it impossible for Jim to unfasten them. At this point, John decided to get the hell out of there, but when he jumped off the sagging stage, he accidentally landed on the light board, which fell to the ground with a shower of sparks. The stage was now swarming with fans, and police officers and security guards were picking them up bodily and tossing them off the stage with no more care than stevedores take tossing heavy bundles of cargo into the hold of a ship. Unfortunately, one of the guards grabbed Jim by mistake and threw him, still clutching the microphone, off the stage and into the center of the audience. As John Densmore described it, "Jim was now in the middle of the auditorium, leading a snake dance with ten thousand people following him. I looked down from the balcony, and the audience looked like a giant whirlpool with Jim at the center."

Bill Siddons picks up the story again. "And so the show kind of self-destructed. And I'm settling up and I'm talking to the policemen. And there's this cop, this lieutenant, who wants seventy-five bucks for his hat that he said Jim had thrown into the audience. So I got him his money. And there were three or four cops I was talking to about the show, and they said, 'Well, you know, it's kind of stupid, but he only hurt himself by doing this show.' I said, 'Yeah, what was so bad about it?' 'Well, you

IN THE NAME AND BY THE AUTHORITY OF

The State of Florida

Claude R. Kirk, Jr., GOVERNOR OF FLORIDA

ISSUED BY
GOVERNOR
APR 23 1969

To the Executive Authority of the State of _California_

Whereas, It appears by the annexed documents, which are hereby certified to be authentic, that _James Morrison_

stands charged with the crime of _Lewd and Lascivious Behavior, Indecent Exposure, Open Profanity, Drunkeness_

committed in the State of Florida, and it appearing and I hereby certify that the said _James Morrison_

(was, were) present in the State of Florida at the time of the commission of said alleged crime, and it appearing that _James Morrison_

thereafter fled from justice, and (has, have) taken refuge in _California_

Therefore I, _Claude R. Kirk, Jr.,_ Governor of the State of Florida, have thought proper, and in pursuance of provisions of the Constitution and laws of the United States, to demand the surrender of the said _James Morrison_ as fugitive from justice, and that _he_ be delivered to _Lt. Stephen Bertucelli and/or_ _Sgt. Paul Rosenthal, DS_ who is hereby appointed agent on the part of the State to receive _him_

Given Under My Hand, and the Great Seal of the State affixed at the City of Tallahassee, the Capital, this _18th._ day of _April_ A. D. 19 _sixty-nine_ and of the Independence of the United States of America the One Hundred and _ninety-third_

"Fugitive from justice," April 1969.

know, there was no songs, he was yelling at the audience the whole time, it just wasn't a very good show.' I said, 'Oh, okay!' I paid the cop, and we got in the car and left. I didn't know anything had happened. That was Saturday night.

"Sunday, we were all supposed to go to Jamaica. Well, I guess the band was going to Jamaica and I was going back to L.A. and Vince was going back to Boston. So Monday morning, Vince calls me from Boston. He'd picked up the local newspapers on the way onto the plane and read the papers, and there was a story about the show. And Vince read me the historic story where the writer had decided to call the local police chief and the local head of the circuit court or whatever judge and ask them, 'How do you let stuff like this go on in your community?' And they all went, 'Well, we won't! We're gonna prosecute!' And he ignited the political monster. And by Monday or Tuesday it was out of control. And on Wednesday they put out a warrant for Jim's arrest. And Jim and his lawyer, Max Fink, and I went down to Miami to post bail. And that was kind of the beginning of the nightmare."

While the wheels of his professional demise were being put into motion, Jim was in Jamaica, oblivious to the havoc he had left in the wake of his drunken performance in Miami. Whatever conflict had led to Pamela leaving Jim at the airport in Los Angeles before the Miami concert was apparently still alive, because she also refused to join Jim and the others in Jamaica. The big, romantic plantation house that Bill Siddons had rented for the couple was occupied by Jim and a few servants who stood silently by, waiting to carry out Jim's wishes. Later Jim would try in his own way to punish Pamela for her absence by telling a group of friends, in front of Pamela, how terribly frightened and forlorn he had been in Jamaica all by himself. "How come you never told me about this before?" she asked indignantly. Jim, knowing that Pamela was more upset at feeling left out of his confidence than at the thought of him pining for her in Jamaica, summoned a calculatedly sad smile and said quietly, "Well, I don't talk about everything all the time."

But as much as he wanted to milk the image of his solitary confinement to try to pull a little guilt out of Pamela, the truth was that Jim was alone for all of twenty-four hours or less in Jamaica before he went looking for company. After all, why wallow in solitude in the absence of your woman when you can just as easily go borrow someone else's?

Julia Densmore Negron recalls, "Jim arrived like a day later, in the middle of the night, drunk, and scared the shit out of everybody." Julia and John and Robby and his wife, Lynne, had all rented a house together near the water. Julia remembers that Ray and Dorothy had chosen to go off by themselves to Guadeloupe rather than stay with the others. Still furious over Jim's behavior in Miami, John was especially peeved at Jim's intrusion on their vacation. "Most of the time there was a real animosity toward Jim," Julia explains, "or this kind of love/hate thing going that was so intense that it was hard to be around Jim with John there. He was uptight. Robby was much looser about it, but Robby's just a much looser guy. John was just very uptight about it all the time."

Of course, worrying about irritating John and Robby had never taken up a great deal of Jim's time. "[Jim] hung around on his own with us for a while and drove John and Robby crazy," says Julia. "Jim and Lynne and I would sit around on the balcony all day having drinks, and John and Robby wanted to go diving. They didn't want him there, they didn't want us girls going barhopping with Jim around Jamaica. It was shrinking their groove, definitely. Because Lynne and I were up for a party, and Robby and John were very straight in those days. They still are."

Whatever groove John and Robby might have had going disappeared completely when Bill Siddons called to let them know that a warrant had been issued for Jim's arrest labeling him a fugitive from justice because he had fled the scene of a crime. Never mind the fact that no one in Florida had even decided that a crime had been committed until four days after the concert, or that Jim had "fled" to a vacation that had been planned long before the Miami gig. Upon hearing the news, the fugitive immediately caught the next flight to Los Angeles, leaving the others to wonder what this would mean for The Doors. They wouldn't have to wait long for the answer.

Almost immediately after the Dinner Key concert, a "Rally for Decency" had been held in Miami, attended by 30,000 outraged citizens, all seemingly united in their condemnation of what really amounted to nothing more than one drunken twenty-five-year-old's successful attempt to make a fool of himself in public. Plans for the East Coast tour rapidly went up in smoke, with one city after another canceling in the wake of the negative publicity generated by the Miami fiasco. "They couldn't get a job," remembered Paul Rothchild. "Promoters all over the country were canceling the shows as fast as The Doors could answer the telephone." John Densmore was especially livid at Jim's latest and most reprehensible act of irresponsibility. "John was on the rag all the time about the whole thing after Miami," says Julia Negron. "He'd never shut up about it: 'We've lost a million dollars in shows!' and 'Jim's just a pain in the ass!' I mean he really complained all the time."

Not that there wasn't anything to complain about. It's not easy to realize that everything you've worked for and dreamed of could be taking a quick trip down the crapper contingent on whether or not a couple of teenagers had been scarred for life by the sight of Jim's dick supposedly making its Miami stage debut. In the context of the nineties, when a well-known rock musician can capriciously drop his pants onstage at a venue like Madison Square Garden without anyone in the audience blinking (or covering) an eye, it seems absurd that Jim unzipping his fly could cause such a furor. But with "lewd and lascivious behavior, indecent exposure, open profanity, and drunkenness," as with comedy (and isn't it a fine line?), timing is everything.

"None of us really thought anything of it at the time," says Bill Siddons, "except that it was a very weird show. In listening to the tapes subsequently, much of the concert that I didn't hear, it was quite clear that the Living Theatre was a big part of that show." Julian Beck's Living Theatre was a confrontational performance group that involved the audience by trying to provoke reactions from them. It was a style Jim had been practicing on those around him his whole life. "Jim attended four days of the Living Theatre at USC about a week prior to this gig," says Siddons, "and what he had done was taken much of what he had been in-fluenced by in the previous week and kind of integrated it into his stage show. And it had nothing to do with rock and roll, but it was so indica-tive of the frustration he was having as a performing artist."

Cheri Siddons echoes Bill's sentiments. "It was never 'The Doors!' right? It was never that," she says. "I mean the crowd was always scream-ing, 'Jim! Jim! Jim!' And he looked at me once and said, 'Cheri what do they want from me? They don't know me, they don't know who I am. What do they want?' I mean that was the crux of it to me, right there. I always compared Jim to Mick Jagger because Jagger would be one person when he was backstage, and when he got onstage, he became the star—he knew how to make that switch. Jim couldn't make that distinction, that was too much for him. And he didn't even have the desire to make it. Somehow everyone got to Jim more. Everyone was sucking more, everyone wanted more, I don't really know what it was. Maybe because Jim was prettier, deeper—it could've been a lot of reasons. But I think somewhere in the middle of it, he didn't want to play anymore and yet this whole cog wheel was going around him; everyone was counting on him, everybody's livelihood, the record company, the band . . . everybody was there wanting him to do this."

What are you doing here?
What do you want?
Is it music?
We can play music
But you want something & someone new

"Jim was kind of being worshipped into a box," says Bill Siddons, "and he was really victimized by it. *'Okay, you're the crazy Jim Morrison! You've got to jump off the stage and reappear in a cloud of smoke!'* And the audience came and the audience was hungry and the audience wanted their show, goddamn it! But he was taunting the audience, going 'What are you here for? Is this what you came to see? I mean, what do you want from me?' He was really after the audience. But it was a bunch of teenagers that wanted to party, and here was this tormented artist who was kind of doing his Van Gogh impression. [Jim] created a monster that got out of control and started to eat him." And like his alter ego, the Steppenwolf:

It happened to him as it does to all; what he strove for with the deepest and most stubborn instinct of his being fell to his lot, but more than is good for men. In the beginning his dream and his happiness, in the end it was his bitter fate.

CHAPTER

12

Attorney Max Fink had seen Jim Morrison through any number of delicate situations, but this time the odds against him looked insurmountable. At first, Fink had hoped that the case would never have to go to trial. According to Margaret Fink's transcript of an interview with her husband, Max had called in a favor from an old friend who happened to be a close friend of California's governor, Ronald Reagan. Not only did Max's friend get Reagan to agree not to extradite Jim, but he said Reagan had agreed to arrange for a full pardon. Jim was ecstatic at the news, saying that Reagan's actions on his behalf were "enough to make me a Republican."

Unfortunately, his elation was short lived. Suddenly Reagan reneged, no doubt on the recommendation of his advisors, who recognized the move as politically suicidal. Though the governor wrote Max a conciliatory letter full of apologies for his change of heart, to Jim it was nothing more than betrayal wearing a smile; he was livid, and Reagan's name couldn't even be mentioned around him after that or he would erupt into profanity.

Eve Babitz once wrote, "If you're allergic to strawberries and you eat them, you break out in hives. If Jim drank scotch, he broke out in fuckups." If that were true, then Miami was proving to be a near fatal attack. In the year preceding the Miami concert, in addition to releasing a new album, *Waiting for the Sun,* and appearing on TV's popular *The Smothers Brothers Show,* The Doors had played over thirty live shows, including performances on tour in Europe and in the United States, as well as a sold-out concert at New York's Madison Square Garden. But in the year since the debacle at the Dinner Key Auditorium, The Doors made only twelve live appearances, few of which lived up to the prestige of their previous bookings.

It was when Max Fink hesitated over representing Jim in a case of this nature, especially in a state as conservative as Florida, that Jim allegedly told Fink the source of his bitter feelings toward his parents, hinting that he had deliberately chosen to self-destruct in his father's home state as a means of revenge. Though alarmed that Jim's apparent premeditation of his actions might leak out and hurt his client even more, Max saw Jim's revelation as a possible way to create a more sympathetic defense if the subject of Jim's professed abuse was brought up in court, and he suggested as much to Jim, a move the attorney immediately regretted. Jim didn't even bother to comment on Max's proposal, though his response clearly indicated his feelings on the matter: Morrison silently stood up and slowly walked out of the room. The subject was never touched upon again.

It took some doing, but Max, worried about the state of Jim's mental health in the wake of this widespread public condemnation, as well as Jim's professed history of abuse, finally convinced the singer to see a psychologist. Pamela had been seeing a psychiatrist for years, ever since the first onset of Jim's fame, and she had urged Jim on several occasions to come with her. Paul Rothchild had also tried to get Jim to seek professional help on more than one occasion. "Oh! Everybody tried!" Rothchild recalled. "I tried a lot, especially when he brought up repeatedly his problems getting hard," said Rothchild, referring to Jim's increasing bouts with impotency, a problem not uncommon in alcoholics, which both Pam and Jim had spoken about with Paul. "I don't need to pay anyone to tell me what I already know," was Jim's usual reply to such suggestions. But Max held firm and made an appointment for Jim, an appointment Jim did keep.

Unfortunately, the session didn't accomplish quite what Max had hoped it would. Instead of opening his psyche to the psychologist, Jim instead challenged the doctor to a chess match, a game which Jim won. He never visited the doctor again. "How can I take advice from someone who can't even win a chess game?" he asked facetiously. Jim also told Max that he felt the doctor himself had serious psychological problems. Living up to Jim's diagnosis, the psychologist committed suicide a few years later.

Even though The Doors' performance schedule had tapered off dramatically after Miami, Jim took pride in many of his own accomplishments in 1969. At the end of March, he had recorded some of his poems, without musical accompaniment, at Elektra Studios. It was another in a series of moves Jim had been making toward leaving The Doors (Elektra's attorneys had, in fact, drawn up agreements to that end, though they had yet to be executed). *Feast of Friends,* a film made by Jim, Paul Ferrara, Babe Hill, and Frank Lisciandro and produced by The Doors, won a first prize documentary award at the Atlanta Film Festival in May. That same month, Jim made his debut as a spoken-word performer when he read his work *An American Prayer* at a fund-raiser for Norman Mailer's New York mayoral campaign in New York City. But nothing he did could shine through the shadow that had been cast by his behavior in Miami and the looming trial.

While Max worked to hammer out a defense for Jim's seemingly indefensible actions, Jim seemed equally intent upon working for the prosecution. On November 11, 1969, two days after pleading not guilty to the charges leveled against him in Miami, Jim and Tom Baker decided to fly from L.A. to Phoenix to catch a Rolling Stones concert. En route, the two got drunk and harassed a flight attendant to the extent that they were arrested upon arrival in Phoenix, and Jim was charged with interfering with the flight of an aircraft.

Max was livid at Jim's wanton carelessness so soon after the Miami debacle, and he told Jim he could find himself another attorney. But Jim insisted that the stewardess who was pressing the harassment charges against him had actually come on to him but "she had a fat ass and I wasn't taking," he explained. "Hell hath no fury like a twat scorned," Jim told his attorney. Max's resolve to cut Jim loose over the indiscretion didn't last long. One day a huge package arrived in the mail at Fink's office. Inside was a replica of a prison, like a miniature doll's house, with a jail cell made out of Popsicle sticks and a little sign that read "Morrison Hotel." All was forgiven.

So Max started to build yet another defense strategy for Jim, one which ended up being unnecessary. During the preliminary hearing in Phoenix, Jim and Max ran into the stewardess in a bar. At Max's suggestion, Jim went over to the woman's table, returning an hour later with a pleased grin on his face. "I told her her ass really turned me on and I couldn't control myself," he laughed. "She's coming up to my room later." Jim must have shown her a good time, because she later agreed to change her story. That was one down.

Nineteen sixty-nine turned into 1970, and The Doors were once again picking up more prestigious bookings—at New York's Felt Forum, at the Winterland in San Francisco—and they also released a new album in February. But as the year progressed and the trial in Miami drew closer, Jim's emotional and physical state steadily deteriorated, and his attorney began to worry about the singer's increasing apathy toward the trial and his career.

In Los Angeles, when Max hadn't heard from Jim for a while, he went to Jim and Pam's apartment on the pretense of having Jim sign some interrogatories. The attorney was stunned at his client's appearance. Jim

Onstage at Winterland,
San Francisco.

looked like "a skeleton with a big beer belly." Jim hadn't shaved or bathed; he had a scruffy beard and his body reeked. The apartment look as though a bomb had been dropped there. When Max asked where Jim had been keeping himself, Jim replied that he'd been sleeping for the past week. When asked about Pamela's whereabouts, Jim replied, his voice devoid of emotion, "I looked over at her sleeping, and she looked so much like my mother I told her to leave."

Jim, who usually took great interest in whatever papers Max asked him to sign, instead just scrawled his name on the documents placed before him without bothering to look at what he was signing, telling Max he didn't care what they were. When Max failed to persuade Jim to get dressed and come to dinner with him, he gathered up the papers Jim had signed and turned to leave. But as he reached the door, Jim called to him. Max turned back, hoping Jim had changed his mind about dinner. Instead, Morrison murmured sadly, "They're all shit, you know Max?"

Max redoubled his efforts and was able to lure Jim out of the house by promising to let Jim drive his Rolls Royce, thinking it might cheer him up. As they got under way, Max gritted his teeth, trying to decide which was more dangerous—bailing out the door of the speeding car, or staying put and taking his chances with Jim's erratic driving. Jim also wanted to stop for every hitchhiker they saw, saying, "I was in that boat once, Max."

By the time Jim and Max arrived at the Chinese restaurant, Max felt that Jim's spirits had lifted a bit. While they waited to place their orders, Max told Jim a joke about a man who goes to a Chinese restaurant to eat every night and always gives the waiter a hard time, complaining about the service, sending the food back. One day the man goes into the restaurant and, feeling remorseful for his past behavior, tells his waiter, "Chang, I feel bad about the way I've been treating you and I won't do it anymore." Chang replies, "Okay, and I no more pee in tea." Jim cracked up, the last of his psychic storm clouds seeming to roll away. When the waiter came to take their order, Jim said to him earnestly, "Please don't pee in the tea."

Jim ate like he hadn't eaten in days. But when the meal was finished and the tea arrived, the mood once again turned somber. "Pam taught me how to read tea leaves," Jim said, swirling the dregs of his tea in the cup and watching as the leaves settled on the bottom. He remained silent for several moments, his eyes riveted on the leaves, until Max playfully prodded him for the his interpretation of the leaves' message. Without taking his eyes from his cup, Jim replied, "Death."

It was Saturday night, and Jim was bored. The trial had begun, and Jim seemed to be spending most of his time in Miami either looking for trouble, getting into trouble, or trying to get out of trouble. Max had been invited to a black-tie affair at the posh Fontainebleau Hotel, and having nothing better to do, Jim asked if he could tag along.

Typically, Jim was a standout in the older, largely conservative gathering. Aside from being the youngest person there by far, everyone else was in formal wear; Jim was in blue jeans and a corduroy jacket. Morrison quickly spotted a stunning blonde somewhat closer to his own age, though still several years older. The next thing Max knew, his client had disappeared—and so had the blonde.

Jim Morrison wasn't the only one in Miami because of legal problems. Famed and feared Mafia crime boss Meyer Lansky was also in town facing two indictments—one a felony, one a misdemeanor—for possession of drugs without a prescription. In the context of the wrenchingly violent world over which Lansky reigned supreme, these charges were little more than nuisance. But they were enough to have put Lansky—and his gorgeous blonde mistress—in the same city, on the same night, at the same hotel, attending the same party, as Max Fink and Jim Morrison. The following day, Max received a call from an "associate" of Lansky's who told him, "Tell that Morrosky kid if he ever pulls that again he'll be singing on two stumps with a high falsetto." Even Max, who was no stranger to the harshest realities of the world, was shaken up by the call, but Jim was thrilled. He made it a point to see Lansky's mistress as often as he could the rest of the time he was in Florida; there was nothing Max could say to dissuade him.

Even more problems loomed on the horizon for Jim, not the least of which was a woman Jim had seen on and off who flew to Miami to announce that she was pregnant. As she seemed determined to have the child, Max advised Jim to deny it, drag her through the courts, and wash his hands of her completely. Most of all, Max counseled, tell her it couldn't possibly be his.

Babe Hill had come down to Miami to keep Jim company through some of the trial, and Jim told him briefly what was going on. "He just told me that this woman's claiming that they're married and claiming they've got a kid and things like that," says Hill. Babe asked Jim if he had actually married her, and Jim conceded it was possible, saying, "I don't know what I did! I was drunk. Maybe I did, but there was no emotional involvement with her."

"Jim had like a stable, you might say," Babe says, "Not one-night stands, but certain women he was fond of if Pam wasn't around—she was gone quite a bit of the time—or if they were fighting or something. Whatever was convenient, a place to crash, a soft shoulder." Jim told Babe he was going to have to see this woman, but he never talked about the result of their confrontation. Says Hill, "Jim's attitude was, I was indiscreet in my past, and now I have to go pay for it. He didn't put it like that, but that's what it amounted to, because he was such a gentleman. He would never just tell anybody just to fuck off. So, whatever it was, he had to see her and he saw her. Didn't talk to me about it."

Once that distraction was behind him, Jim had another unexpected encounter with his past. Sitting in a coffee shop at the hotel having breakfast, Jim and Max suddenly heard someone squeal "Jimmy!" from across the room. The pair turned to see an enormously obese woman heading in their direction. She and Jim spoke for a few moments and, after she left the shop, Jim turned back to Max, his face red, and said, "Max, she was my first," going on to explain that she used to be one of the cutest girls in high school. The woman reappeared later while Jim and Max were at the barbershop having their hair trimmed, and she asked Jim if he would have the barber sweep up the clippings from his hair so she could take it home with her as a souvenir.

It was one of the realities of his celebrity that Jim had always had a hard time accepting: To many, even some of those who had known him before his days with The Doors, he had stopped being Jim Morrison and had become instead a commodity, an attraction, a collectible. But Jim told the woman to go ahead and take what she wanted. What else could he do? After all, he wasn't a human being. He was a star.

The trial was grueling, and prejudiced to the point of being a joke. The trial judge had let Max Fink know early on that $50,000 could make the entire matter go away instantly. Max declined, feeling that the amount was exorbitant. As a result, Max found it difficult to say anything more controversial than "Good morning" without being overruled.

Jim tried to lighten the proceedings with his usual skewed brand of humor. One morning Max found Jim sitting outside the courthouse steps. "The trial's been postponed," Jim told his attorney. "Terry [the prosecutor] was arrested last night for exposing himself to a ten-year-old in his car." Max was stunned, but Jim's delivery was completely credible. Then the singer couldn't hold it in any longer and burst into laughter, giving away the joke.

Jim also sent to Max's hotel room the "gift" of a beautiful young woman in reparation, he explained to Max, for Jim's having hit on Max's girlfriend once. Max was amused until the "gift's" mother called to let Max know that her daughter was only fifteen years old. Jim had known

"They were drugged on their own boredom."

the girl was a professional, but hadn't known how young she was, or that her mother was a career litigant who used her daughter as bait. Though Max hadn't "unwrapped" Jim's "gift," in Jim's current situation, even the threat of trouble had to be averted at all costs. Deals were made, money changed hands.

Bryan Gates had followed Jim's career from a distance, mainly through items in the media, so he knew about the proceedings in Miami and took an afternoon off work to sit in the courtroom one day. Jim instantly recognized his former hitchhiking companion and said, "For god's sake! I never thought I'd see you ever again in my life! I can't believe you're here! C'mon out here! Let's catch up!" Bryan immediately asked about Mary Werbelow, and Jim told him of their breakup. But then he told Bryan about Pamela, referring to her as "a woman who was on the same wavelength as him, someone who understood him, someone he understood," says Gates. "He said that he hoped that this relationship, unlike his relationship with Mary, would not dissipate into nothingness."

The two spent a little time reminiscing, and, says Gates, "It was a wonderful forty-five minutes, but then he had to go back into the trial." Jim invited Bryan to join him and some friends that night in Miami Beach, so they could spend more time catching up on the years that had elapsed since they had seen each other last. But their lives had taken very different turns, and Bryan knew they could never converge again. "We were living different lives then," Gates says sadly. "He was a rock singer and I had two babies at home. So I never went." It was the last time Bryan would ever see his friend.

Jim took two breaks from the trial to perform with The Doors, first in California, where Jeff Morehouse's mother came to see him. "She told me she went to see him because Clara and Steve hadn't seen him in a long time," recalls Jeff. "Jim had refused to see [his parents] at a concert when they had gone to see him." So Jeff's mother went to check up on the Morrison boy for his parents. Jim greeted her warmly and presented her with a copy of the book of poetry and musings, *The Lords and the New Creatures,* that had been published by Simon and Schuster earlier that year. Underneath the book's dedication—"To Pamela Susan"—Jim wrote "To Jetty Morehouse, Jim Morrison."

A week later The Doors performed at the Isle of Wight Festival in England, but the show seemed a pale imitation of the group's usual fiery presentations. Max noticed that Jim had lost a lot of his spontaneity and didn't seem as patient with the other Doors as he once had been. Though his three bandmates had flown to Miami for the trial to show their support for Jim, testifying convincingly on his behalf, Jim told Max that he felt that they were secretly enjoying his predicament, that there was a smugness now in their attitude toward him. After the Isle of Wight Festival, Jim told the press that it might be his last live performance.

Despite the fact that Max had finally given in and paid off the trial judge (though at a fraction of what the judge had originally asked), the jury returned a guilty verdict on the misdemeanor charges that had been brought against Jim, though they came to the conclusion that he was not guilty of the felony charge. The judge told Max that another substantial payment would get Jim a suspended sentence, but Max instead filed an appeal. Jim Morrison, a twenty-six-year-old rock star, still faced the possibility of six months in jail for allegedly having pulled his pants down in public.

The charges filed against Meyer Lansky were dismissed. The insidious crime boss, who had recently been called "Public Enemy No. 1," walked away a free man.

Jim had ambivalent feelings about his own verdict. After all they'd

**"I saw her get just a little more
outrageous as time went on . . ."**

been though, it wasn't over yet. With this still hanging over his head, Jim would have to put a lot of his plans on hold, including going solo. If the case were to wind up in appellate court, he would need the others, for the time being anyhow. With this in mind, more than one person suggested that Jim get out of the country for a while, lay low, and put some distance between himself and the other Doors. By that time the relationship between the band members seemed to be hanging by a fraying thread.

Even so, the group began recording a new album a few weeks later. Paul Rothchild had just finished producing Janis Joplin's album *Pearl,* and the contrast between the excitement and energy he'd felt in those sessions and the torpor he witnessed in his sessions with The Doors was staggering. "They were drugged on their own boredom," Rothchild said. "Just totally bummed out." When Paul found himself actually falling asleep over the control panel, he knew it was time to say good-bye. "Ever see anyone walk away from a million dollars?" he asked engineer Bruce Botnick. And then Paul proceeded to do just that. The Doors would produce their last album with Jim themselves, assisted by Bruce Botnick.

On his twenty-seventh birthday, a few of Jim's friends gathered at Village Recorders and listened as Jim, assisted by engineer John Haeny, recorded several of his poetic works without musical accompaniment, save for a tambourine he wielded during some of the pieces. The atmosphere was festive, even more so when Haeny presented Jim with a bottle of whiskey for his birthday. The bottle was passed around, and Jim talked his friends into reading some of his work for the microphone. By the end of the evening, several reels had been filled, and Jim was feeling better than he had in months. "This was incredible," he said.

At Jim's request, Pamela had made herself scarce during the Miami trial. He knew she would be bored, and Pamela didn't pretend otherwise. Instead she had stayed alone in L.A., at one point going for days without eating and winding up in the hospital to be treated for malnutrition. She, too, was exhausted by all the had been happening in Jim's life, in their life.

give me your love, your
tired eyes, sad for
delivery

Jim's sentence was under appeal and he was free on $50,000 bond; he and Pamela began talking seriously about leaving the country for good. To Pamela, it seemed their only chance at redemption, to remove themselves completely and physically from everything and everyone that she blamed for dragging them down. "If you don't leave here," she told him, "I'll leave without you."

Soon our voices must become
one, or one must leave.

On December 12, Jim performed on stage with The Doors for the last time. By the time the dismal show was reaching its conclusion, Jim's pleas for someone to "Light My Fire" were sounding more than a little desperate. The Doors canceled their remaining shows and called an end to their live performances.

The next few months were spent tying up loose ends in preparation for the move to Paris. Jim seemed to be weighing things more seriously, and was speaking with hope of the future, as well as about his feelings for Pamela. Leon Barnard, The Doors' European publicist, remembers the last time he saw Jim, at lunch with Kathy Lisciandro in Los Angeles, during which Jim was uncharacteristically open about his personal feelings. "He began talking about changing his identity and the fact that he was maturing at the age of twenty-seven and that he viewed things differently," says Barnard. "He said that Pamela was the one who had gotten under his skin, that she was his cosmic mate. He considered her to be his cosmic counterpart. He felt that he couldn't live without her, that she was the one that he always returned to and she was the complement to his existence; that he was considering going to Paris and writing screenplays and giving up the whole superstar persona thing, that it had reached its conclusion."

But the mature Jim still retained his mischievous sense of humor. Pamela had gone on to Paris to find a place for them to live, and Jim was planning to join her in a few days. On one of his last evenings in L.A., Jim and Babe Hill paid a visit to Pam's sister, Judy, and her husband, Tom. The group started drinking, and Jim began phoning people at random and asking them if they believed in magic, a subject that had come up over dinner earlier. Most people told Jim he was nuts, or simply hung up on him without bothering to answer his question. But finally Jim called one of Judy's neighbors, who replied immediately, "Oh yes, I believe in magic! Magic is the spark of my life, it means everything to me!" When Jim hung up the phone, he was thrilled with the man's passionate response. He had Judy find an envelope while he fished all the money he had out of his pockets—about $80. He then put the money in the envelope, ran out, and slipped it under the man's door. Returning to Judy's apartment, he called the man back and said, "Magic has just left you a gift underneath your door." And hung up.

CHAPTER 13

"The weather finally turned sunny today after a month of gray. Paris is beautiful in the sun, an exciting town, built for human beings."

The letter to Doors accountant Bob Greene that Jim was dictating to his assistant, Robin Wertle, seemed to sum up not only Paris's weather, but the current climate of Jim's life as well: the first tentative rays of sunlight finally breaking through the clouds after a seemingly endless stretch of gray.

Jim was twenty-seven when he joined Pamela in Paris in March 1971, but he told friends before leaving the States that inside he felt forty-seven, and his outer appearance did nothing to belie his words. Threads of silver had appeared in his dark hair, which had grown past his shoulders, merging with a shaggy beard that was also now streaked with gray. His steady weight gain was compounded by the ever present layer of bloat caused by his chronic alcoholism. The stress of the trial, together with a viral infection he'd picked up a short time before, had triggered Jim's childhood asthma, leaving him with a deep cough that he was making worse by chain-smoking.

But Paris was proving to be good for Jim, and in a matter of weeks his physical appearance reflected that benefit. He and Pam were living without pressures, without schedules, traveling anywhere that caught their fancy, coming back only when it pleased them to do so. Later, remembering an excursion from Paris to Morocco, Pamela said, "I woke up one morning and saw this handsome man by the hotel pool, talking to two young American girls. I fell instantly in love with him. Then I realized it was Jim. I hadn't recognized him. He had got up early and shaved his beard, and he was so lean from losing so much weight, he seemed a new man. It was so nice to fall in love again with the man I was already in love with."

Pamela, too, was doing well. Where Jim had lost some of his excess pounds, away from the stress of their lifestyle in L.A., Pamela had gained some much-needed weight. Typically at least twenty pounds underweight, eating out with Jim most nights at the numerous sidewalk cafés Paris had to offer had caused Pamela's weight to creep over the hundred-pound mark for the first time in her life.

But there was more than just physical healing going on in Paris. Jim had also made the first tentative steps toward bridging the chasm that had so long existed between him and his parents. Alain Ronay, Jim's French-born friend from UCLA, stayed with Jim and Pam in Paris for a few weeks and remembers an evening Jim spent recounting affectionate, funny stories about his father. "The stories were really tender and warm," says Ronay. "I wish his parents could've heard it." Jim's mother had expressed concern about her son's physical condition, reports of which had filtered back to her from various sources during Jim's last few months in the States, and her concerns had gotten back to Jim through reciprocal channels. Admiral Morrison was now assigned to the Pentagon, and Jim had Pamela call his parents in Washington to let them know that Jim was "in fine shape and he was getting better and taking care of himself." Pamela called the Morrisons again a short time later to let them know that she and Jim were looking forward to seeing them as soon as they got back to the States. Even using Pamela as an intermediary, Jim was taking the first difficult steps toward gaining control of his past in order to move on to the future. For the first time, he began talking about having children.

"Most of the time [Jim] was very calm and he wasn't drinking very much," says Ronay. "He wrote practically every day. I really felt that he'd totally reclaimed himself." As they had before Jim became famous and their lives grew so hectic, Jim and Pamela would often stay up all night long drinking wine, Jim using Pamela as a sounding board for his work. "Pamela told me that he would keep her up nights, reading poetry—his poetry, Ezra Pound's poetry," recalled journalist Ellen Sander. "And they'd be drinking and she'd be falling over and he would say, 'Stay awake!' And he would read her poetry and poetry and more poetry." As they had done several times before in the States, the couple obtained another marriage license.

Tere Tereba, one of the people who had acted as models at the Themis photo shoot, was impressed with the obvious overall improvement in Jim when she ran into the couple in Paris in late June. "Jim looks better than he has in a while," Tere wrote of their meeting, though she noted that the French food was keeping Jim from being "the gaunt shadow that prowled L.A. as the 'Lizard King.'" Jim had given up his leather pants in favor of the kind of clothing he'd worn when he was a college student: button-down shirts, chinos, and sweaters. "He is clean-shaven," Tere wrote, "and except for the long brown hair framing the soft, childlike face, he could be mistaken for a college senior from Middle America."

Pamela had first run into Tere having lunch at a sidewalk café one Saturday, and had invited their old friend to visit her and Jim the next day at their apartment on rue Beautreillis, on the Right Bank near the place Bastille. When Jim had first arrived in Paris in March, he had stayed only one night with Pamela at the elegant Hotel Georges V before declaring it a little overdone for his maturing tastes. "It's like a New Orleans bordello," he complained. So the couple had spent a few weeks at the more modest Hôtel du Nice, where Jim had again experienced problems with—and rejected medical treatment for—his asthma, before moving into the spacious though sparsely furnished apartment just off the rue St. Antoine that Pamela had arranged for them to sublet. Jim seemed pleased with Pamela's choice. "Can't get anything like this in L.A.," he'd said.

During Tere's visit to the apartment, Jim confirmed what Pam had already told her the previous day, that they were having a marvelous time in Europe and that both of them loved Paris, even though neither could speak the language. Jim showed Tere some of the writing he had been working on, including a handwritten book which he said would soon be ready for publication. "He wants to be immortalized," said Pam.

Tere suggested they all have dinner at La Coupole, where philosopher Jean-Paul Sartre often dined and where literary couples such as the Hemingways and the Fitzgeralds used to meet in their time. Jim and Pam had never been to the restaurant, so they let Tere be their guide. "Where Scott and Zelda once held court," wrote Tereba of their arrival that evening at the historic café, "Jim and Pam entered unrecognized."

Over dinner, Jim spoke of some offers he had had to do stage and screen work, offers which he was planning to turn down in favor of spending more time on his writing. He also told Tere he had quit drinking. "It looks like the 'Lizard King' has reformed and is seriously attempting to be an American writer in Paris in the romantic tradition of the expatriates of the twenties," Tere later wrote. Jim and Pamela also regaled Tere with tales of their travels together in the past few months, particularly the month they had spent in Morocco where, they both agreed, they'd taken some fabulous footage with Pamela's Super 8 movie camera. "One of the reasons I like Paris so much is that it's so centrally located, not very far from anywhere, not like L.A.," Jim explained to Tere. "We also went to Corsica, but it rained every day we were there except one, so it got to be sort of boring."

17 rue Beautreillis, Paris.

Like much of their travels, the trip to Corsica had been a whim sparked by nothing more than a drunken meeting and a particularly tasty bottle of wine.

Gilles Yepremian, a Parisian college student, had met Jim, in a manner of speaking, outside the trendy Rock and Roll Circus. Gilles had just left the club and recalls, "I see this guy knocking on the door, having a fight with the security guy." To the bouncer on duty, Jim was just another belligerent drunk who had been thrown out of the club. But Gilles recognized the American singer and told the guard that he would handle the situation. Jim let himself be led away by this French stranger.

Because Gilles was living in his parents' home at the time, he took Jim to the nearby apartment of his friend, journalist Herve Mueller. Herve's girlfriend, Yvonne, answered the door, extremely annoyed at Gilles for waking them from a sound sleep in the middle of the night.

"What do you want?" she said angrily, thinking Gilles was simply look-ing for a place to crash for the night. "If you want to sleep, then go and sleep!" But Gilles pointed to Jim standing rather shakily behind him in the hallway and said, "No, I've brought Jim Morrison." Herve shouted, "Shut up!" from the next room, thinking Gilles was joking. But as Herve came out of the bedroom to deal with the situation, Jim walked past Gilles into the apartment and, to the astonishment of all present, kept right on walk-ing into the bedroom, where he passed out on Herve's bed. Gilles went home, and Herve and Yvonne spent the night in a sleeping bag.

Jim finally woke up around noon the next day, and Herve explained to him where he was and how he had gotten there. By this time Jim was starving, so he offered to treat the couple and two of their friends to a late breakfast at the posh Alexander, a restaurant near the Hotel Georges V. Unfortunately, by the time they arrived they were too late for breakfast, but the group decided to wait the half hour until the lunch service began, and they ordered bloody Marys to tide them over. While the rest of the group followed their bloody Marys with lunch, Jim followed his with a bottle of scotch, washing that down with a bottle of cognac.

What do you do with a drunken rock star? No one knew exactly where Jim was living, nor how to get in touch with the woman he kept mumbling about. "He just wanted to be telling us about Pam," says Mueller. "There was a little apartment on rue Beautreillis, he said, and they were just back from Morocco." It wasn't really enough information to do them any good, so Herve and Yvonne ended up taking Jim back to Herve's flat. Jim made a scene at the apartment building, refusing to move out of the stairwell and screaming obscenities at no one in particular before Herve was finally able to calm him and get him to bed.

The next day, "I drove him back to rue Beautreillis, which is when I met Pam for the first time," Herve recalls. "I remember thinking, God, she must be worried!" But if Pamela had been concerned, she showed little sign of it when Jim and Herve walked in the door. "Oh, he's been with you," was all she said about Jim's two-day absence. It was clear to Herve that either Pamela was used to such occurrences or she had at least learned to mask her true feelings about them from outsiders.

A few days later, a newly sober Jim brought Pamela to lunch at Herve's flat, where he was able to properly thank Gilles for the first time. "I'll never forget that lunch," says Mueller, "because Jim didn't get drunk. We talked about everything. We talked just briefly about The Doors and he said for him it was over, he'd left those days behind. He said, 'I'm twenty-seven—that's too old to be a rock and roll star.'" Though more ambiguous about his decision, Jim expressed similar sentiments the few

Pam and Jim with Herve Mueller and friend, Paris, 1971.

times that he spoke to Bill Siddons on the phone. "I spoke to Jim on three separate occasions," recalls Siddons. "He always seemed to be in good spirits, happy that he'd gone there, and optimistic." Jim told Bill that he was fine, that he and Pamela were living together and doing well, but he grew somewhat evasive when talk would inevitably turn to The Doors. "We talked to him about coming back," says Siddons, "and all we ever got was 'Ah! No plans! I'm having a great time. Maybe someday we'll do another record, but no plans!' Jim was completely noncommittal about The Doors' future every time I talked to him."

John, Robby, and Ray seemed less ambiguous about Jim's future with the band. "I remember sitting in The Doors' office one day when Jim and Pam were in Paris," says Cheri Siddons, "and the three of them were all saying, 'Well let's just dump Jim and let's make an album without him. Who's going to tell him? Who's going to tell him we don't want to work with him anymore?'" Cheri was furious at the group for their apparent lack of gratitude to Jim for all he had done for them. In spite of the problems he had caused, it was Jim, after all, who had made The Doors famous. "I was just so indignant, so angry!" Cheri says. "I said, 'I'll tell him!'" But her indignation seemed to make little impression on the group and the subject wasn't broached in front of Cheri again.

Herve thought that Pamela seemed relieved by Jim's feelings on the matter. "I remember that he honestly wanted to settle in France," Herve recalls. Jim and Pam talked briefly about perhaps buying a house in the French countryside. "She wanted to find an old church or chapel and turn it into a house," says Mueller. "She said, 'Of course we couldn't spend more than . . .' and I don't remember the figure she gave, but Gilles and I looked at each other; it was an enormous amount at the time, like sixty grand."

Neither Pam nor Jim drank more than a sociable amount of the wine that was offered to them. "Oh, this is good!" Pam said after taking a sip, "What is it?" When told that it was Corsican wine, she turned to Jim and said, "Can we go there?" Pamela loved to travel, and Jim was ready for another adventure, so he said, "Sure! We'll go next week."

But, as Jim and Pam explained to Tere, their Corsican experience was dampened by the weather, so now they were back in Paris, planning more and better adventures—a few days in London the following week, and a possible trip to Switzerland later on. Jim seemed amazed when Tere expressed her happiness at the thought of returning to the States in a few days. "I won't be back in the States until September at the earliest," he told her.

The excursion to London the following week was cut short when Jim's asthma once again flared up. This time his breathing was affected to the point where a doctor had to be been summoned to the couple's hotel room in the middle of the night. Again the doctor wrote out a prescription for asthma medication, but whether Jim followed through with this course of treatment is doubtful. He had filled a similar prescription for asthma medication at a pharmacy in Los Angeles shortly before he left for Paris, but his drinking at the time was so heavy, it's likely that remembering to take his medication on a regular basis was nearly impossible for Jim.

The following Friday, while Pamela used one of Jim's poetry-filled notebooks to make a list, complete with sketches, of the outfits she wanted to take with her on their next trip (*silver mini, silk paisley suit and hat, Indian suit, moccasins, feather fringe, hair beads . . .*), Jim dictated to Robin his letter to Bob Greene. In the letter Jim explained to Bob that he and Pamela had decided they wanted to stay on in Paris indefinitely, asking for an informal financial statement letting them know how long they could go on living there at their current rate. Jim also asked Bob's help in turning Themis over to Judy and her husband, saying that Judy and Tom could get a loan to buy the business outright, all but a few personal things that Jim and Pam wanted to keep. After instructing the accountant to send Pam's parents $100 for the care of their dog, Sage, as well as inquiring on the status of credit cards Jim had requested both in his name and Pamela's and asking for $3,000 to cover "house bills," Jim closed by saying simply: "Later. Jim."

Robin wasn't planning to stop at the post office until the next morning, so she typed up the letter and dated it "3 July 1971."

In Los Angeles the following Monday, Bill and Cheri Siddons were awakened at 3:00 A.M. by the ringing of the phone next to their bed. Bill hesitated a moment before lifting the receiver to his ear, and Cheri gave voice to the first thought that came into her head: "Jim's dead."

BALTIMORE MORNING SUN

Elegy in a Paris Graveyard
by Mike John

James Douglas Morrison, twenty-seven, lead singer of The Doors, died in Paris on July 3. He went there in pursuit of his girlfriend, and ended up making her the beneficiary of his considerable estate, according to a spokesman for Elektra Records. He was buried in that city, in the "Poet's Corner" of a cemetery. Doors manager Bill Siddons said he died of natural causes, relating to a respiratory illness. This is, of course, how it had to be. Drugs were out of the question. Morrison was a drinker, to put it mildly. He lived like there would be no tomorrow; getting sick and not taking care of himself is entirely feasible for him. It had to be this way . . .

That was the day the Dodgers beat San Francisco ten to nothing, they beat up on Juan Marichal." Babe Hill likes to assume an almost casual air when speaking of Jim Morrison's death. But just as the flash of an atomic bomb sears the images of those obliterated by the blast onto whatever remains standing, so, too, are the trivial details of that weekend in 1971 permanently etched in Babe's memory.

"I was staying on The Doors' boat down in Oxnard," Hill says. "That same night that Jim died, I was drunk out there. I was so drunk that I fell out of my truck down by this guy's house where I was hanging out, down on the beach up there. Oh, I was bombed! We went driving around in the back of this truck and I was drinking wine and it was just crazy! Wild! And then Monday I went back to town and found out Jim had died that Saturday. I was over at Frank and Kathy's when Bill Siddons called and told us."

While Jim's death affected Babe deeply, he saw an inevitability about the event that only seemed to add to its tragic nature. "I've seen friends of mine drink or drug themselves to death," he says, "and you look at their lives and their potential and their talent, and you think, what a waste. But I think that what Jim wanted he wouldn't have achieved, he wouldn't have attained. To be known as a good poet. It's one thing to be able to respect your peers, your fellow poets. But I mean, to be known as a rock star and not to be known as what you really think you are is kind of hard to put up with. I couldn't speculate what else he expected to achieve or be in his life other than that."

RECORD WORLD

Jac Holzman, President of Elektra, has issued the following statement: Jim Morrison was an artist of stellar magnitude who was able to retain a bemused and detached perspective on his aura, his art, and his stardom. His exciting qualities as a performer and writer are universally known to the fascinated public for whom Jim was always news. Jim admired those people who stretched their lives to the fullest, who lived out on the edge of experience. He possessed special insights into people, their lives and into the dark corners of human existence. But beyond his public image, he was a friend to many, and those of us at Elektra who worked with him and The Doors so closely over the past five years will remember him as one of the kindest and most thoughtful people we have known. He is already missed.

Paul Ferrara cried when he heard of Jim's death, but he also felt an overwhelming anger at his friend's disregard for life. "Jim and I used to argue a lot about his excesses," says Ferrara, "and he would make excuses that nothing matters, it doesn't matter. And I would say, 'Yes it does, you're going to fucking kill yourself!'" A story comes to mind that reminds Paul of Jim's feeling of invulnerability. "One night," recalls Ferrara, "Jim was driving—he had a Shelby Mustang—and I think Babe was in the front seat, I was in the back, and I think Frank [Lisciandro] was with me. From the Whisky a Go-Go, if you head east on Sunset eventually you come to a street called Halloway that dips down and goes to La Cienega. There's like six or seven stoplights. And somewhere down west of the Whisky, Jim floored the car and went screaming through every light regardless of color for like six or seven blocks. He literally just pushed his foot to the floor and that was it, man! I mean we must've been going about a hundred miles per hour; that car was *fast!*" As much as the story illustrates and reminds Ferrara of his anger at Jim's foolishness, it also makes him grow wistful for those dangerous times. "I had great times after that," he says, "after Jim died. But my life was never the same again."

TIME MAGAZINE

Died. Jim Morrison, twenty-seven, lead singer of The Doors and the third big rock star to die within ten months; in Paris. Although Morrison at times drank heavily, he did not have a reputation as a drug user, and he died of heart attack . . .

The day after he returned to the States, Bill Siddons met with the three remaining members of The Doors to tell them what had transpired in Paris. Recalling the group's reaction to the news, Siddons says, "It was pretty businesslike. Wasn't a lot of tears, it was just, 'Oh, okay.' None of us ever really believed Jim would make it to thirty, so as much of a shock as it was, it was a shock tempered by knowledge of Jim's completely erratic behavior patterns. So we just kind of did what we had to do and, you know, took a couple of months off and dealt with all the details, following through with this. There was a lot of outrage with not having a public funeral and having, you know, a lot of access with more depth to it. But it was our intent to keep it quiet, and we did it as best we could and granted as few interviews as possible that was necessary to keep it relatively quiet. But of course in that circumstance it's not quiet, it's worldwide."

NEWSWEEK

Death Disclosed: Jim Morrison, twenty-seven, rock superstar, the lead singer of The Doors. Though his manager fueled suspicion by keeping Morrison's death a secret for six days—until after his burial last week—there was no evidence of a drug connection as in last year's deaths of Janis Joplin and Jimi Hendrix, nor was Morrison's fifth-a-day booze habit officially a factor; police listed a heart attack as the cause after Morrison was found dead in the bathtub of his apartment in Paris, where he had been living as a writer in recent months . . .

"John told me," says Julia Negron, then married to John Densmore. "But it's weird—he didn't tell me 'til like a day later. I don't think Robby told Lynne either. I think they couldn't figure out how to tell us or something. Or they had to meet about it—I don't know what the hell. But we were driving to the office, and on the way John said, 'We're going to the office to meet because Jim is dead.' And I thought, *you idiot,* because everyone had heard that rumor before a million times. But he said, 'No, really. Billy went to Paris and Jim's definitely dead.' So John told me. He was fairly matter of fact about it, but maybe he didn't know how I'd react."

THE MIAMI HERALD

Morrison and Miami: Beginning of the End
by Lawrence Mahoney

. . . Morrison, a royal figure of the drug-oriented counterculture, was not a man for narcotics himself. He drank heavily and dismissed LSD as "a new kind of wine." So Jim Morrison, who called Florida his home, is dead and buried in France at twenty-seven. His life ended, the Paris police say, in a bathtub. The end of an American enigma.

"That was a bad day," says Bryan Gates, recalling the day he read about Jim's death in a Florida newspaper. The report seemed to come such a short time after Jim's departure for Paris, a move that had filled Bryan with hope. "It pleased me from the point of view of well, maybe he's going to make it. Maybe he's going to use that celebrity as the springboard he always talked about to intellectual significance, a place in the literary history of the United States. I was essentially cheering for him when I learned that he had sloughed it off and gone to Paris." But reading the reports of Jim's death such a short time later, says Gates, "I felt that all of us had been cheated of his potential. I really couldn't understand it! He seemed to have just broken through from the madness of American celebrity. He may have then gone on to calmly realize his potential, he may have had some sort of contribution to make beyond anything that we could have imagined. Yet—mysteriously, snuffed out in such a strange, uncharacteristic manner. To believe the press reports, that this fellow, who had lived so close to death all his life by his penchant for pushing things to the edge, could possibly pass on as a result of respiratory problems and, of all places, in a bathtub? To me, it was just overwhelmingly sad."

LOS ANGELES TIMES

Rock Star Jim Morrison Dies
by Tom Paegel

. . . Morrison, who sometimes called himself "The Lizard King," had a reputation as a heavy drinker. Last year, he was fined $600 for disturbing other passengers aboard an airlines flight. He was accused of violating several safety regulations and of excessive drinking and using loud and lewd language. Morrison leaves his wife, Pamela, his parents, a brother and a sister.

"I guess I heard it the same time everyone else did," says Jeff Morehouse of the death of his childhood friend. "I also talked to my parents about it; they had talked to the Morrisons. The only thing I heard from my family about his family was that they were very, very torn up, they were distressed. It was one of those things that was absolutely unexpected for everybody. It was basically a tragedy." For years Jeff refused to discuss his friend or what had become of him. "I didn't want to talk about it," says Morehouse. "I guess I just didn't want to admit that I was never going to see him again. I always imagined I would see him in another four years, always imagined that that's how it would be, and obviously it won't. I didn't even want to think about it." But Jeff has come to accept his friend's death, and remembers him as he saw him last. "He was a rebel at the right time. A very visible rebel. But he is the same person in my mind as the last time I saw him that Christmas in California."

WASHINGTON POST

Singer Jim Morrison Reported Dead;
Parents in Arlington Not Notified
by Timothy S. Robinson

Jim Morrison, raucous lead singer of the rock group The Doors, died Saturday in Paris, according to wire service reports. The reports said Morrison, who was 27, died of natural causes. However, Morrison's parents, R. Adm. and Mrs. Steve Morrison of Arlington, said early this morning they had not been notified of their son's death. . . . Wire services said the death was announced by Bob Gibson, of the public relations firm of Gershman, Gibson and Stromberg, which represents The Doors. They quoted Gibson as saying he could give no explanation of the delay in announcing the death. According to the Associated Press, Gibson said he learned of Morrison's death from William Siddons, the singer's personal manager. . . . Morrison's parents said they had not heard of Gibson, but confirmed that Siddons was the singer's manager. "If Bill Siddons said it, it's true," Adm. Morrison said. "If you get in touch with him, call us . . ."

15

Cheri Siddons waited anxiously, scanning the steady stream of faces emerging from the plane that had just arrived from Paris as she tried to calm her fretful ten-month-old daughter. The arrivals gate was bathed in an aura of joyous anticipation as each emerging passenger was greeted by warm smiles and wrapped in joyous embraces by their waiting loved ones. But soon all the happy passengers had come and gone, leaving only Cheri, her daughter, and an older woman whose face seemed to reflect the weary watchfulness of Cheri's own. Cheri approached the woman and asked, "Are you Pamela's mother?" When Penny Courson nodded her assent, the two women fell into each other's arms, instantly bound by a common grief.

For Cheri, it was the first time she had been allowed to vent some of the deep pain she was feeling over losing a dear friend. "When Jim died," she explains, "nobody was allowed to know for three days, and it was a horrible, horrible time. If you can imagine losing somebody you love and not being able to tell anybody. So by the time we got to the airport, Penny was the first person I could connect with." By now, word had leaked out through various sources that this time, rumors of Jim Morrison's death were not premature. As soon as Bill came off the plane with Pamela, the group would have to face the prospect of dealing with the press, making an announcement none of them wanted to acknowledge was true.

Cheri and Penny sat and talked as they waited for Bill and Pam to emerge from the plane. Pamela's father, whom Cheri had not noticed previously, kept to himself as the women talked. Penny took the opportunity to ask Cheri a favor. "She knew that we had to go to this press conference," says Cheri, "and she asked me if I would do her a favor and have Billy say that Jim and Pam were married. And I did that, and that's how it was reported in the papers." The marriage license obtained in Paris would end up being another one that Jim and Pam would never execute.

Finally, a weary Bill Siddons appeared with Pamela at his side. "She'd been through so much," Cheri says, "and she just seemed haggard, white as a ghost, very raw, very exhausted." Though it was getting late, the group stopped at one of the airport cafés for a little while before they had to face the ordeal that still lay ahead. Whereas Cheri had always found Pamela's attitude toward her to be extremely cold, tonight all of Pamela's defenses seemed to have been left in Paris. "She really spoke openly without any of her airs or protection or whatever she felt that she needed," Cheri recalls. "What was amazing was that she was so compassionate toward me. Literally that girl had never looked me in the eye, never given me the time of day before. But that night she looked at me, specifically, across the table and she said, 'Cheri, he died peacefully, he had a smile on his face.' And that was meant woman to woman, that was very directly meant for me."

It was nearly 10:00 before Pam left with her parents, and Cheri, Bill, and their sleeping child headed for the publicist's office to try to put together an official statement that would satisfy the question sure to be on everybody's minds: What had happened in Paris?

According to the reports filed by the French fire brigade and police officers who were called to deal with the situation, the death of Jim Morrison held little of the mystery that would later be built up around it. Lt. Alain Raisson's fire brigade was the was the first on the scene and he filed the following report:

> *This morning at 9:20 a.m. I went as commander of my unit to 17 rue Beautreillis, Paris 4th, the third floor, right-hand-side flat in answer to a report of "asphyxiation." When we reached the flat, the door was opened by a young woman who could not speak French and who took us to the bathroom. In this room there was a man in the bath, completely naked and heavily built. His head was above the water, resting on the edge of the bath. The bath was full of water, slightly pink in color, and his right arm was resting on the side of the bath. The water was still lukewarm, as well as the body. Together with my men, I took the body out and laid it on the floor of the bedroom where I started giving heart massage but I immediately realized that the victim was dead and I had the body placed on the bed.*

In a brief addendum, Lt. Raisson noted:

When I went into the bathroom, there was some water on the floor beside the bath and the dressing gown of the person who opened the door to us was wet.

Pamela, finding Jim unconscious, had tried desperately to lift him out of the bathtub, but he weighed nearly twice as much as she did, making the task impossible for her to manage alone.

The term *asphyxiation* used in the report could refer to a number of serious breathing difficulties, including choking and suffocation. In situations such as these, the fire brigade "resuscitation unit" responds to the emergency, as they had done in this instance.

Next to arrive at the scene were the police, whose report to the state prosecutor was written by Police Superintendent Robert Berry. In reading the statement, it is helpful to note that the somewhat jarring word *concubine* is simply a term employed by the French as a legal definition for a live-in lover who has the same rights as a wife. As a legal term the word has none of the derogatory implications it has in English. After identifying the deceased, "MORRISON, James Douglas," as an American writer who had been living at the present address since March 1971, as well as listing Jim's date of birth and giving his home address as The Doors' office in Los Angeles, Superintendent Berry made the following report:

On July 3rd between 8:30 a.m. and 9:00 a.m. Miss Pamela COURSON—Mr. MORRISON's concubine—noticed that her boyfriend who had got up in the middle of the night, apparently around 4:00 a.m. in order to have a bath, had not returned to bed. Miss COURSON went to the bathroom and saw that Mr. MORRISON was in the bath unconscious, with his head above the water and resting on the side of the bath. Miss COURSON, who does not speak French, telephoned a couple of compatriots and friends, Mr. RONAY and his girlfriend Miss DEMY, temporarily in Paris at 86 rue Daguerre, who came right away and called the Fire Brigade and Police.

The Fire Brigade men took Mr. MORRISON's body out of the bath, the water of which was still lukewarm, and tried to massage his heart, without any success. Inquiries brought to light that Mr. MORRISON had been feeling faint in the middle of the night; according to his concubine he was breathing with difficulty and decided to have a hot bath. According to Miss COURSON's statement he started vomiting and she collected this vomit in a container which she rinsed afterwards before going back to bed, thinking that

"We are going to 17 rue Beautreillis in Paris, 4th
Arrondissement, Staircase A, third floor flat on the
right hand side . . ."

*the vomiting would have helped and that he would return to bed
after his bath. She went back to sleep. Nothing suspicious was
noticed on the spot either in the flat or on the body, which bore no
trace of blows, lesions or needle marks.*

*Dr. Vassille conducted the medical examination and concluded
that death was by natural causes due to heart failure, which could
have been caused by a change of temperature, following a bath,
causing the classical "myocardial infarction," a case of sudden
death.*

*It is significant that Mr. RONAY and Miss COURSON had
already noticed that Mr. MORRISON had been suffering from
respiratory problems for several months and that he looked unwell.
Despite the advice given to him, Mr. MORRISON had always
refused to see a doctor.*

It was true that Jim only saw doctors when it was absolutely necessary, and
then no one doctor in particular. When Jim would pick up an occasional

venereal disease, Max Fink sent him to an old friend of his, a gynecologist in the Wilshire district who would treat Jim quietly, after regular office hours. Most of The Doors and their wives used the services of Dr. Arnold Derwin, who would later be cited as an authority on why Jim's death could not have been caused by respiratory distress, based on the fact that Derwin himself had not been aware of Jim's existing asthma condition, nor had Jim seemed ill the last time Dr. Derwin had seen him. But Derwin had no access to Jim's past medical records, nor was Jim likely to provide an accurate history, assuming one had been requested. At the time Jim left for France, Derwin had not seen the singer for a year or more, making it unlikely the doctor would be able to speak with any authority on Jim's physical condition at that time.

Another report was filed by police officer Jacques Manchez, which largely concurred with what had already been reported by the superintendent:

> We are going to 17 rue Beautreillis in Paris 4th Arrondissement, Staircase A, third floor flat on the right hand side. At the scene we note the presence of firemen from the Sevigne Brigade and the Police Emergency Services bus of the 4th Arrondissement.
>
> The fire chief informs us that he took the body of Mr. MORRISON, the tenant of the flat, from the bath, and that his body was placed on the bed in the bedroom after having tried, without success, to resuscitate him by heart massage.
>
> We then go to the bedroom where we find the body of a young man, quite heavily built, lying on the bed. The body is covered with a bedspread which we removed; he is lying on his back, completely naked, with his arms by his sides. His eyes are half closed and his mouth is slightly open, a trickle of blood coming from his right nostril and his left nostril obstructed by a clot. The body is still supple and bears no trace of trauma or lesions of any kind.
>
> We do not notice any signs of disorder in the room where we are. Continuing on with our observations, we go to the bathroom where we find the bath in which Mr. MORRISON's body lay before it was taken to the bed by the firemen. This room is connected with the bedroom by a secondary corridor which also leads to the kitchen. The bath is situated on the left hand side in front of a bidet, on the right hand side there is a wash hand basin and a little cabinet. The outside dimensions of the bath are 1 metre 50 × 65 centimeters, inside the bath there is still some slightly pink colored water. The bath is 35 cms. deep and the water is 19 cms. deep. The water is still

Form FS-192
(1-19-01)

DEPARTMENT OF STATE
FOREIGN SERVICE OF THE UNITED STATES OF AMERICA

REPORT OF THE DEATH OF AN AMERICAN CITIZEN

FINAL

American Embassy, Paris, France, August 11, 1971
(Place and date)

Name in full __James Douglas MORRISON__ Occupation __Singer__

Native or naturalized __BORN ON December 8, 1943 AT Clearwater,__ Last known address
Florida

in the United States __8216 Norton Avenue, Los Angeles, California__

Date of death __July__ __3__ __5:00 a.m.__ __1971__ Age __27 years__
(Month) (Day) (Hour) (Minute) (Year) (As nearly as can be ascertained)

Place of death __17, rue Beautreillis, Paris 4, France__
(Number and street) or (Hospital or hotel) (City) (Country)

Cause of death __Heart Failure__
(Include authority for statement)

As certified by Dr. Max Vassille, 31, rue du Renard, Paris, France

Disposition of the remains __Interred in Pere Lachaise Cemetery, 16th Division, Paris,__
France on July 7, 1971.

Local law as to disinterring remains __May be disinterred at any time upon the request of__
nearest relative or legal representative of the estate. See Decree Law of December
31, 1941, Journal Officiel, January 26-27, 1942, Page 378.

Disposition of the effects __In the custody of Pamela Courson, friend.__

Person or official responsible for custody of effects and accounting therefor __Rear Admiral George S.__
Informed by telegram: __Morrison, father.__

NAME	ADDRESS	RELATIONSHIP	DATE SENT
N/A			

Copy of this report sent to:

NAME	ADDRESS	RELATIONSHIP	DATE SENT
Rear Admiral George S. Morrison	Chief Naval Operations	Father	August 11, 1971
	OPO 3B - Room 4E 552		
	Pentagon, Washington, D.C. 20350		

Traveling or residing abroad with relatives or friends as follows:

NAME	ADDRESS	RELATIONSHIP
Miss Pamela Courson	17, rue Beautreillis	Friend
	75 - Paris 4, France	

Other known relatives (not given above):

NAME	ADDRESS	RELATIONSHIP
Unknown		

This information and data concerning an inventory of the effects, accounts, etc., have been placed under File 234 in the correspondence of this office.

Remarks: __U.S. passport number J.900083, issued at Los Angeles, California,__
on August 7, 1968 cancelled and returned to father.

Filing date and place of French Death Certificate: __July 3, 1971 at the Town Hall__
of Paris 4, France.
(Continue on reverse if necessary.)

Mary Ann Meysenburg
Mary Ann Meysenburg
(Signature on all copies)

[SEAL]
No fee prescribed.

Vice Consul .... of the United States of America.

MORRISON, James Douglas

Report of the Death of an American Citizen.

lukewarm. On the floor next to the cabinet we notice a container, yellow/orange in color and empty. We leave this room to go to the lounge where we find three people, two women and a man, they are all American; a policeman tells us that it is Pamela COURSON, Mr. MORRISON's girlfriend with whom he lived, Mr. Alain RONAY, compatriot and friend of the MORRISON-COURSON couple and Miss Agnes DEMY, Mr. RONAY's concubine . . .

Through Mr. RONAY, Miss COURSON tells us that her friend got up this morning around about 4:00 a.m. to have a bath because he was not feeling well. Miss COURSON had gone back to sleep and when she woke around about 8:30 a.m. she realized that her friend had not come back to bed. She had then gone to the bathroom and seen her friend unconscious in the bath with his head outside the water. She had tried to take him out of the bath but couldn't do it because of Mr. MORRISON's height (1 metre 86).

Alain Ronay had been helping Pamela by acting as interpreter for the many questions she was being asked, but the steady stream of French was making a difficult situation even more untenable for her. "You could say anything and I wouldn't understand it," she said to Ronay. "I'm sorry, but how can I understand you? I want to know everything you say from now on." After that, Alain took pains to make sure he translated everything that was said so Pamela could understand what was going on around her.

That afternoon, Pamela was at the fourth arrondissement police station to once again relate the events leading up to Jim's death. With Alain again acting as translator, Pamela gave the following statement:

I am Mr. MORRISON's girlfriend and have been living with him for five years. Last March, I came to France with my friend. During a previous short stay I had found rented accommodation at the address 17 rue Beautreillis, third floor, right hand side. My boyfriend was a writer but mostly he lived on a personal fortune.

Before living at rue Beautreillis, my boyfriend and I lived for three weeks at the Hôtel de Nice, rue des Beaux Arts, I think, and while we were there my friend was sick, he was complaining of difficulty in breathing, and he also had coughing fits at night. I called a doctor to the hotel who prescribed pills for asthma, but my friend didn't like to see doctors and never looked after himself seriously. [In answer to a question from the officer taking the statement: I cannot say precisely who the doctor was, and I didn't keep the prescription. During a previous stay in London, my friend had already experienced the same problems.]

Last night I had dinner with my friend . . . I am not explaining myself properly—I didn't have dinner last night, my friend went out to a restaurant on his own, probably in the area. When my friend came back from the restaurant, we both went to the cinema to see the film Death Valley. The cinema is beside the Metro Station Le Pelletier, I think it is called Action Lafayette. We came back from the cinema around 1:00 a.m., I did the dishes and my friend watched an amateur film from a projector. My friend looked in good health, he seemed very happy. However, I have to say, my friend never used to complain, it wasn't in his nature. We then listened to records; I should say that the record player is in the bedroom and we were both listening to the music lying on the bed. I think we went to sleep at 2:30 a.m. approximately, but I can't say exactly because the record player stops automatically. [In answer to a question from the officer taking the statement: No, we didn't have any sexual intercourse last night.]

Round about 3:30 a.m. I think, because there was not a clock in the bedroom and I didn't notice the time, I was woken by the noise my friend was making with his breathing. His breathing was noisy and I thought he was choking. It was noisy. I shook my friend, I slapped him a few times to wake him, I shook him and he woke up. I asked him what was wrong, I wanted to call a doctor. He got up, walked about in the bedroom and then told me he wanted to have a bath. He headed towards the bathroom and ran his bath. When he was in the bath he called me and said that he felt sick and felt like vomiting. On my way I picked up an orange colored bowl. He vomited food into the bowl I was holding. I think there was blood in it. I emptied the contents then my friend vomited into the container again, only blood this time and then a third time blood clots. Each time I emptied the bowl down the wash basin of the bathroom, then I washed the bowl. My friend then told me he felt strange but he said, "I don't feel sick, don't call a doctor, I feel better. It's over!" He told me to "go to bed" and said that he was going to finish his bath and would join me in bed. At this time it appeared to me that my friend felt better because he had vomited and his color had returned a bit. I went back to bed and I immediately fell asleep. I was reassured.

I don't know how long I slept. I awoke with a start and I saw that my friend wasn't lying next to me. I ran to the bathroom and saw that my friend was still in the bath, a little blood was running from his nostril. I shook my friend, thinking he would wake up. I thought he had fainted and was unconscious. I tried to get him out of the bath but I couldn't. Then I phoned up Mr. RONAY. He came with his girlfriend, Miss Agnes DEMY, and they called, I think, the Fire Brigade or the Police.

Alain was also asked to give a statement in which he explained:

I have known Mr. MORRISON since 1963, he was one of my friends. Mr. MORRISON came to see me in London on the 5th of June last month, when I was on holiday there. He was with Miss COURSON. I knew that my friend had been living with Miss COURSON for several years.

Ronay goes on to say:

I was with Mr. Morrison the whole of yesterday afternoon and I left him around 6:00 p.m. I thought he looked unwell and I told him. He said that everything was fine. As a matter of fact, he never used to complain. I went for a walk with him yesterday afternoon, he told me he felt tired . . .

Alain concluded his statement by saying that he and Pamela were going to make the funeral arrangements.

It took three days for all the necessary reports to be filed and formalities to be honored before the body could be released for burial and funeral arrangements made. Alain accompanied Pamela to the *pompes funèbres municipales,* the city funeral directors, to arrange for the polished oak coffin, shroud, coffin nails, and all the other harsh realities the situation demanded. Pamela may have given her consent to all the choices made that day as they were translated to her, but the signature on the release form, while Pamela's name, does not appear to be in Pamela's handwriting, suggesting that perhaps either Robin or Agnes went along that day and signed in Pamela's place. Ronay also accompanied Pamela to Cimetière du Père-Lachaise where a double plot, apparently the only size available, was purchased for the interment.

By the time all the necessary arrangements had been made, Jim's body had been in the apartment three full days. Because it was July and the apartment had no air-conditioning, the body had been packed in dry ice, which was delivered to the apartment in great chunks several times over the weekend, to help delay decomposition. The man delivering the ice warned that the summer heat would soon make the situation untenable, and particularly discouraged Pamela from lingering near the body. But the

Funeral director's instructions. The name at the
bottom is Pamela's, but the signature is not.

iceman's warnings couldn't dissuade Pamela from spending as much time as possible with Jim, holding his hand, talking to him, and spending the night next to him. She told Alain that having Jim in the house made her feel more secure, saying, "If it were up to me, I'd keep him here forever."

By Monday, gossip had begun circulating throughout Europe that something was very wrong with Jim Morrison. Elektra's London office began receiving calls from the press asking for confirmation of Jim's death. Rumors of Jim's death had come and gone frequently over the years, but it was usually fans who were telling tales among themselves. Now the calls were coming from reputable journalists, and Clive Selwood, a representative of Elektra's British subsidiary, decided it was time to alert Bill Siddons. Bill, sleepy and tense on the other end of the phone, promised Clive he would look into the matter and get back to him.

"I finally got Pamela on the phone around 10:00, 10:30 Monday morning," says Siddons, "but she wouldn't admit it. I just remember her being evasive." Pamela had always had a healthy suspicion of anything or anyone connected with The Doors, and Bill was no exception. Siddons continues: "I finally said, 'Pamela, I am your friend. You may not see me as that sometimes, but if Jim has died, I want to help you through whatever you have to go through. I want to come there and assist you, not as a representative of The Doors, but as your friend.'" Bill's instant understanding of her evasions, together with his kind tone, melted the last of Pamela's defenses, and, dissolving into tears, she told him the truth. Bill assured her he would be on the next plane to Paris.

Siddons arrived in Paris early Tuesday morning, too early, he felt, to go directly to the apartment. Instead, he decided to stop at a sidewalk café on rue St. Antoine and have some coffee while he waited for time to pass. As he sat and sipped his coffee, Bill began to see, at least in part, why Jim had felt so comfortable in Paris. "I learned a lot about the French culture as all these workmen came in and had their morning drinks of alcohol at six A.M.," he says.

Bill needn't have been concerned about visiting the apartment too soon. By the time he arrived, representatives of the funeral home had already been there to wrap Jim's body in its shroud and place it in the coffin Alain and Pamela had selected. "Pamela let me into the apartment," says Siddons. "It was a fairly simple old place, not big but reasonably spacious. The only alarming thing was that the casket was in the bedroom. Jim was with us."

Bill found Pamela to be "distraught and depressed," he says, "but she was coherent, not screwed up in any way, not crying all the time, just trying to manage the details of how to handle this situation. I have a lot

Jim's gravesite at Père-Lachaise cemetery,
Paris, as it looks today.

of forgiveness for people who are in mourning. Pamela wasn't like Miss Orderly-I've-Got-It-Together. She did what she had to do. She was just getting by."

Pamela explained to Bill what had happened, and asked that no press releases be issued until everything had been taken care of. Everyone was well aware of the hailstorm of publicity that would break around the news of Jim's death, and no one wanted to face the storm's ferocity before it was absolutely necessary. "I was quite impressed with how they handled the whole thing," Bills says of the concerted effort by Pamela, Alain, Robin, and Agnes to handle all the details while keeping word of the situation from the press. Bill agreed to remain silent until they returned to the States. "I think that the goal in Paris was to avoid the kind of giant scenes that happened with Jimi and Janis," he says, "so we just did everything we could to keep it as quiet and low-key as possible."

The next morning at 9:00, a small van arrived to transport the coffin the short distance to Père-Lachaise cemetery. Attending at the graveside were Pamela, Bill, Alain, Robin, Agnes, and a friend Agnes had brought along. Included with the funeral package was a small group of paid "wailers" who accompanied the small funeral procession. As the civil service was being conducted, these professional mourners, dressed in black and draped in veils, seemed consumed by abject grief, rocking back and forth, moaning, wailing, sobbing. Later, Pamela told her mother, "I almost wanted to giggle, it was so absurd. I just knew Jim would've gotten the biggest kick out of that!"

Pamela and Bill spent the rest of the day in preparation for their return to the States. "I helped her pack up the apartment," says Siddons. "Twenty-five little boxes that we shipped back." They returned to Los Angeles the following day and were met by Pamela's parents and Cheri.

After leaving the airport in Los Angeles late that night, Cheri and Bill drove straight to the office of the publicist, who had been alerted of their arrival. Bill told the publicist and another writer there what had happened, and each wrote a press release, with Bill choosing the one he thought most appropriate. The next day the statement appeared in newspapers under Bill's name, saying, in part:

> I have just returned from Paris where I attended the funeral of Jim Morrison. Jim was buried in a simple ceremony with only a few friends present. . . . I can say that Jim died peacefully of natural causes—he had been in Paris since March with his wife, Pam. He had seen a doctor in Paris about a respiratory problem and had complained of this problem on Saturday—the day of his death. I hope that Jim is remembered not only as a rock singer and poet, but as a warm human being. He was the most warm, most human, most understanding person I've known. That wasn't always the Jim Morrison people read about—but it was the Jim Morrison I knew and his close friends will remember . . .

Stories immediately began to spring up around the cause of Jim's death, the most prevalent being that he had died of a drug overdose. "I thought he OD'd," Mirandi Babitz recalls of her initial reaction to the news of Jim's death. "It was like everybody was ODing at that point." But there was no basis for this speculation beyond the fact that Jim had been a rock star, and didn't all rock stars die in some exciting, provocative way? No story seemed too far-fetched for anyone to believe (including the scurrilous rumor that Pamela had murdered Jim, to which Siddons responded, "To me there was absolutely never one-thousandth of a percentage of a chance that that was the case; she loved the man"), no conspiracy theory too tangled to be assigned credibility. Yet no matter how ridiculous the speculation became, the only story people seemed quick to dismiss was the official version: that Jim, asthmatic since childhood, had suffered a respiratory infection that triggered his condition, leading to heart failure.

It is a fact that nearly a dozen Americans die exactly this way every day, and that the death of 260 to 350 Parisians each year is blamed on the city's extremely poor air quality, particularly during the summer months. Why, then, was it so hard for people to accept that an already ailing alcoholic asthmatic in Paris in the summer might possibly have died from just this combination of factors? Because Jim Morrison had led a noisy life, how could anyone believe his death would prove to be any less raucous?

A consultant for the American Lung Association, Lenore Coover, R.N., M.S.N., is a member of the Chicago Asthma Consortium and has been working exclusively with asthma patients for the past twenty years. Coover, for one, sees nothing unusual in the officially reported account of Morrison's death. "Many years ago," says Coover, "people were dying from asthma, but the cause of death was very often listed more in terms of, say, their heart stopped, a cardiac arrest," as was the case with Morrison. "In fact," Coover continues, "a lot of times these people did probably die from asthma, more than was recognized, but it was just not being reported in that way."

Jim's chronic alcoholism also made possible a number of mainly liver-related physiological conditions, such as esophageal varices, which could have accounted for some of the blood noticed by Pamela and, later, by the fire brigade rescue squad and the medical examiner. Given Jim's lifestyle, there is also a good possibility Jim may have had a stomach ulcer, which could provide another explanation for the blood in his vomit.

Jim's desire to sit in a hot bath also, according to Coover, falls into a recognized pattern. "Always people tend to go back to whatever was done for them as a child," Coover explains. As any mother knows who has ever been awakened in the middle of the night by the sound of her child's hacking cough due to croup, a common home remedy to ease congestion is to either turn on a hot shower and cradle a baby near the resulting steam or, for older children, to have them sit in a hot bath. For adults like Jim who consistently ignored prescribed medications to treat their ailment, when a serious attack suddenly occurs, they often draw on memories of childhood cures to pull them through. "Whatever treatment was done when they were younger is so soothing, they'll try that, especially when they're feeling really bad," says Coover.

But Jim Morrison was larger than life, and as a result it seems important to many that his demise be made to seem larger than death. To those who cared about Morrison the most, however, the persistent speculation on the cause of their friend's death is of little consequence. "Jim died of a heart attack in the bathtub," says Bill Siddons, who maintains he was given no reason to doubt the official findings of the medical examiner. "To me what caused the death was never as significant as the life that preceded it." Elektra Records executive Steve Harris echoed Bill's sentiments when he was quoted in the *Baltimore Morning Sun,* saying, "When you say the name Hemingway, people think of what he did, not of how he died. That's the way I would like it to be with Jim. He just died."

CHAPTER

16

Bill Siddons doesn't remember seeing Pamela again for months after they parted at the airport that night in 1971. "She came back and disappeared," he says. With the help of her friend, publicist Diane Gardiner, Pamela had done exactly that.

No one knows how to garner attention like a publicist; that is, after all, what they do. But because publicists are so finely attuned to the inner workings of the media, there is also no one who knows how to dodge the press quite so well. This time, though, it was to a member of the press Diane turned for assistance in keeping Pamela out of the public eye.

"I didn't believe Jim was dead," says journalist Ellen Sander. Though Jim and Ellen had, in time, become friends, as a writer for the *Saturday Review,* the *New York Times, Vogue,* and other publications, Sander had written about Jim and The Doors several times, usually not kindly. After their concert at the Singer Bowl in 1969, Sander wrote, "The Doors should rest in peace, not do an overlong encore. It hasn't lit anyone's fire in a good long time." She had also referred to Jim once in print as "Mickey Mouse de Sade." But despite Ellen's past criticisms of Jim's work, Diane felt confident that Sander had the integrity to keep Pamela's whereabouts a secret.

"Obviously Diane thought that I could be trusted," says Sander. "One of the things that they were trying to avoid was the press, and I was the press." But Sander, seven months pregnant and home working on a book, was on hiatus from her official press duties. So Ellen's house in Bolinas, just north of San Francisco, seemed a logical hiding place to Diane because, as Ellen puts it, "I think she figured it was someplace nobody would look for Pamela."

When Ellen heard Diane's voice on the phone that day in July 1971, she was positive that she had been right in her secret belief that Jim's death had been a giant hoax, and that soon she would be let in on the joke. "Diane called me, and she said, 'we're at the San Francisco airport, and we need to come over there,'" recalls Sander. "I could just hear in her voice it was really important. Then she said, 'I've got Pam with me.' And I said fine. I figured that they would have Jim in the trunk alive—this is what I really thought! I did not believe he'd died." But a short while later, it was only Diane and Pam who stood on the doorstep. "When I opened the door and I saw the two of them, their faces crumpled up from crying so much," Ellen says, "I knew instantly that he was dead. I just knew instantly."

The three women spent that week at Ellen's house, hiding from the world and comforting each other. Above all, Ellen and Diane encouraged Pamela to express her grief. "She was devastated," Ellen recalls, "and I was glad that she was there, because she could just fall apart and it wouldn't matter. Nobody was going to accuse her of anything or hound her about anything. We just grieved together."

Ellen's prior contact with Pamela had only been as an addendum to Jim. "Half the time when I saw Jim, Pamela was with him," says Sander. "Otherwise he was alone or he was with guys. I can't say I knew her well." Over time, Ellen's impression of Pamela, though based only on this slight social contact, grew into admiration. "First I thought she was kind of silly and dumb," Ellen explains, "but I learned that she was no dummy at all. She was like a Gracie Allen. She would just make these clever quips—I wish I could think of one! She had a very lyrical, high-pitched voice; she was pretty, she was sweet—I never heard her say an unkind word about anybody, which impressed me. Sweet-needy. That's my description of her. She was sweet and needy."

But even though they had never exchanged more than public pleasantries before, during that week in Bolinas, Pamela opened her heart to Ellen, who patiently listened and shared her sorrow. "She only confided in me because I was there, not because I was me," Sander hastens to clarify. "She was so devastated, and I think she trusted that I wouldn't tell anybody if she asked me not to—not because she was hiding any information, but because she needed permission to babble without having to be accountable for what she said. She was just overflowing with grief, sorrow, and regrets. So she talked, she babbled, we cried a lot, all of us. We took walks and were quiet. She was just in a state of abject grief. A lot of the conversation was about what was she going to do."

Unfortunately, Pamela had no idea exactly what to do. There was no going back but, without Jim, how could she possibly think about moving on? She was barely twenty-four years old and the only man she had ever loved had just made a shocking exit from her life. How was she supposed to handle that? What was she supposed to do? "Well," says Sander, "she was not thinking of doing anything. She was just talking like Jim was her life. She kept looking at my stomach and saying, 'I wish we'd had a baby. I wish I was pregnant too.' She was devastated about what had happened and what was going to happen to her." In short, says Sander, "She was just behaving as you would expect somebody to behave who had recently found their lover dead."

Pamela made no calls that week, though Diane made several, one to someone with whom both she and Pamela spoke; Ellen has no idea who this person was. "The only thing I overheard was Diane saying that she wasn't going to say where they were," says Sander, though she adds that she doubts the person was either from The Doors' camp or a member of Pamela's family. "Pam acted as if she had no family," Ellen says. "She said she had no idea where to go and what to do." Then Pamela looked at Ellen and said, "I have no one but you."

Ellen also hastens to refute Pamela's rumored heroin addiction while she was in Paris, and after. "When she stayed with me, I did not see her do anything like that. And if she was a heroin addict in Paris—it's awfully hard to hide it. It's not like you can put it down for a week. I saw no evidence of any kind of hard drug usage while she was at my house, and I was with her almost constantly." January Jensen, who lived in nearby Sausalito and was to become Pamela's confidant, echoes Ellen's observation. "During the time that she was here in Sausalito, she wasn't doing anything but smoking pot every now and then."

After leaving Ellen's house with her assurances that they could return if they needed to, Diane and Pamela had gone on to rest in the shadow of the ancient redwoods at nearby Muir Woods. Then, unable to face the prospect of going back to Los Angeles and the same people and circumstances she blamed for Jim's demise, Pamela settled instead in Sausalito, a peaceful artist colony on the northern shores of the San Francisco Bay, not far from January's house. "The Sausalito scene was like a parallel scene to L.A., but it was not the same people," explains Jensen. "So Pamela kind of migrated up there to still be in touch but to be totally removed from anybody she knew with the exception of two or three people."

Pamela lived in Sausalito for a year, alone save for Sage, the golden retriever she had shared with Jim. "Pamela was lost without Jim, totally lost." says Jensen. She would occasionally visit January, saying, "You don't mind if I just hang out, do you?" January didn't mind, and asked Pamela if she wanted to talk. "No," she replied, "I just need a different place to sit."

"She'd just sit," says January. "Just sit there with a forlorn look on her face."

At times, Pamela also seemed lost in desperate denial of her tragedy. Preparing to leave January's house one day, she said to him, "You know, I should probably get home because Jim's gonna call." January hugged her reassuringly and said, "Right, honey." Ellen Sander had observed similar behavior from Pamela earlier, and wisely attributed it to the savage grief by which she was gripped. "I think if you give Pam credit for that pain," says Sander, "then you can understand her behavior."

Is there a moon in your window
Is madness laughing
Can you still run down beach
rocks bed below w/out him?

More disturbing to friends was Pamela's seeming inability to summon the will to go on with her life without Jim. January met Pamela by chance in Sausalito one day, and she asked him if he'd have a drink with her. He suggested a couple of places they might go, but Pamela preferred privacy, so they bought a bottle of wine at the corner store and went back to January's house instead. As they sat and drank their wine, Pamela said, "You know, I just have no desire to live without Jim; I can't live without him." January said, "C'mon now!" and gave her a big hug. "I knew what she was feeling," he says.

But no one could really fathom the depths of Pamela's despair over the loss of Jim. Many of his friends felt remorseful that they had not somehow convinced Jim to take better care of himself. "Everybody's response was *I wish I'd done something*," says Ellen Sander. "I wish I'd taken that guy and throttled him around the neck and made him understand that he was mortal. But Jim thought he was impervious to death or that he had conquered it, that death wouldn't matter to him."

But Pamela's remorse over the matter was paralyzing. Though she had summoned medical assistance for Jim more than once while they were overseas, now Pamela had to live the rest of her life regretting that she'd finally let him have his way when he refused medical treatment that last night of his life. *Maybe if I hadn't listened to him,* she thought, even though Jim had never heeded the advice of any of the previous doctors who had been called. *Maybe if I hadn't fallen asleep,* as though the mere force of her watchfulness could have held death at bay. As a twenty-four-year-old in Paris, she had held the world in her hands, facing an ever brightening future with the man she loved. Now, at twenty-five, she was back in

Last Will and Testament

of

JAMES D. MORRISON

573952

I, JAMES D. MORRISON, being of sound and disposing mind, memory and understanding, and after consideration for all persons, the objects of my bounty, and with full knowledge of the nature and extent of my assets, do hereby make, publish and declare this my Last Will and Testament, as follows:

FIRST: I declare that I am a resident of Los Angeles County, California; that I am unmarried and have no children.

SECOND: I direct the payment of all debts and expenses of last illness.

THIRD: I do hereby devise and bequeath each and every thing of value of which I may die possessed, including real property, personal property and mixed properties to PAMELA S. COURSON of Los Angeles County.   BK1979 PG0430

In the event the said PAMELA S. COURSON should predecease me, or fail to survive for a period of three months following the date of my death, then and in such event, the devise and bequest to her shall fail and the same is devised and bequeathed instead to my brother, ANDREW MORRISON of Monterey, California, and to my sister, ANNE R. MORRISON of Coronado Beach, California, to share and share alike; provided, however, further that in the event either of them should predecease me, then and in such event, the devise and bequest shall go to the other.

FOURTH: I do hereby appoint PAMELA S. COURSON and MAX FINK, jointly, Executors, or Executor and Executrix, as the case may be, of my estate, giving to said persons, and each of them, full power of appointment of substitution in their place and stead by their Last Will and Testament, or otherwise.

In the event said PAMELA S. COURSON shall survive me and be living at the time of her appointment, then in such event, bond is hereby waived.

I subscribe my name to this Will this _12_ day of February, 1969, at Beverly Hills, California.

ADMITTED TO PROBATE

AUG 17 1971

JAMES D. MORRISON

Jim's Last Will and Testament.

California, alone, left with nothing but a dry handful of torturous memories and half-lived dreams. And regrets. So, so many regrets.

Pamela's reaction to the news that her sister had dyed her light brown hair the same shade of red as Pamela's seemed to reflect her growing despondency. "She's trying to be me, isn't she?" Pamela complained to a friend. "Why would anyone want to be me?"

With Bill Siddons help, Pamela had designed a headstone for Jim's grave. Bill diagrammed the design and sent it, along with enough money to cover the expense, to Agnes Varda for implementation. In his letter, Siddons wrote:

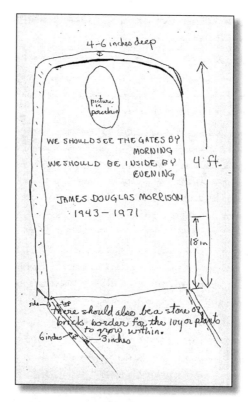

The original plan for Jim's gravesite, drawn by Bill Siddons, designed by Bill and Pam.

Dear Agnes:

Pam asked that I write to you and ask you to take care of getting the stone made up and placed on Jim's grave. It is the last order of business and you're the one Pamela trusts to do it 'cause she loves you and you've been so good. I have enclosed a diagram taken from the one Pam left me with explanation and if you have any trouble, call me collect. I'm not much of an artist but I hope this makes it fairly clear. Pam wanted all lettering in capitals and the same size letters thru-out. The stone should be approximately 4 feet high by 6 inches deep, arched at the top with the enclosed picture put to porcelain at the top of the stone. Below the picture goes the quote, name, and dates as drawn. We should leave 18 inches at the bottom clear so the plants will not obscure the name . . .

"I have no idea why it was never done," says Siddons.

During his life, Pamela had fought to protect Jim from those she felt were taking unfair advantage of his talents. Since his death, as his sole heir, she had spent much of her time fighting to keep lawyers and members of The Doors from cashing in on what she felt were unfair claims against Jim's estate. Cut off from the cash-on-demand existence she had enjoyed with Jim, Pamela had been getting by financially with her parents' assistance during the two and a half years it took for the myriad lawsuits connected with the estate to be settled. By this time, Pamela had returned from her self-imposed exile in Sausalito and had been living in Los Angeles for over a year.

While the pending litigation had posed many problems, including financial and emotional hardship, there was also a singular benefit to the protracted legal wrangling: it gave Pamela a reason to live. Growing up, Pamela had fought—if in a passive way—against her parents, peers, and school authorities. While she was with Jim, she had fought with him and for him, struggling to provide a barrier between Jim and those she feared could take him from her, take him from his ideal vision of himself. After Jim's death, the struggle continued, this time over dollars and cents. There was no spirited courtroom drama involved in these fights, but rather a relentlessly grinding machine fueled by demands and accusations and innuendo; ream after ream of court papers, endless filings, repeated depositions. It had taken a couple of years, but the day finally came when the machine seemed to grind to a halt. Settlements were made, agreements were reached. Everything that had been Jim's was now Pamela's. There was nothing left to fight about, nothing left to fight for. Her entire life, it had been Pamela versus somebody or something. Suddenly, it was Pamela versus . . . Pamela.

CHAPTER

17

Randy Ralston was a handsome twenty-three-year-old film student attending UCLA. Originally from Iowa, he was an attractive combination of movie-star good looks and midwestern manners. On this particular day in 1973, he and his friend George had stopped by the Cafe Figaro in Beverly Hills with hopes of indulging in their favorite pastime: meeting girls.

"We had just arrived and ordered a beer at the bar," Ralston recalls. "And as soon as we sat down at our table, I noticed a girl sitting alone, giving me some eye dalliance. So I immediately got up and went over and introduced myself and said, 'Would you like to join us?'" All eyes seemed to be fixed on them as the slender, attractive young woman, her vivid red hair cut just above her shoulders, picked up her hot fudge sundae and followed Randy back to his table. "I'm Pamela Morrison," she said, introducing herself to George and Randy.

"So she sat down and we started talking," says Ralston. "I told her I was studying filmmaking at UCLA and she said, 'Oh, my husband did that!'" Randy and George exchanged disappointed looks at the mention of a husband, but then Pamela added, "My husband died; he was a poet."

"She got a little melancholy about saying he was a poet," says Randy, "so we didn't make anything of it. She said, 'I have some films that we shot in Europe that I want to see, but I don't have a projector.'" Randy owned a projector, which seemed to make George the odd man out in this trio. So Randy and Pam dropped George off at his house, then went to Randy's place and watched some of his films from UCLA before proceeding, projector in hand, to Pamela's place in the canyons of Beverly Hills. "She had a lovely house, a big Spanish-style place," says Ralston, "and I thought, Not only is she beautiful, but a rich girl to boot."

Randy set up the projector on the stairs, using the white stucco wall as a screen. The Super 8 films were short, about three minutes each, and largely out of focus. "She was really mesmerized by them," Randy says, and she insisted that he run them again and again. Pamela was the star of the films. Her husband, she explained, acted as cameraman. One showed her at a Corsican cemetery, cavorting among the graves after an obviously cross exchange with the unseen cameraman. "He told me, 'This is a *motion* picture, you have to *move*!'" she explained. She hadn't felt like moving at the time, but when he turned the camera away from her, she had obliged in order to regain his attention.

Another film showed a crowded flea market in France. Pamela, wearing a dramatic hooded cape, smiled amidst hanging dolls and musical instruments and all manner of wares being peddled from tents and tables. At one point, she took control of the camera, and Randy got his first glimpse of the man who, up to this point, had been filming Pamela. His wide, round face was clean shaven, and his thick brown hair, streaked with gray, was neatly combed and hanging down to his shoulders. A blue sweater tied loosely around a colorful button-down collar shirt made him look rather collegiate, and he seemed to shy away from the camera trained on him. "That's my old man," Pamela said.

"His face was like a pumpkin, it was so bloated," Randy says. "And I think it maybe disappointed her that I didn't recognize who he was."

If Pamela was disappointed that Jim went unrecognized, she never clarified his identity for Randy. Instead she just had him reload the projector and play the films again. And again. And again. "It was very, very late by the time we were through watching the films, in the middle of the night," recalls Ralston. "I finally told her that I had to let the projector cool down, because the bulb was very expensive." Randy wondered then if Pamela would ask him to leave, but instead she said, "Let's go to bed now."

The next morning seemed idyllic to Randy. "We woke up in the morning and she fixed breakfast," he says. "She fixed bacon and eggs and squeezed orange juice, and we sat and fed the birds outside the window." But the idyll was short lived. After breakfast, Pamela said, "Could you do me a favor?"

"I was completely smitten with her, there's no doubt about it," says Randy, who told Pamela, "I'll do anything in the world, I'll move mountains, what do you want?" To which she replied, "I'm being evicted from here, and I have to move out—today."

So, despite the fact that it was Saturday and they had prior plans to "go to the beach and look at bikinis," Randy and George instead found themselves renting a truck and loading it with all of Pamela's possessions. "It was all of Jim's possessions, all his books," says Randy, though he didn't realize it at the time. "I didn't know that she was Morrison's widow, and we didn't pay much attention to what she had; we just wanted get the job done."

When Pamela started barking orders at them as though they were hired hands, Randy was quick to set her straight. "Pamela, look, we're doing you a favor here and you'd better act accordingly," he told her, "because we'll drop your shit right here and leave if you don't stop acting like you're the queen bee and we're the worker bees." She was immediately contrite and, says Ralston, "started acting helpful and sweet and did not give us any more of the bossiness for the rest of the day."

Though Pamela knew that she had to be out of the house that day ("She made it sound like her landlord was being really mean to her," says Ralston, "but I don't think she'd paid the rent in two or three months"), she didn't seem to have any clear idea of where it was she wanted to go from there. So, twenty-four hours after first meeting him, Pamela moved in with Randy.

"We had a great time," says Randy of their first few days together. "We cooked, we sat in the backyard. We would eat gourmet food, we would go to the movies, we would walk Sage in the park. I like to do yoga, and she would encourage me to keep up my routine of morning and evening meditation, and going to play tennis and stuff like that. It was pretty idyllic." And then one day a Doors song came on the radio, and once again the idyll ended.

While the song was playing, Pamela asked Randy, "What do you think of The Doors?" Randy said, "I love The Doors! I thought Jim Morrison was the greatest!" Randy's words seemed to send Pamela into a deep depression, which Randy couldn't understand. "When I told her that I had really idolized Jim so much," says Ralston, "she got into a blue funk, and I didn't know why. And she stayed in a blue funk to the point where she became very moody and morose and didn't want to leave the house. And I thought, What is the deal here? What's wrong with her?"

Pamela's mood would brighten temporarily, but then she would sink into depression once again; Randy had no idea the cause of these mood swings. "She would get happy and we would go out to eat, go to a movie, and then she would get morose again," he says. "She wouldn't even want to leave the house then, she would just sit brooding over—I didn't know what." One day she took Randy out to the rental truck, where most of her possessions were still stored, and she showed him a list of bank accounts."I think at the time the FDIC max was $20,000," says Ralston, "and she

**Pamela with Randy Ralston at Diane
Gardiner's house, 1973.**

showed me a list of what looked like accounts in banks all over town, each
with $20,000 in them. And at the top of the list I saw, "The Probate of
James Douglas Morrison."

But Morrison is a common name, and Jim had been out of the
spotlight for a very long time; Randy still didn't make the connection
between this moody girl living in his house and the singer who had died
over two years ago. At twenty-three, Randy's main concerns were sex and
fun, and obviously this woman couldn't be relied upon for either. "I was
getting kind of tired of her," says Ralston. "If she was going to be this
moody, and if she was not going to make love with me every time I wanted
her to, of course I was getting a little bent out of shape. It would bring me
down, the fact that she was so morose all the time." When Pamela's mood
didn't improve, says Ralston, "I just said, 'Get the fuck out! Get your shit
and split. I don't need you bringing me down.' Because she did. So she
left."

A few days later Pamela called to let Randy know that she had found a new place, an apartment on Sycamore, and she was sorry to have caused him any trouble during her stay. To make up for it, she said, she wanted him to be her guest at a concert at the Palladium, and asked him to pick up her friend, Diane Gardiner, on the way, as Diane would be attending to the concert with them. "Pamela wanted me to know who she was," Randy explains, "so she had me pick up Diane, and Diane told me who Pamela was before we went to the concert."

Indeed, it was a much different Pamela Randy observed at the concert that night than the lonely little girl he'd picked up at Cafe Figaro just a short time before. "She was all dressed up and looked unbelievably gorgeous," says Ralston. "It was bizarre. Diane would be whispering in my ear as people came up to pay homage to Pamela, the rock and roll princess." The biggest names in the record industry stopped to speak to Pamela, who, says Ralston, would occasionally throw him triumphant little glances. "She really wanted me to know who I'd thrown out of my house," he says.

Randy saw both Diane and Pamela on and off in the following months. "She would call me to come over and show the films," Randy recalls. "My films from UCLA and her films. And she would have parties, little soirées, where there would be old friends of hers, I guess, guys and girls who were like, you know . . . just our group. We'd smoke pot, we'd drink fine wine, we'd watch movies, we'd listen to music, stuff like that."

One night Randy and Pamela went out together, prowling the nightspots of Los Angeles. "We went to Tiny Naylors and ate cheeseburgers, fries, malts," he recalls. "She stole the salt and pepper shakers, and I said, 'What are you doing that for?' She just laughed." It was one of the few nights Randy remembers that he was able to broach the subject of Jim without Pamela turning instantly melancholy. "That night I asked her a lot about Jim," Randy says. Pamela laughed and said, "Oh! Jim was a wild man! I couldn't do anything to control him! He was always out of control!" She told Randy that Jim would never change his pants, so she'd have to steal them while he slept to get them cleaned. Randy asked her, "Did he do a lot of drugs?" And Pamela said, "No, but do you know what he really liked? Alcohol. Alcohol was his favorite."

"I asked her question after question because I wanted to know all about him," says Ralston. "And she said one time—I believe it was one of the first parties for The Doors, right after they first became a success—Jim was drunk and climbed up on the table and urinated in the punch bowl right in front of the *Life* magazine photographers."

"It embarrassed me to tears!" Pamela said of the incident, but Randy didn't think she'd been as horrified as she pretended. "So many guys would bow and scrape at her feet," he said. "I think that quickly bored her. But she said she and Jim *fought!* And she would throw his fucking clothes out the window, and throw his books out the window. It was one fight after another. And just the way she talked about it," says Ralston, "I could tell she loved the fact she couldn't control him."

At one point, Randy and Pamela took a trip to Las Vegas with another couple and even talked briefly about getting married, though it never amounted to more than talk. "We always were really very enamored of each other," Randy says. "But I don't think anybody could fill the boots of Jim Morrison. I don't think there was any guy who could do that in her life for her."

CHAPTER

18

I t was December 1973. The phone conversation began in a light-hearted manner, Pamela's voice giggly and full of life, hammer-ing out the details of a camping trip she and Randy were planning to take. The scenario was a familiar one: Pamela stating what she wanted, Randy vetoing her ideas, then, without Randy ever realizing what had happened, Pamela not only getting what she originally wanted but even more, all the while making it seem like Randy's decision.

"What do you think we should get to camp?" Pamela asked Randy. "Do you think we should get a tent, and a cot and a heater . . . ?"

"Well, we should definitely have a tent," Randy said. "The cot, no; heater, no."

"Why not a heater? We might freeze to death out there!" Pamela's giggles made freezing to death sound like the most fun idea ever.

"I've stayed in five-degree weather up in Yosemite with just a tent," Randy reasoned. "A tent is enough to keep the wind out, and you're dressed warm and you have a warm sleeping bag, that's all it takes."

"Well, what about a cot to keep you off the ground?" Pamela responded, still laughing.

"Well, you might as well stay home if you're going to do all that shit!"

"Well if you had a cot it would be very easy to make camp because you wouldn't have to lay on the ground." Pamela couldn't stop giggling at her own convoluted reasoning. "Then if you're laying on the ground, and what if ants and bugs and stuff start crawling . . . don't they crawl all over you and everything when you lay down?"

"It's too cold for ants and bugs to live," Randy laughed, but his resolve seemed to be wavering, so he changed the subject instead of continuing the debate. "I think we oughta have a fuckin' armored truck, I'm afraid of some ax murderer or something."

Pamela's reply, delivered in that tiny, disarmingly childish voice, had the same impact it would coming from an adorable five-year-old: "Well, we can take my pistol."

It wasn't long before Randy had conceded to Pamela's wishes for a tent, a cot, a heater, as well as Sage, who would be brought along as an "early alarm" to guard against Randy's dreaded ax murderers. "It would be nice if we could do something like backpack in and set up the tent and cots and the heater, and then kind of leave Sage in charge, you know?" Pamela told Randy.

"I don't know how you're going to leave him in charge, but . . ." said Randy, skeptical.

"Well, if we went way out in the desert where no one was, wouldn't . . . no one would know we were there," Pamela reasoned.

"I guess that's right, yeah."

"So we'd just leave Sage and tell him to stay."

This notion made them both laugh, because, as Randy was quick to remind Pamela, they had once done something similar at a restaurant, commanding Sage to "stay" while they went in. Apparently having the same regard for authority as his owners, the golden retriever had immediately set off on his own adventures and it had taken Randy and Pamela a while to find him.

"Well, he really needs to be out in the country," Pamela continued, "so why don't we get an old army tent, and I'm going to get a cot—No! An air mattress!"

Randy never had a chance.

But the lighthearted mood of the conversation changed rapidly when Pamela began talking about her family. She had recently made a trip to Utah with her sister, after which Judy had said some things about Pamela to their parents that Pamela found extremely hurtful. "She knew that if she mentioned any of that, I wouldn't go home for Christmas," Pamela told Randy, obviously still hurt and angry.

"So you're not going home for the holiday?" he asked.

"No. What am I gonna do?" she asked sadly. "Let's spend it together."

"Well, I'm going to be up here, so . . ."

Pamela started crying softly and said, "I'm writing a letter to my father." She then read Randy the letter she had drafted explaining to Corky why she didn't feel she could come home for the holidays. "Dear Dad," she began. "Thank you more than words can say for everything." As

Pamela read the letter she had written, it went on to tell her father that her trip to Utah had been "such a sad experience" and that she had decided it would be best for her "not to be close to those who hurt," referring, apparently, to her sister. Randy doesn't remember now exactly what it was that Judy had said or done to cause Pamela such anguish, but it had obviously been something Pamela found unforgivable. "Even now I feel quite wounded by the memory," she wrote, "I cannot resolve this hurt."

After reading the last few lines of the letter to Randy, Pamela said, "And that's all. I'm not going home."

Randy felt that Pamela was making a mistake, and urged her to reconsider her decision to spend the holidays away from her family. "Well my sister's going home, Randy, and saying all these shitty, trashy things about me," Pamela said, weeping softly. "How can my own . . . you know, I don't want to go—no."

Randy knew Pamela was only trying to strike back at her sister, so he urged her again, "Think about it. I think it'll hurt your dad more."

"Probably," she said sadly, "but I can't stand being near my sister."

Though Judy had betrayed Pamela in some way to both parents, it was only her father to whom Pamela addressed the anguished letter expressing her gratitude for his help, and her despair over her sister's transgression. "It was a turbulent thing with her mother," Ralston recalls. "Sometimes she would have normal conversations with her mother just like any daughter would have, and everything would seem to be hunky-dory, and then they would have spats."

But sometimes the situation would go beyond customary mother/daughter quarreling. Randy once overheard a phone conversation in which Pamela seemed to be taking great delight in regaling her mother with the sordid details of something rather unsavory she had recently done. Randy was shocked. "I said to Pamela more than once, 'Do you like to hurt your mother or what? Why would you tell your mother things that would definitely upset her and do emotional injury to her?'" But Pamela would never provide Randy with an explanation for her behavior. "I think that she somehow took delight in inflicting emotional pain on her mom," Randy says, "but I don't know why."

Pamela turned twenty-seven that month, and the following month, January 1974, all the obstacles keeping her from Jim's estate were finally cleared. She bought a new car, a yellow VW, and started making plans for the future. Things seemed to be looking up. Then in April, attorneys for The Doors filed another lawsuit against Jim's estate, claiming that Pamela was not allowing them to deduct from her share of the band's royalties $250,000 that had been advanced to Jim before his death. Though Doors

The apartment at 108 N. Sycamore St.

accountant Bob Greene told the press, "It's not a real lawsuit," it felt real to Pamela. "Jim's been dead for three years and they still haven't squeezed enough out of him," Pamela complained to a friend. The legal machine seemed to be revving up again.

Babe Hill had recently returned to Los Angeles from New Mexico, where he had been working on a construction job. Since he'd been back in town, he had been staying temporarily with Tom Baker. Neither Babe nor Tom had heard from Pamela in over a year, so they were both surprised and delighted when she called them one evening in late April.

"She was cheerful and optimistic," says Babe, "and talked of getting some land somewhere in the country, maybe Colorado." Babe had been one of Jim's most trusted friends, and had in the past stayed at Jim and Pamela's place and looked after things while the couple was traveling. "She said that maybe we could get together again and I could caretake the place." Pamela spoke with both Tom and Babe, and "the conversation ended with a breakfast date among the three of us," Babe recalls.

The next morning, Tom called Pam's apartment to find out where she wanted to meet them for breakfast. But the phone was answered instead by a distraught Penny Courson, who informed Tom that her daughter was dead.

The report of the Los Angeles Police Department noted that a five foot, five inch, red-haired, green-eyed Caucasian female weighing 115 pounds and wearing a red print blouse and pants died of an apparent accidental drug overdose sometime between 10:00 P.M. and midnight on Thursday, April 25. John Mandell (referred to by police as Witness 1, or W-1), though not romantically involved with Pamela, had been living with her for a few months, and his friend, Clifton Dunn (referred to by police as Witness 2, or W-2), had been staying with them for a short time. The Investigating Officer (I/O), based on his conversation with John and Cliff, gave the following report:

I/O arrived at 108 N. Sycamore St. #1 and was met by unit 7A1 ofcrs. Brophy #16772 & McLoud, who had rec'd an Amb-OD call at this location.

I/O interviewed W-1, Mandell (boyfriend) who states that when he arrived home from work on 4–25–74 at approx. 1730 hrs, he obs'd decedent and her girlfriend, Dianne Gardner [sic] in a drunken condition. Decedent kept asking W-1 to buy some heroin for her but he refused.

Dianne Gardner left the apt. at approx. 1830 hrs. and W-1 and W-2 went out at approx. 1930. They returned at 2130 and W-1 started cooking some food. Decedent was lying on a studio couch in the living room. She was in a prone position and W-1 thought that she was sleeping off her drunk. At approx. 2345 hrs. W-1 tried to awaken decedent so she could eat and at that time obs'd there were no vital signs. W-1 called the police and RA 61 responded and pronounced death at 2400 hrs.

Wit-2 had been living at the residence for approx. 2 weeks and Wit-1 had been living with decedent since Jan. of this year. W-1 stated that the decedent had been under a Dr's care for a bladder infection and possibly an asthma condition and that decedent had been using heroin for approx. one year.

I/O's investigation revealed decedent in a supine position on the studio couch with no apparent indication of trauma. An apparent fresh needle mark was obs'd in decedent's inner lt/elbow. A hype syringe was found on the table in the living room but no other narcotic paraphnelia was obs'd.

W-1 stated that decedent was married to Jim Morrison (also died approx. 2 years ago) who was a rock singer for the "Doors" and that she was very despondent over litigation regarding settlement of the estate. Decedent had threatened suicide in the past but had not made any attempts to Wit-1's knowledge.

Two of decedent's handguns were located in the bedroom closet and booked evidence at Wilshire Prop. under above DR.

CME Coroner G. Greene removed decedent to County Morgue.

The guns referred to in the report were a .22 caliber Ruger and a .380 caliber Mauser, both licensed in Pamela's name. Because the cause of Pamela's death was still under investigation, and because the police suspected that John Mandell was a narcotics user, the guns were taken from the scene as a precaution.

The police report was filed shortly before 1:00 A.M. on April 26. At 3:25 A.M., the LAPD placed a call to the police department in Orange, requesting they send someone to the Courson house to inform them of their daughter's death. There were only seven or eight people on duty at the Orange Police Department at that time of the morning, and they were having a shift party for which they had distributed T-shirts bearing the slogan "Let's do somebody good!" The words were deceptive, as they had nothing to do with spreading sunshine but referred instead to catching the bad guys and, in the police vernacular, "doing" them. The officer assigned to Beat 17 was pulled away from the festivities and, five minutes later, informed Corky and Penny that their younger daughter had been found dead.

Later that day, Corky answered questions for the death certificate, indicating that his daughter was to be cremated and her ashes buried at Père-Lachaise in Paris, with Jim. It's unclear why Pamela's ashes were, instead, interred at Fairhaven Memorial Park in Santa Ana, California, eight months later. There was speculation that Jim's parents refused to have Pamela's remains buried with Jim, somehow blaming Pamela for Jim's chosen lifestyle. But the Morrisons knew that their son had been behaving in a similarly unorthodox and self-destructive manner long before he met Pamela, and, if anything, credited Pamela for Jim's overture toward reconciliation with his parents, as well as his decision to leave the band. Speaking on behalf of Admiral and Mrs. Morrison, attorney Brian Manion said, "The Morrisons tell me that they've never had any discussions whatsoever with the Coursons regarding Pamela's ashes. But they also said to me that they would be perfectly willing to have her ashes joined, as it were, with Jim. They have no animus about this at all."

The Coursons arranged a memorial service the following week honoring both Jim and Pamela. The Morrisons did not attend, nor did Robby Krieger and John Densmore ("We were invited not to come," says

Pamela Susan Morrison, 1946–1974.

Robby with a wry grin, though he doesn't say why). Ray Manzarek was there, however; he played the organ.

But the memorial service did not lay to rest questions about the circumstances surrounding Pamela's death. One Los Angeles police officer, who asked to remain anonymous, noted recently that at the time Pamela died the police were not likely to spend much time investigating. "At that time, in that place," he said, "if it looked to us like someone had died of a drug overdose, frankly we thought they deserved it and we didn't waste our time on it." The Coursons were furious over the apparent lack of interest demonstrated by the police, and hired a private detective to look into the matter.

When Randy Ralston heard of Pamela's death, he immediately called Diane Gardiner to see if she could give him any further information. "Diane very calmly said, 'Oh, yes, I had dinner with her that night.'" She indicated to Randy that she and Pamela, as well as a few friends, went out to a nice restaurant for dinner, at the end of which Pamela had stood up and said, "It's time for me to go be with Jim now."

"It was like Pamela's bon voyage party," says Ralston. "That's what Diane made it sound like."

"Pamela really knew she wanted to die at the age of twenty-seven the way Jim died," Diane told Randy, "so we all knew that this was what she wanted to do. We knew she was going to go home and overdose and commit suicide, and that's just the way it was." Randy had been distraught, but, he said, "Diane was so calm about it that she calmed me down."

Diane's initial explanation to Randy didn't fit very well with the story John Mandell had told the police, though Mandell himself later gave a somewhat rearranged version of his original statement to the medical examiner. Gardiner, too, later recanted her story, telling Randy rather inexplicably, "Oh, darling, I just had to tell you that."

The Coursons wanted the matter investigated as a murder, feeling their suspicions were shored up by a break-in that occurred during the memorial service, in which some items of Jim's were stolen from Pamela's apartment. The autopsy report also revealed an agonizing irony: a young woman completely healthy in every way save for the single needle mark in her arm and the lethal dose of heroin that had caused her heart to stop. Dr. Michael W. Kaufman, a pathologist analyzing the report, later wrote, in part:

> The decedent's weight, state of nutrition, and state of hydration would indicate that she was living a normal existence. Of significance was that examination of the endometrium was in the secretary phase and that the ovaries demonstrated evidence of recent ovulation. This evidence of ongoing reproductive functioning is frequently absent in drug abusers and in individuals with malnutrition or other chronic illnesses. The liver, likewise, did not show changes suggestive of alcohol abuse on either a chronic or acute basis. The lungs did not demonstrate changes which would be expected in chronic intravenous drug abusers. The examination of the skin only disclosed the one fresh injection site, and there was no evidence of acute or external trauma.

Mandell's statement to the police that Pamela had been using heroin for "approximately one year" seems to corroborate January Jensen's and Ellen Sander's observations that Pamela was not using heroin during the year she lived in Sausalito, and is also confirmed by Dr. Kaufman's report which, simply stated, indicates that if Pamela had been using drugs, either it wasn't a chronic condition, or she had just begun her use again after a long recess. "Yes, I can substantiate that," Dr. Ackerman says in response to this assessment of Kaufman's report. "She did use, but it was not a heavy habit, kind of light use. She didn't start [using heroin] until after

"I came back for you Jimmy,
Love Pam."

Jim died. I can't tell you how soon after, but it wasn't very heavy use, just enough to be worrisome."

It was also within that one-year window of time that Pamela had befriended Randy Ralston. Randy had observed Pamela's heroin use, particularly in the last few months before her death, and her association with those selling the drug—an increasing recklessness which could explain the presence of John Mandell, a reputed drug pusher, in Pamela's home, as well as support Diane Gardiner's original story that Pamela simply wanted to be with Jim, by whatever means possible. Dr. Ackerman concurs: "I think if anything, it was suicidal behavior on her part to join Jim, to be with him in death."

The Coursons either dismissed or could not accept the theory that their daughter had taken her own life, and they continued trying to make a case for murder, naming at least one person they felt strongly could have been the culprit, a theory that went nowhere. Jim's erstwhile brother-in-law, Allan Graham, a few years ago claimed that the Coursons had tried to have him indicted for Pamela's murder at one point because, Graham says, the week before Pamela died he had threatened her life. As it is unclear why Graham, who seemed to have been the object of nothing but Jim's contempt during his life, would have had any contact at all with Pamela three years after Jim's death, his claims regarding the Coursons' accusations appear to be baseless.

But in spite their gnawing doubts about the cause of their daughter's death, the Coursons' investigation weakened and was eventually dropped. No matter what foundation their suspicions might have had, no one was willing to give much weight to what appeared to be nothing more than the concerns of two seemingly overwrought parents who apparently could not accept the death of their child.

Cheri Siddons and Penny Courson had forged a bond that night in 1971 while they sat at the Los Angeles airport waiting for Bill and Pamela to return from Paris. After Pamela's death, Penny began calling Cheri on the phone periodically. "She would be crying and moaning and talking about her daughter," says Cheri, "and I would listen to her. It went on for a couple of years. I felt so sorry for her!" Though she had a good deal of sympathy for Penny and her situation, it was difficult for Cheri, the mother of two, to listen to Penny's raw anguish over the loss of Pamela. "The death of this child did this woman in," Cheri says, "and I don't know that she ever recovered from it." During one of these conversations, Corky took the phone from his wife. "You know," he said to Cheri, his voice tired and sad, "it's just not normal for a child to precede their parents into death."

Whatever its cause, those who had known Jim and Pamela expressed sadness at her passing. But most also felt about the tragedy a certain inevitability—a circuit closed, a half once again made whole. After all, hadn't they heard this story before?

"It's a tragedy that Pam died," Ray Manzarek says, voicing the opinion held by most who knew the couple. "But Pamela and Jim are going to go down in the history books as great lovers, and people are going to be writing plays about them. It's *Romeo and Juliet*, it's *Heloise and Abelard*. It's Jim and Pam."

The film, slightly shaky and out of focus, begins with a close-up of red flowers in a clear vase sitting next to two black-and-white photos in frames placed on a gravestone. The camera then pans to a crucifix, and zooms in on a bust of Christ. *The scene cuts to Pamela, slowly walking between an aisle of gravestones. Her head is bowed, and her long red hair shields her face from view for a moment, before she slowly looks up to stare pensively into the camera. A moment later, an extreme close-up of her face, again slightly out of focus, shows Pamela pouting in the direction of Jim, who is operating the camera. It is easy to make out the words she speaks as she tells him, "I don't want to move." So the camera pans away from the uncooperative subject, who changes her mind suddenly and runs back into the camera's range, reclaiming the scene by dancing wildly among the gravestones, her hair flashing about her like a flaming banner.*

All at once, Pamela disappears behind a mausoleum, but Jim anticipates her moves, and the camera catches her reappearance, running from behind the marble monument and continuing her wild dance. Abruptly the film goes into slow motion, and Pamela seems to be swimming through a thick liquid as she comes around the front gate of the churchyard. Then, just as suddenly, she is in full motion again, laughing at Jim as she whirls about. He follows her every move; she anticipates his every need. At this moment they are a team, in perfect synchronization, vibrant young lovers playing among the gravestones.

And then the film goes to black.

In conclusion, darling, let
me repeat: your home is still
here, inviolate & certain
and I open the wide smile of
my remembrance. This to you
on the anniversary of our first
night. I know you love me
to talk this way. I hope
no one sees this message
written in the calm lonely
far out languid summer afternoon
W/ my total love

Smart, *funny, charming, mysterious, private, beautiful, trouble-some, irresistible* . . . If I took all the adjectives their friends used to describe Jim and Pamela, mixed them together in a hat, and then pulled them out one by one, I'd be hard pressed to determine which word had been used to describe which person. In fact, Jim and Pamela seemed so perfectly patterned after each other that what differences they did have somehow only served to highlight their similarities. "They were the same person as a man and a woman," Ray Manzarek said of the couple, and the truth of his observation was reinforced for me over and over again the more people I talked to and the more stories I was told.

Their friends told me a lot of stories about Jim and Pamela—as individuals and as a couple—so many stories that I wasn't able to include all of them in this book. There were small anecdotes I found amusing, like this one from January Jensen:

"Yeah, one time we were over at Pam's apartment on La Cienaga, and it was early in the morning—I don't remember how early or what we were doing up that early—but she decided that we had to go shopping. Both Jim and I had on black—you know I used to make his clothes—we both had on black goatskin pants. So she took us to this boutique and got us these, what she called white angel shirts. And the two of us—Jim looked at me and I looked at him, and he said, 'It's gonna take more than shirts to make angels of us!' Which was true!"

And there were recollections that evoked more disturbing visions of the effects of Jim's chronic alcoholism, like this one from Julia Densmore Negron:

"Well, the first time I met him I didn't really meet him. He was lying on the floor under a bench in an airport. He'd passed out. He was drunk, and I don't know if he'd fallen or they'd put him there or what, but he was under a bench along a wall in some airport in the midwest. And Billy Siddons or someone had rolled two of those big cigarette urns up in front of him so he couldn't get out if he woke up. And I remember John going, 'There he is! There's our big lead singer!' And I just thought, oh, god!"

I think both of these stories help to illustrate the paradox that has so frustrated many of Jim's friends over the years. As Paul Ferrara stated: "When he wasn't drunk, he was the gentleman, he was the angel dude. But

he had his threshold, and once he passed it, he was obnoxious." Unfortunately, it has been the obnoxious Jim who has drawn most of the attention in the media since The Doors first took the stage, and it's the obnoxious Jim who seems to exert his will among fans today, thanks in large
part to biographers and moviemakers who see Jim's drunken antics as
somehow more entertaining or commercially viable than the gentler side
of his character better known to his friends. When Cheri Siddons first saw
the script of Oliver Stone's 1991 movie The Doors, she expressed just such
a concern to Stone, telling him that the Jim she knew—and she had known
Jim quite well—was not the incessantly dark and dangerous character
Stone had drawn, but a loving, compassionate, funny man who, only when
he had been drinking, could sometimes become this dark shadow of his
true self. Stone's response to Cheri's concerns was typical: "*That* Jim
would make a boring movie," he told her, "and I don't want to make a
boring movie."

Stone seemed to feel even less obligation to portray Pamela as anything more than a caricature of a mythical rock star's girlfriend. "The
Doors would have liked to see more of the foursome in the movie and for
me to have dropped Pamela completely," Stone told the *Orange County
Register* in 1991. "They didn't care much for Pamela. In fact, most of the
people I talked to felt that she was pretty much of a nightmare." Stone
didn't really need much persuasion to avoid the bother of researching the
real woman and her real relationship with "*that* Jim." Instead, he simply
tried to make Meg Ryan look as much like Pamela as possible physically
(though one *Doors* insider observed "It's probably the only movie in
history where the lead actors don't even come close to being as beautiful
as the people they're portraying."), while the character's words and actions
seemed to bear little or no resemblance to anything Pamela might have
said or done in real life. "That was just some other person, that's all," says
Julia Negron of the character Meg Ryan plays in *The Doors*. "I just
remember the one scene where she walks on the plane in the movie and
says, 'Hi, Pamela Morrison, ornament' or something. And I thought, 'Who
is that supposed to be? Anybody I know? I don't think so!' There's no way
in the world she would have ever said anything like that! And not with a
smile on her face, with that attitude. No way."

But then who wants to be bored by the truth, right?

The most unfortunate thing about this type of license being taken
in the media with the lives of real people—even in a movie that is not billed
as a documentary—is that audiences tend to believe that what they're
seeing on screen or on the printed page, because it is about people who
actually lived, must be true. This has been driven home to me time and

again by fans who have approached me, particularly online, to ask about or comment on the publication of this book. "Are you going to tell the story about the golden mike?" one person asked me. When I expressed my ignorance on this particular subject, he went on to tell me, very matter-of-factly, that Jim had had a special microphone made, all of gold, which he carried around with him in a special briefcase. Jim refused to perform without his golden mike. "Where did you get this information?" I asked the fan, bemused. "I think I read it in a book about Jim once," he replied, rather vaguely. And because the story had taken on the veil of authenticity often inferred by publication, this person had not hesitated to believe that a man who couldn't even bring himself to keep track of a wallet wouldn't go anywhere without his golden mike.*

Aside from the myth that both Pamela and Jim were drug addicts, a subject I feel I've addressed adequately in the body of this book, probably the feeling among fans that disturbs me the most is the rage continually expressed against Jim's parents, and sometimes Pamela's parents as well. "I'm so pissed off that those horrible people got all of Jim's money!" one fan wrote, referring to Jim's parents.

Though apparently representative of the opinion of the majority of Morrison's fans, there are a few things wrong with that statement. For one thing, the Morrisons did not get all of Jim's money. When Pamela died intestate, her estate—which included all of Jim's estate—automatically went to her parents, a legal action which was contested by the Morrisons. Court papers filed at the conclusion of this dispute in January 1975 stated: "It is hereby agreed that the estate of Pamela shall be deemed to consist entirely of the former community property of Pamela and James, and such estate shall be distributed in accordance with the provisions of California Probate Code Section 228, to wit, one-half thereof in equal shares to George and Clara, as the parents of James, and one-half thereof in equal shares to Columbus and Pearl, as the parents of Pamela."

Another problem with that statement, and the many others like it I've heard or read over the years, is the presumption to judgment against either set of parents. Despite stories told or secrets revealed, no one ever truly knows what goes on within a family unit. I've done six years of research for this book—waded through truckloads of paper, talked to hundreds of people—but I cannot in any definitive way tell you what transpired between these children and their parents; it's all open to interpretation and misinterpretation and subject to the frailties of human

---

*The object in question was actually a seldom-used prop purchased and owned by Doors roadie Vince Treanor.

memory. But I do know that Jim was in the process of reconciling with his parents when he died, so whatever animosity may or may not have existed between these people, obviously Jim had moved past it. So why can't his fans? Max Fink said something once that I find quite perceptive. "If Jim had been brought up differently, he wouldn't have been Jim. He wouldn't have had the same drive, or for that matter the pain that enabled him to touch people in his songs." Think about it.

Another thing that I've noticed from my interaction with Jim's fans is the natural tendency to judge Jim and Pamela's actions, as well as the reactions of those closest to them, by today's standards rather than by the standards of their own era. In the late sixties/early seventies when Jim and Pamela were struggling with their own demons and each other's, we had not yet gone through what's been called the "Oprah-fication of America." People did not go on national television and air their dirty laundry; personal problems, real or perceived, were kept within the home or within the individual, where they often festered. Alcoholism was seen as a character flaw rather than the disease we know it to be today. Women who worked outside the home were still an exception rather than a rule. So if Jim kept certain traumas from his past or aspects of his adult lifestyle a secret; if Jim's bandmates turned a blind eye as his alcoholism escalated; if Pamela was supported by Jim's income—none of these things seem particularly unusual when viewed in the context of the era in which they took place.

While I tried to speak with as many people as possible to gather information for this book, there are those I did not interview. Patricia Kennealy felt she had said all she wanted to say on the subject of Jim and Pamela in her book *Strange Days*. John Densmore had also published a book, *Riders on the Storm*, about his life with The Doors, which I felt rendered pursuit of him for an additional interview redundant. I did not speak to anyone who demanded a list of questions in advance (a request which usually means that the person is concerned with squaring his or her story with others who may be asked the same questions; I was not interested in a collaborative effort to rewrite the past), nor did I speak to anyone who demanded cash payment in exchange for their memories. For example, one woman who was said to have been a close friend of Pamela's initially said she would talk to me only if I were willing to meet her price. When she was told that it is my policy not to pay for information, she said in that case these memories of her friend were "just too painful to discuss."

While doing the research for this book, I was reminded time and again that memories of the past are subjective at best. A good example is a little dispute I had with Paul Rothchild. You probably noticed that this book is dedicated to Paul, so obviously we were good friends and I trusted him absolutely; Paul had no reason to lie to me about anything, nor would I ever suspect he would. Which is why it was so frustrating when Paul told me in one of our early interviews that late in her life Pamela had become obese, ballooning up from about 96 pounds to nearly twice that. "She went the Jim route completely," he told me. "Jim turned his Michelangelo beauty into a grotesque fat man, she turned her Botticelli beauty into a grotesque fat lady. She had nothing appealing about her."

I was stunned! Of course I immediately set about trying to get confirmation of Paul's recollection, confirmation I never found. It is true that at the time of her death, Pamela was 115 pounds—the ideal weight for her height, but twenty pounds heavier than she had been before she and Jim left for Paris. Though she was always slender, never even a pound overweight, over the years Paul's memory had multiplied this twenty-pound gain several times until, in his mind, she was remembered as obese. When I pressed him, he told me that he had seen her in this condition about six months before she died. But the photo you saw of Pamela earlier in the book, with Randy Ralston at Diane Gardiner's house, was taken within that time. Does she look like "a grotesque fat lady" to you? Of course not. Was Paul lying to me? No, but his memory was lying to him. These are the tricks memory can play on all of us, and it is always wise to remember this when either writing or reading a book about real-life events of long ago, or even last week.

While Jim's death had made headlines worldwide, Pamela's death was quietly marked by a tiny news item in the April 27, 1974, Los Angeles Times, headlined, "Widow of Rock Star Morrison Found Dead," as well as by a touching (though factually flawed) obituary by Judith Sims in Rolling Stone. After her death, Pamela's father and his friend Preach Lyerla traveled up and down the state of California recovering abandoned vehicles. Just as she and Jim had both done during Jim's lifetime, "[Pamela] drove cars or vans or whatever until they mechanically went bad," explained Lyerla, "and then she'd leave that one to be fixed and just buy another car and never pick up the old one." Preach remembers recovering about six vehicles that had, for one reason or another, been left in Pamela's wake. "That was Pam," he laughs.

Despite some people's wishes that her remains be interred with Jim's in Paris, Pamela's ashes remain in Santa Ana, California, marked only by a tiny brass plaque bearing the simple legend, "Pamela Morrison, 1946–1974." Rumors have been running rampant for years that, after numerous complaints from the families of those interred near him, Jim's remains have been legally "evicted" from Père-Lachaise by court order because of the mindless destruction by visitors to Jim's grave over the years. Despite these rumors, however, the Morrisons, as recently as August 1996, have stated unequivocally that there are absolutely no plans to disturb Jim's body.

In an interesting side note, the *Bon Homme Richard,* the ship Jim's father commanded aboard which Jim was subjected to an unwelcome haircut, was built in 1943, the same year Jim was born, and, ironically, was taken out of commission the day before Jim was—July 2, 1971. But don't worry, you may still be able to occupy the same seat Jim did when he visited his father that day in 1964. Castaways Casino at 1690 North Decatur in Las Vegas, Nevada, has hatches, portholes, lanterns, and phones from the *Bonnie Dick,* and Gladstones 4 Fish of LA Walk in Universal Studios, California, has tables, chairs, serving carts, and bar tops made from wood from the ship's flight deck.

The Doors, who were inducted into the Rock and Roll Hall of Fame in 1993, continue to thrive, at least financially (the three surviving band members tried to go on performing as The Doors without Jim, but gave up in 1973). This phenomenal ongoing success was probably best summed up by John Densmore, who wrote in his book *Riders on the Storm,* "The size of the checks I have signed over to Julia [Densmore Negron, his first wife] twice a year at royalty time have shocked me, but they indicated that if she was doing well by me, I was doing obscenely well. The Doors myth marches on."

Yes, it certainly does. But please let's all try to remember that at the core of this burgeoning myth there remains always the simple truth of two young people in love (and they were very young—another fact that, unfortunately, people tend to overlook). My friend Dan Salomon was doing a little light reading one night and came across this passage from Rimbaud that immediately reminded him of Jim and Pamela.

> *One fine morning, in a land of very gentle people, a superb man and woman shouted in the public square: "Friends, I want her to be queen!"*
>
> *"I want to be queen!"*
>
> *She laughed and trembled.*
>
> *He spoke to his friends of revelation, of ordeals terminated. They leaned on each other in ecstasy.*

They were indeed sovereigns for a whole morning, while all the houses were adorned with crimson hangings, and for an entire afternoon, while they made their way toward the palm gardens. *

They were sovereigns for a whole morning, and an entire afternoon, and maybe even longer. I hope they found the palm gardens.

Don't you?

---

* "Royalty," *Illuminations* by Arthur Rimbaud.

SOURCES

CHAPTER ONE

Interview with Ray Manzarek.

Interview with Jeff Morehouse.

No One Here Gets Out Alive, Jerry Hopkins and Danny Sugerman, Warner Books, Inc., 1980.

"Remembering the Lizard King," Sandy Barnes, *Alexandria Gazette Packet,* March 21, 1991.

Interview with Stan Durkee.

Interview with Richard Sparks.

A Feast of Friends, Frank Lisciandro, Warner Books, Inc., 1991.

Jim Morrison: The Truth About His Turbulent Life and Mysterious Death, Margaret Fink (unpublished manuscript).

Interview with Paul Rothchild.

Admiral and Mrs. George S. Morrison.

Interview with Bryan Gates.

Interview with Thomas Bruce Reese.

Interview with Chris Kallivokas.

Interview with Nick Kallivokas.

CHAPTER TWO

"The Girl With No Brownie Uniform" by Charlene Estes Enzler.

Interview with Charlene Estes Enzler.

Interview with Abner Weed, Jr.

Mount Shasta: Home of the Ancients, edited by Bruce Walton, Health Research, 1985.

Birth certificate of Pamela Susan Morrison, Shasta County Recorder.

Weed: Evolution of a Company Town, Abner E. Weed, Jr., master's thesis, California State University, Chico, 1974.

"White and Gold," Weed High School, 1932–1936.

Interview with Charles and Madeline Andresen.

Birth certificate of Judith Courson, Cook County Recorder.

Great Lakes Naval Training Station.

Interview with Preach Lyerla.

Interview with Barbara Marko.

The California Indians: A Source Book, complied and edited by R. F. Heizer and M. A. Whipple, University of California Press, 1971.

Interview with Randall Jahnson.

Orange Public Schools.

Orange High School Yearbook, 1961–1964.

Interview with Barbara Stewart Noble.

Interview with Kendall Niesess.

Interview with Tamsyn Griffith.

Interview with Annette Burden.

Interview with Charlotte Greenwald.

Interview with David Hart.

Interview with Thomas Murphine.

Interview with Jim Carnett.

Capistrano Union Public Schools.

Anne Spinn, Librarian, *The Newport Beach/Costa Mesa Daily Pilot.*

Dr. W. O. Hendricks, Director, Sherman Library.

CHAPTER THREE

Do You Believe in Magic? The Second Coming of the Sixties Generation, Annie Gottlieb, Times Books, March 1987.

Fire in the Streets: America in the 1960's, Milton Viorst, Touchstone, 1979.

"Birth of the Go-Go Boom," Laura C. Smith, *Entertainment Weekly,* January 13, 1995.

Break On Through: The Life and Death of Jim Morrison, James Riordan and Jerry Prochnicky, Wm. Morrow & Company, 1991.

Riders on the Storm, John Densmore, Delacorte Press, 1990.

Interview with Randall Jahnson.

Interview with January Jensen.

Interview with Ray Manzarek.

Interview with Jeff Morehouse.

Interview with Bryan Gates.

Interview with Mirandi Babitz.

Los Angeles City College.

Interview with Babe Hill.

Warhol, David Bourdon, Abrams, 1989.

The Doors, Carolco Pictures, 1991.

Interview with Julia Densmore Negron.

Interview with Madeline Andresen.

Interview with Preach Lyerla.

Interview with John Phillip Law.

"Interview with Morrison," John Carpenter, *Los Angeles Free Press,* July 19, 1968.

CHAPTER FOUR

Interview with January Jensen.

Interview with Ray Manzarek.

A Feast of Friends, Frank Lisciandro, Warner Books, Inc., 1991.

Interview with Paul Ferrara.

Interview with Danny Sugerman.

Interview with Mirandi Babitz.

Interview with Paul Rothchild.

Interview with Jac Holzman.

Interview with Robby Krieger.

Linda McCartney's Sixties: Portraits of an Era, Linda McCartney, Bullfinch Press, 1992.

Riders on the Storm, John Densmore, Delacorte Press, 1990.

"Artaud Rock: Dark Logic of the Doors," Bill Kerby, *UCLA Daily Bruin*, May 24, 1967.

Moonlight Drive: The Stories Behind Every Doors Song, Chuck Crisafulli, Carlton Books Limited, 1995.

I'm With the Band, Pamela des Barres, Wm. Morrow & Company, 1987.

Take Another Little Piece of My Heart, Pamela des Barres, Wm. Morrow & Company, 1992.

Interview with Christopher Jones.

Interview with Robby Krieger.

CHAPTER FIVE

Interview with Randall Jahnson.

Moonlight Drive: The Stories Behind Every Doors Song, Chuck Crisafulli, Carlton Books Limited, 1995.

Break On Through: The Life and Death of Jim Morrison, James Riordan and Jerry Prochnicky, Wm. Morrow & Company, 1991.

Riders on the Storm, John Densmore, Delacorte Press, 1990.

"The Doors Open Up," Pete Johnson, *Los Angeles Times*, February 26, 1967.

"The Doors Open Wide," Richard Goldstein, *New York* magazine, March 19, 1967.

"Doors, A Way in and a Way out, Rock on Coast," Robert Windeler, *New York Times*, November 20, 1967.

Interview with Bill Siddons.

Jim Morrison: The Truth About His Turbulent Life and Mysterious Death, Margaret Fink (unpublished manuscript).

Interview with Ray Manzarek.

Interview with Robby Krieger.

CHAPTER SIX

Interview with Randall Jahnson.

Steppenwolf, Herman Hesse, Holt, Rinehart and Winston, Inc., 1957.

Moonlight Drive: The Stories Behind Every Doors Song, Chuck Crisafulli, Carlton Books Limited, 1995.

Jim Morrison: The Truth About His Turbulent Life and Mysterious Death, Margaret Fink (unpublished manuscript).

Interview with January Jensen.

Interview with Paul Rothchild.

Interview with Paul Ferrara.

Riders on the Storm, John Densmore, Delacorte Press, 1990.

Interview with Ray Manzarek.

Interview with Mirandi Babitz.

Interview with Anne Moore.

Interview with Kendall Niesses.

Interview with Rich Linnell.

Interview with Preach Lyerla.

Interview with Bill Siddons.

A Feast of Friends, Frank Lisciandro, Warner Books, Inc., 1991.

Interview with January Jensen.

CHAPTER SEVEN
Interview with Randall Jahnson.

CHAPTER EIGHT
Interview with Ray and Dorothy Manzarek.
City of Los Angeles.
Interview with January Jensen.
Interview with Cheri Siddons.
Interview with Paul Ferrara.
Interview with Dr. Paul Ackerman.
Interview with Bill Siddons.
Interview with Mirandi Babitz.
Interview with Babe Hill.
Interview with Anne Moore.
Interview with Julia Densmore Negron.
Interview with Rich Linnell.
Interview with Raeanne Rubenstein.

CHAPTER NINE
Jim Morrison: The Truth About His Turbulent Life and Mysterious Death,
   Margaret Fink (unpublished manuscript).

CHAPTER TEN
Interview with Christopher Jones.
Interview with Mirandi Babitz.
Edie: An American Biography, Jean Stein, Knopf, 1982.
Interview with Paul Rothchild.
Interview with John Phillip Law.
Strange Days: My Life With and Without Jim Morrison, Patricia Kennealy,
   Dutton, 1992.
Interview with Anne Moore.
Interview with Penelope Truex.
Interview with Cathy Weldy.
Interview with Eve Babitz.
Interview with Cheri Siddons.
Interview with Babe Hill.
A Feast of Friends, Frank Lisciandro, Warner Books, Inc., 1991.
Interview with John Phillip Law.
Interview with Paul Ferrara.
Interview with Ray Manzarek.
Moonlight Drive: The Stories Behind Every Doors Song, Chuck Crisafulli,
   Carlton Books Limited, 1995.
Interview with Bill Siddons.
Interview with Larry Gustin.
The Buick: The Complete History, Lawrence R. Gustin and Terry B. Dunham,
   Automobile Quarterly/CBS Magazine, 1980.

Riders on the Storm, John Densmore, Delacorte Press, 1990.
Last Will and Testament of James D. Morrison.

CHAPTER ELEVEN
Interview with Bill Siddons.
Riders on the Storm, John Densmore, Delacorte Press, 1990.
"Jim Morrison Is Dead and Living in Hollywood," Eve Babitz, *Esquire,* March
    1991.
Interview with Paul Rothchild.
A Feast of Friends, Frank Lisciandro, Warner Books, Inc., 1991.
Interview with Julia Densmore Negron.
The Doors: The Illustrated History, Danny Sugerman, Wm. Morrow & Co.,
    1983.
Steppenwolf, Hermann Hesse, Holt, Rinehart and Winston, Inc., 1957.

CHAPTER TWELVE
Jim Morrison: The Truth About His Turbulent Life and Mysterious Death,
    Margaret Fink (unpublished manuscript).
"Jim Morrison Is Dead and Living in Hollywood," Eve Babitz, *Esquire,* March
    1991.
Moonlight Drive: The Stories Behind Every Doors Song, Chuck Crisafulli,
    Carlton Books Limited, 1995.
Interview with Paul Rothchild.
Little Man: Meyer Lansky and the Gangster Life, Robert Lacey, Little, Brown,
    1991.
Interview with Babe Hill.
Interview with Bryan Gates.
Interview with Jeff Morehouse.
Interview with Herve Mueller.
A Feast of Friends, Frank Lisciandro, Warner Books, Inc., 1991.
Interview with Randall Jahnson.

CHAPTER THIRTEEN
Letter from Jim Morrison to Bob Greene, July 3, 1971.
Interview with Bob Greene.
"Goodbyes," Tere Tereba, *Crawdaddy.*
Interview with Cathy Weldy.
Interview with Ray Manzarek.
No One Here Gets Out Alive, Jerry Hopkins and Danny Sugerman, Warner
    Books, Inc., 1980.
Interview with Herve Mueller.
Interview with Gilles Yepremian.
"Jim and I: Friends Until Death," Alain Ronay, translated from Italian by Joel
    Brody, *King* magazine.
Admiral and Mrs. George S. Morrison.

Interview with Ellen Sander.
Interview with Bill Siddons.
Interview with Cheri Siddons.
Interview with Rich Linnell.
"Fascination 1–2-7" documents, courtesy of Paul Rothchild.

CHAPTER FOURTEEN

"Elegy in a Paris Graveyard," Mike Jahn, *Baltimore Morning Sun.*
Interview with Babe Hill.
The Doors: The Illustrated History, Danny Sugerman, Wm. Morrow & Co., 1983.
Interview with Paul Ferrara.
Milestones item about Jim Morrison's death, *Time,* July 12, 1971.
Interview with Bill Siddons.
"Transition" column, Jim Morrison obituary, *Newsweek,* July 21, 1971.
Interview with Julia Densmore Negron.
"Morrison and Miami: Beginning of the End," Larry Mahoney, *Miami Herald,* July 10, 1971.
Interview with Bryan Gates.
"Rock Star Jim Morrison Dies," Tom Paegel, *Los Angeles Times,* July 9, 1971.
Interview with Jeff Morehouse.
"Singer Jim Morrison Reported Dead: Parents in Arlington Not Notified," Timothy S. Robinson, *Washington Post,* July 9, 1971.

CHAPTER FIFTEEN

Interview with Cheri Siddons.
Report of the Los Angeles Police Department in the death of Pamela Susan Morrison.
Jim Morrison: The Truth About His Turbulent Life and Mysterious Death, Margaret Fink (unpublished manuscript).
Interview with Dr. Arnold Derwin.
Interview with Cathy Weldy.
"Jim and I: Friends Until Death," Alain Ronay, translated from Italian by Joel Brody, *King* magazine.
Pompes Funèbres Municipales order, July 6, 1971.
Interview with Bill Siddons.
Interview with Randall Jahnson.
Interview with Mirandi Babitz.
"France Scrambling to Fight Air Pollution," CALSTART News Notes, April 10, 1996.
Interview with Lenore Coover, R.N., M.S.N.
National Center for Health Statistics.
National Asthma Education Program.
"Blunted Perception and Death from Asthma," Peter J. Barnes, D.M., D.Sc., National Heart and Lung Institute, *New England Journal of Medicine,* May 12, 1994.
"Preventing Deaths from Asthma," A. Sonia Buist, M.D., Oregon Health

Sciences University; William M. Vollmer, Ph.D., Kaiser Permanente Center
for Health Research, *New England Journal of Medicine,* December 8, 1994.
American Lung Association.
"Elegy in a Paris Graveyard," Mike Jahn, *Baltimore Morning Sun.*

CHAPTER SIXTEEN
Interview with Bill Siddons.
Interview with Ellen Sander.
Interview with January Jensen.
Interview with Danny Sugerman.
Letter from Bill Siddons to Agnes Varda.
Interview with Randall Jahnson.
Interview with Preach Lyerla.
Court file in the probate of Pamela Susan Morrison.
Interview with Randy Ralston.

CHAPTER SEVENTEEN
Interview with Randy Ralston.
Court file in the probate of Pamela Susan Morrison.
Interview with Ray Manzarek.
Interview with Babe Hill.
Los Angeles Police Department, Death Report, Pamela Susan Morrison.
County of Los Angeles Registrar-Recorder/County Clerk, Certificate of Death,
    Pamela Susan Morrison.
Admiral and Mrs. George S. Morrison.
Interview with Robby Krieger.
Interview with Mirandi Babitz.
Interview with Barbara Marko.
Los Angeles Police Department, Wilshire Division.
County of Los Angeles, Case Report, Pamela Susan Morrison.
County of Los Angeles, Autopsy Report, Pamela Susan Morrison.
County of Los Angeles, Medical Report, Pamela Susan Morrison.
Fairhaven Memorial Park.
Forest Lawn Hollywood Hills Mortuary.
Interview with Bruce Ramm.
Interview with Alan Graham.
Interview with Dr. Paul Ackerman.
Interview with Randall Jahnson.
Interview with Cheri Siddons.

PHOTO CREDITS

Frontispiece: © Edmund Teske/Michael Ochs Archives/Venice CA; *page 2:* private collection; *page 4:* courtesy of Jeff Morehouse; *page 6:* courtesy of Jeff Morehouse; *page 18:* courtesy of Thomas Bruce Reese; *page 20:* courtesy of Thomas Bruce Reese; *page 28:* Fernand Amandi Collection; *page 37:* Fernand Amandi Collection; *page 38:* courtesy of the U.S. Navy; *page 45:* photo by Patricia Butler; *page 46:* courtesy of Charlene Enzler; *page 49:* courtesy of Tamsyn Griffith; *page 52:* photo courtesy of Tamsyn Griffith; *page 54:* courtesy of Sherman Library; *page 66:* The Archives of Andy Warhol Museum, Pittsburgh Founding Collection, Contribution, The Andy Warhol Foundation for the Visual Arts, Inc.; *page 73:* courtesy of Dan Rothchild; *page 75:* © Tom Monaster Photography; *page 76:* photo by Chuck Schiesser; *page 78:* courtesy of Baron Wolman Photography; *page 94:* photographer unknown; *page 108:* courtesy of Anne Moore; *page 121:* © Lisa Law Productions; *page 127:* photo by Chuck Schiesser; *page 128:* photo by Chuck Schiesser; *page 130:* courtesy of Christopher Jones; *page 133:* courtesy of Lawrence R. Gustin; *page 148:* © Baron Wolman Photography; *page 152:* © Edmund Teske/Michael Ochs Archives/Venice CA; *page 154:* photographer unknown; *page 160:* photo by Patricia Butler; *page 162:* © Gilles Yéprémian; *page 174:* photo by Patricia Butler; *page 180:* document courtesy of Michelle Campbell; *page 182:* photo by Patricia Butler; *page 198:* courtesy of Diane Gardiner; *page 204:* photo by Chuck Schiesser; *page 207:* photo by Tamsyn Griffith; *page 209:* photo by Patricia Butler; *page 220:* © Edmund Teske/Michael Ochs Archives/Venice CA; *color insert:* photos © Raeanne Rubinstein.

ADDITIONAL SOURCES

My Sister and I, Friedrich Nietzsche, Amok Books, 1990.

Mr. Mojo Risin': Jim Morrison, the Last Holy Fool, David Dalton, Space & Archer, Inc., 1991.

Wilderness: The Lost Writings of Jim Morrison, Volume 1, James Douglas Morrison, Villard Books, 1988.

The American Night: The Writings of Jim Morrison, Volume 2, James Douglas Morrison, Villard Books, 1990.

The Lizard King: The Essential Jim Morrison, Jerry Hopkins, Scribners, 1992.

The Lords and the New Creatures, James Douglas Morrison, Simon and Schuster, 1969.

Anti-Rock: The Opposition to Rock 'n' Roll, Linda Martin and Kerry Segrave, DaCapo, 1993.

The Doors: The Complete Illustrated Lyrics, Compiled by Danny Sugerman, Hyperion, 1991.

The End: The Death of Jim Morrison, Bob Seymore, Omnibus Press, 1991.

And I Don't Want to Live This Life, Deborah Spungen, Fawcett Crest, 1983.

The New Heroin Users, Geoffrey Pearson, Basil Blackwell, Inc., 1983.

The Sixties: From Memory to History, Compiled by David Farber, The University of North Carolina Press, 1994.

Bound by Love: The Sweet Trap of Daughterhood, Lucy Gilbert and Paula Webster, Beacon Press, 1982.

It Was Twenty Years Ago Today: Anniversary Celebration of 1967, Derek Taylor, Simon and Schuster, 1987.

The Sixties: Years of Hope, Days of Rage, Todd Gitlin, Bantam Books, 1987.

Jim Morrison: Dark Star, Dylan Jones, Viking Studio Books, 1990.

The Death of Rock 'n' Roll, Jeff Pike, Faber and Faber, 1993.

Get the Facts on Anyone, Dennis King, Prentice Hall, 1992.

Be Your Own Detective, Greg Fallis and Ruth Greenburg, M. Evans and Company, 1989.

Alice's Adventures in Wonderland/Through the Looking Glass, Lewis Carroll.

Romeo and Juliet, William Shakespeare.

Rock Eras: Interpretation of Music and Society 1954–1984, Jim Curtis, Bowling Green State University Popular Press, 1987.

Drugs and Addict Lifestyles: Lifestyle Histories of Heroin Users, edited by Patricia Ferguson, M.L.S.; Thomas Lennox, M.L.S.; Dan J. Lettieri, Ph.D., National Institute on Drug Abuse, 1974.

Nietzsche: Philosopher, Psychologist, Antichrist, Walter Kaufman, Princeton University Press, 1974.

California Dreamin': The True Story of The Mamas and the Papas, Michelle Phillips, Warner Books, 1986.

Adoring Audience: Fan Culture and Popular Media, edited by Lisa A. Lewis, Rougledge, 1992.

"The Legacy of Jim Morrison and The Doors," Mikal Gilmore, *Rolling Stone,* April 4, 1991.

"Love Me Two Times," Gregg Kilday, *Entertainment Weekly,* March 1, 1991.

"The Doors: Celebration of the Lizard King," David Cavanaugh, *Select,* May 1991.

"Like Jim Morrison, Working Stiffs from Elvis to Marilyn Are Still Striking It Rich," *People Weekly,* March 18, 1991.

"Last Call for The Doors," *Entertainment Weekly,* December 13, 1996.

"Widow of Rock Star Morrison Found Dead," *Los Angeles Times,* April 27, 1974.

"A Fire Gone Out," Timothy S. Robinson, *Washington Post,* July 10, 1971.

"Testing the Bounds of Reality: Doors Traces Rise and Fall of Rock Legend," Barry Koltnow, *Orange County Register,* March 1, 1991.

"Pam Morrison: A Final Curtain on Her Affair with Life," Judith Sims, *Rolling Stone,* June 6, 1974.

Various reports from the probate file of the estate of Pamela Susan Morrison.

Various reports from the probate file of and legal procedings against James Douglas Morrison.

Agreement between James Morrison, Raymond Manzarek, John Densmore, Robert Krieger, and Elektra Records for Jim Morrison to record as a solo artist.

RECOMMENDED READING

If you're interested in developing a better understanding of Jim Morrison's life and work, you will find the following books a great way to begin.

The Lords and the New Creatures, James Douglas Morrison, Simon and Schuster, 1969.

Wilderness: The Lost Writings of Jim Morrison, Volume 1, James Douglas Morrison, Villard Books, 1988.

The American Night: The Writings of Jim Morrison, Volume 2, James Douglas Morrison, Villard Books, 1990.

A Feast of Friends, Frank Lisciandro, Warner Books, Inc., 1991.

The Doors: The Illustrated History, Danny Sugerman, Wm. Morrow & Co., 1983.

The Doors: The Complete Illustrated Lyrics, Compiled by Danny Sugerman, Hyperion, 1991.

Jim Morrison: My Eyes Have Seen You [Photos], Jerry Prochnicky and Joe Russo.

INDEX